ABOUT THE AUTHOR

Glen Humphries is a journalist and a multi-award-winning writer and author. In 2016 he was named Beer Writer of the Year at the Australian International Beer Awards. His first book, *The Slab: 24 Stories of Beer in Australia*, was the national winner in the worldwide Gourmand food and drink writing award. He has also written a biography of convict brewer James Squire (yes, he was a real person) and an ebook companion to *The Slab* called *The Six-Pack: Stories from the World of Beer*. He can't stand people who refer to records as "vinyls". These days he doesn't go out much to see bands because he's old and staying up after 9.30pm is a challenge. He used to tell people that he was a drummer in a thrash band. That was a complete lie. One which led to him sitting behind a drumkit at a band audition while at university. No, he didn't get the gig. He writes one of these stupidly long "about the author" pieces for each of his books. And it gets harder and harder to come up with dumb things to write. He is sure Blink-182 once played at the Oxford before they were famous, but can't find any evidence to support this claim. He misses not having a functioning CD player in his car. But at the same time is too lazy to actually arrange to get it replaced. Know any good auto electricians who can help him out? He has actually appeared on a Wollongong band's CD – Adam Buckland's *Soundtrack From a Noisy Mind*. He played tambourine on one track. He's also played tambourine onstage with The Culprits, Merry Widows and David Challenger and the Insiders. He is what you call a session tambourine player. He can no longer stand to drink instant coffee.

Also by Glen Humphries
The Slab: 24 Stories of Beer in Australia
James Squire: The Biography
The Six-Pack: Stories from the World of Beer
Beer is Fun!

For more information visit www.lastdayofschool.net

FRIDAY NIGHT AT THE OXFORD

GLEN HUMPHRIES

LAST DAY OF SCHOOL
www.lastdayofschool.net

ISBN: 978 0 64803233 5

Copyright Glen Humphries 2018

Friday Night at the Oxford is first published in book form in 2018 by Last Day of School. Pieces appeared in the *Illawarra Mercury* between 1997 and 2018 and Dragster webzine between 1999 and 2000.
Websites: lastdayofschool.net
For more information, to purchase additional copies or even if you're a crazy millionaire who wants to pay me a salary to stay home and write books email dragstermag@hotmail.com.

This book is copyright. All rights reserved. Except for private study, research, criticism or reviews, as permitted under the Copyright Act, no part of this book may be reproduced, stored in a retrieval system, or transmitted in any form or by any means without prior written permission. Enquires can be directed to the author at dragstermag@hotmail.com. Sometimes I wonder what happened to the economy in The Flintstones' town of Bedrock when dinosaurs became extinct. You know, because the creatures were the backbone of so many industries, such as digging out the quarry where Fred worked. They were also the basis of numerous labour-saving devices, from lawnmowers to dishwashers. The lazy folk of Bedrock owed so much of their comfortable lifestyle to the dinosaur, I reckon. And I reckon their economy totally tanked when all the dinosaurs kicked the bucket.

A catalogue record of this book is available from the National Library of Australia.

This one's for all the Wollongong bands — both those who appear in this book and those who don't.

FOREWORD
"It's *our* dreams in *our* town"

"Don't go in there. That's where all the lesbians hang out."

And so spoke my youth pastor as we walked past the Oxford Hotel one sunny afternoon in the very early part of the nineties.

I had joined the church in my teens, and my Friday and Saturday nights were often filled with wholesome, youth-oriented activities. Besides the usual the bible study and prayer circles, we would also venture out and go the cinema, the bowling alley or go see the occasional Christian rock band playing at a local church hall. On Sundays of course I would go to church and duly listen to the sermon before partaking in communion – usually a small piece of Sao biscuit and some Ribena in a small plastic shot glass.

A few short years later I walked out of the church disillusioned and into the Oxford to find a new group of friends to commune with. Only this time instead of small sips of Ribena, it was schooners of beer. The preacher was now dressed in a black band shirt with and had a Stratocaster slung over their shoulder and the message they shared was one of rock 'n' roll, hedonism and debauchery. That video of Bon Scott in *Let There Be Rock* suddenly made a world of sense.

Of course, my church leader was right. The Oxford *was* where all the lesbians hung out. As well as the hippies, the punks, the stoners, the metalheads, the art students, the jailbirds, the drop-outs … basically anyone rejected by mainstream society.

This unique mix of cultures and subcultures is what made the Oxford legendary. It certainly wasn't the room itself, as many touring musician will tell you. The stage was tiny and the sound average. Rather it was the cross-pollination of ideas that fermented amongst the ragtag bunch of beer swillers.

Whether it was a heated debate about the merits of socialism or what was the best Ramones record, the people who attended the Oxford were generally there for the right reasons: music, booze and friends. It rarely mattered who was playing on any given night. One could head down to Oxford and see someone they knew or maybe someone they didn't. It wouldn't be long though before everyone resembled the cast of *Cheers*, sharing a drink and a having a laugh.

But despite the unique mix of the Oxford clientele, it was also just another live music venue in just another regional town. Wollongong, and indeed Australia, is littered with them. Live music venues come and go. Some survive across generations. Some are just a blip on the radar – blink and you'll have missed it.

Each town has a history of these spaces – all holding a special place within the hearts of those fortunate enough to have darkened their doors. For Wollongong it's Zondraes in the sixties, the Ironworkers in the eighties, Rad right now and naturally, the Oxford – as well as the Youthie and Sunami – in the nineties.

Such spaces are crucial not only for the development of talent, but also for healthy, cohesive communities. So when the Oxford changed ownership in the mid-nineties and a Sydney booking agency swooped in to put strippers on the stage, we all knew the community would suffer for it. When the pub finally closed its doors to make way for apartments, it wasn't long before a bunch of creatives would open a small bar around the corner under the name Yours & Owls and a new generation was born.

Those longing for the Oxford's heyday – those punks, hippies, and other counter-culturalists – have little time to nurse hangovers and shake the tinnitus from their ears. Their days are now filled with family responsibilities, mortgage repayments, jobs they probably hate, and the occasional getaway down the coast. And that's OK. It's someone else's turn now.

And this is where Glen's book comes in. During those heady days, as the chief entertainment writer at the *Mercury*, Glen (or Bear as he is affectionately known) documented his own version of our live music history through a series of brief but informative interviews. These pieces were often in the lead-up to a performance or an album release and show many a wide-eyed aspiring muso talking about their hopes and fears. His subjects could be any kid with a guitar and a dream in any dead-end regional town anywhere in Australia.

But *Friday Night at the Oxford* is about us. It's *our* dreams in *our* town. Some fulfilled, but many lost to the ravages of time.

Perhaps unwittingly, Glen has captured a moment in time. A moment that, unless you were there, may not be of great interest, But for those of us that were, his book is a great way to remember people, the bands they were in and the places we went to so we could watch them play.

In that sense, *Friday Night at the Oxford* is like the Gospel according to Glen. It is our bible; an ancient text whose readings are rich with colourful characters, stories of hope and love, and the occasional tall truth for dramatic effect.

It is also the perfect addendum to the *Steel City Sound* exhibition, for our musical heritage tells the story of us just as much as any other local studies can.

Now, if you'll just turn to Tumbleweed 3:16, I'll begin my sermon for today.

Warren Wheeler
Steel City Sound curator

Glen Humphries

INTRODUCTION
"You'll love it in here"

It was a Friday night that inspired this book. Not a Friday at the Oxford back in the 1990s but one much later, at Wollongong Art Gallery. On Friday November 21, 2014, the *Steel City Sound* exhibition opened at the gallery. A collection curated by Wollongong music scene's don't-call-me-guru Warren Wheeler, it looked back at the last 50 years of the city's music scene. There are several stories about the exhibition in this book.

On that Friday night in late 2014, I headed down to the gallery, both excited to see the exhibition and to catch up with old friends. In the early 1990s I had been the roadie for The Culprits and we had arranged to meet up at the gallery and go out afterwards for dinner and a few beers.

It turns out we were far from the only ones in a buoyant mood that night. Hundreds of other people had turned up to meet with friends and remember the days when they were younger and could stay up way past midnight. The crowd was bigger than any art gallery opening I'd been to, with people spotting names they remembered from gig posters, seeing band T-shirts they once owned but had since thrown away and hearing old songs for the first time in ages.

Bearing in mind this collection has come out three years after the *Steel City Sound* gig, it's not so much the actual exhibition but its underlying message that inspired the book. And that message? This shit's important. This stuff matters to people. The local bands, the music, the venues, the memories. They all matter. In terms of the history of a city, we always talk of the founders, the early explorers, the politicians, the bigwigs and movers and shakers. But the artistic side of the city, certainly the musical side? Well, that usually gets given the short shrift by historians because it's not "important".

But they're wrong. One look at a packed art gallery on that Friday night in November would tell you that.

Friday Night at the Oxford

This book is largely made up of the local band stories I've written for the *Illawarra Mercury* over the years. The bulk come from a period in the early 2000s when I was the editor of the entertainment section - then called *The Beat*, though there are also pieces from before and after that time. Thanks should go to the *Mercury* for allowing me to write so many stories about some of the bands of this city.

I've given the stories a very light edit for any typos that may have gotten through but otherwise they remain as they were when they first appeared in print. Which was sometimes hard to do as there are a few pieces here where my choice of words made me cringe a little.

Early on in the book you'll notice there are a number of stories featuring the same few bands. That's because I was reporting on other rounds at the *Mercury* and didn't get to write many band stories. The only ones I ended up writing were those I pitched, and those were all about bands who were friends of mine. Things changed for a few years around 2003 when I was moved to the job of editing *The Beat* entertainment section, where I got to write band stories every week.

There are also a selection of stories that appeared on the webzine (that's what we called them back then) Dragster in 1999-2000. I'd started it because I'd been moved into sub-editing at work and realised how much I missed writing, so I devised Dragster as a product to scratch that itch. As for the name Dragster, well, I stole that from a local band that featured Dave Curley on vocals.

There are some interesting pieces here; even if I do say so myself. There's a piece about the first time the now iconic HOPE fundraiser was held, as well as another piece which offers a deeper dive into the origins of the event. There is what was meant to be an in-depth retrospective on Tumbleweed, which ended up playing a part in their reformation. And a few pieces covering that wonderful *Steel City Sound* exhibition.

Reading through some of these pieces reminded me of venues that had opened and closed, magazines and websites covering the local scene that only lasted a few months and long gone record labels. I also realised I have no idea how to spell HyTest's name. Is it HyTest, Hytest, or Hy-Test? I'd spelt it all three ways at different times, though

Glen Humphries

for the sake of consistency have gone with HyTest throughout this book.

Despite what the title suggests, the bands in the following pages didn't all play at the Oxford on a Friday night. I chose that name because, for a long time, in the 1990s Friday night at the Oxford was the highlight of my week. Didn't matter what else was going on in my life, didn't matter which band was playing, didn't matter if it was the middle of a stinking hot summer, didn't matter if it was the depths of a marrow-chilling winter, heading down to the corner of Crown and Corrimal streets on a Friday night made me happy. It was a place where I felt like I belonged, a depth of feeling I've not had since. Whether you were gothed up in all black, sported studs, a mohawk and an Exploited back patch or nice pants and your best dress shirt or a Steelers jersey after having watched the team at the showground down the road, you were welcome. Other venues might have been prone to drunken punch-ups but I honestly can't remember a single instance of that happening at the Occy. There never seemed to be any anger or drama, it was just good vibes – a sign that it wasn't the pub itself, it was the people.

Which isn't to say that other generations don't feel that way about other venues, of course they do. That's the shit that's important to them. Friday night at the Occy? Well, that shit's important to me. And if it's important to you too, then hopefully you'll get something out of this book.

In closing, many thanks to Warren Wheeler for graciously agreeing to write the foreword to this book. As you'll soon see, Warren features in Friday Night at the Oxford and that's because he's a real champion of the Wollongong music scene. He might not play an instrument but he's done an enormous amount of work in the local scene.

Glen Humphries
July 2018

Friday Night at the Oxford

Glen Humphries

On a roll but credit is verbal
July 3, 1997

It's a myth. There is no money in rock and roll. Just ask Wollongong band Pounderhound.

Two weeks ago, the band played four gigs in Brisbane (the longest tour the band's been on to date) and came out ahead. To the tune of about eight bucks.

Up there to support a Def Records compilation CD they're on, guitarist/vocalist Tim Ireland said money wasn't the point; rather, it was the first step in gaining a profile outside Wollongong.

"We played four gigs up there, Surfer's Paradise, Brisbane, Lismore, and back to Brisbane," he said.

"No-one knows us from a bar of soap up there. You can't expect a lot of response straight away, but it was still pretty good. People were interested, especially at the last gig in Brisbane.

"We try to put out an energetic vibe. We're an energetic band, and people can pick up on that whether it's their style of music or not."

Something else that will help lift the band's profile is their debut CD, *Twisted Made Complete*, released by Redback Music and due in store on July 7.

The four-piece band, which also includes drummer Danny Glasgow, bassplayer Tim Dennis and guitarist Damien Lane, spent three days recording and mixing the seven-track CD in Sydney.

"We actually planned to do six songs, but ended up with more time in the studio," Dennis said.

That extra seventh song turned out to be *Damocles*, the same song on the Def Records compilation. Both Ireland and Dennis agree the version on *Twisted Made Complete* is the better of the two.

The CD, which features a Berlin Wall painting on its cover, has its tracks listed in a deliberate order.

Twisted Made Complete opens with the more poppy-sounding

Friday Night at the Oxford

Superhero before gradually moving towards darker tracks like *Music Milk* and *Cynical*.

"The darker songs don't necessarily have more depth than the others, they're just a little bit less accessible," Ireland said.

"It's better not to have them in your face straight away."

What stands out on *Twisted Made Complete* is the band's distinctive style, which seems to be a by-product of the way members approach their instruments.

"The way we approach guitar-playing, we don't have a rhythm and a lead guitarist," Ireland said.

"We use the instruments the way we want to use them. What develops is sounds that interweave with each other.

"Every instrument in this band is as important as the others," Dennis added.

"Sometimes all four instruments might be going at the same time, and then other times, they might pair off in different ways."

Pounderhound are the latest band on the Redback Music label; after Zambian Goat Herders, Dettol and Mudlungs. Ireland sees this label as a sign people are becoming more accepting of local bands.

"John and Fiona (at Redback) are just very interested in music in general and in Wollongong music especially," Ireland said.

Pounderhound are playing an acoustic gig at the Hideaway Cafe on July 5 and at the Youth Centre on July 13, 2-6pm with Screamfeeder, Dettol and Karma.

Moshing takes a dive
July 7, 1997

A sweaty crowd of people, tightly packed together, jumps up and down and slams into each other.

Some hoist themselves up on their friends' shoulders and get passed over the heads of the crowd.

Others dodge security staff while climbing onto the stage, only to fling themselves back into the crush of people, expecting hands to reach up and catch them.

For several years, this was a fairly common sight at music gigs. Moshing, crowd surfing and stage diving were the ways fans fed off the energy created by bands. It can be impressive to watch, particularly the writhing mass of flesh in the moshpit, moving and undulating as though it's all one large beast.

This sort of physical appreciation of music is now being actively discouraged by venues and bands, which both see the potential for serious injury.

It isn't the moshing itself that is dangerous; at worst, it usually leads to little more than bumps and bruises. It's the related activities of stage diving and crowd surfing that represent the real dangers: concussions, broken necks and occasionally death.

It should be stressed that these sorts of injuries are not commonplace. Most moshers leave the pit with a few bruises and ringing eardrums.

Steven Harding, St John Ambulance Bulli Division superintendent, said he was yet to see anything as serious as spinal injuries from a concert.

"We see anything from scrapes and scratches to concussion," Harding said.

"We've had people with concussion from diving off stages and then no-one actually catches them."

Harding has been with St John Ambulance for 10 years and has treated people during a rave at Bass Point, as well as gigs at Thirroul Surf Club and Thirroul Skating Rink.

He said 25 per cent of injuries he treated resulted from stage diving or crowd surfing. Most of the time, the patients got back into the mosh after they'd been treated.

"Sometimes your patients allow you to treat them and, when you go to send them to hospital, they don't want to go," he said.

"So they go back into it (the moshpit). In that type of situation, we get them to sign a release form, stating that we're no longer liable for whatever happens to them from then on."

To the outsider these sorts of activities may seem pointless, but

Friday Night at the Oxford

"mosher" Jason Lee believes there's several very good reasons for it.

"The reason we do it is out of frustration and relief but it's also about fun and getting into the music," he said.

"You can mosh to anything really. More or less it's with the heavy bands, heavy metal and punk, but I've seen moshing going on at most concerts these days."

Now 24, Lee has been moshing since he was about 14 years old. For him, it is almost "a '90s style of dancing", but one where the steps may differ from one country to the next. Lee's been in the pit both in Australia and the US and has noticed two distinct styles of moshing.

"In the Australian style, the crowd is packed in like sardines and everyone jumps around and jostles each other," he said.

"There's a lot of camaraderie in the crowd, people look after each other. If you fall down, someone will pick you up. If you're tired, the crowd will push you out to the back of the pit."

In the US style, Lee said, there's a group of people five or six rows deep at the front of the stage, and a big "mosh circle" moved around the pit, behind those at the front of the stage. If you wanted to join the circle, you simply jumped in. The rest of the crowd stood back, well clear of the mosh circle.

Lee has crowd surfed and stage dived numerous times without harm and believes any injuries that do occur are due to the "poor judgment" of the person.

"There are risks, but no more than riding a skateboard on a skate ramp or something like that," he said.

"If you want to do it, you have to take that risk, but if you use good judgment, it'll be okay. I've only seen a handful of people get hurt in the 60 international concerts I've been to."

However small the potential for serious injury is, it has still made the entertainment industry change its attitude to crowd surfing and stage diving. Venues, facing the very real prospect of being sued by an injured patron, have been banning both stage diving and crowd surfing.

Waves nightclub has had a ban on these practices for close to two years, on the advice of the club's insurance company.

One of the partners in Waves, Kevin Cooney, said the insurance company acted after a case in Victoria, where a patron sued a venue over a moshpit incident.

"It's just an insurance nightmare," he said.

"It's like all these public liability things. If someone gets up and dives into the crowd, and then the crowd parts, the liability goes back to the hotel."

Waves has "never had any problem" with injuries from the mosh or crowd surfing and stage diving, which may in part be due the measures taken to prevent or restrict these activities.

To stop stage divers, a "punter barrier" is placed across the front of the stage and five security staff stay behind it for the gig.

The tactic has proved so successful Cooney won a bet over it with Mike Patton, lead singer with US band Faith No More.

Like the majority of bands that play at Waves, Faith No More said they didn't want any stage divers. After hearing that would not be a problem at Waves, Patton bet Cooney $10 that at least one person would get on-stage during the night.

"In the end, he paid me the $10 because no-one got on-stage," Cooney said with a laugh.

"He said to me that was a first for any gig they'd done. He paid me in US dollars, too."

Cooney admitted crowd surfing was "difficult to stop" but said Waves took a flexible approach to it.

"We wouldn't normally throw someone out if they've been crowd surfing once or twice," he said.

"But with repeat offenders, we ask them to leave or we might put them out for a couple of songs. We'll say 'look, you can go back in but take it easy'."

Moshing can be very draining on people's energy levels, which may be why the majority of moshers are young; usually in their teens or early 20s.

Many of these people, especially those under age, would attend all-ages gigs at the Wollongong Youth Centre. Youth Centre entertainment co-ordinator Frank Mincone said, like Waves, the centre discouraged both crowd surfing and stage diving.

Friday Night at the Oxford

Moshing itself did not pose much of a problem, Mincone said, because there was an unwritten code of conduct among moshers.

"We feel that a lot of young people that do it are pretty much aware of the other people around them, even though it might seem pretty chaotic to the outsider," he said.

"It's pretty much a rule that you look out for the person next to you. If someone falls down on the floor, you lift them up and make sure they're all right."

Mincone said any injuries from Youth Centre gigs were minor compared to other moshpits he'd seen.

"There's been very few injuries," he said. "That could include something like someone with a swollen eye or a swollen nose because someone accidentally hit them, but there's nothing major.

"I've been to other venues where things can get quite hairy. You see people coming out of the moshpit with blood pouring out of their face."

As well as venues discouraging stage diving, Mincone said a lot of bands didn't like it either. This was partially because stage divers tended to trip over guitar leads or knock over microphone stands while they were onstage.

"Some bands, they may be really hardcore, but they really prefer their stage space to be respected," he said.

"They encourage interaction with the crowd, but some bands get really disappointed about the whole stage diving thing.

"The feeling is it's just an exhibitionist thing and it's not really about being there and watching the band. It's something that people do to show off."

Sydney punk band Frenzal Rhomb play the style of music best suited to moshing; loud and fast, though singer Jay Whalley confirms that "there's a few tunes in there every so often".

While he is more than happy to play music to mosh by, Whalley prefers it when people dance at a Frenzal Rhomb show.

"I really love playing shows where people actually dance," he said.

"That's really good because you know they're actually getting into the music, but you can never be sure with a big mosh.

"You don't know whether it's the intensity of the gig or the speed we're playing rather than the actual songs we're playing."

Whalley was once a stage diver himself but gave it away when he snapped his collarbone after the crowd failed to catch him.

He said there weren't many venues that still allowed stage diving but the venues handled the problem in different ways. For example, the Metro in Sydney had what Whalley called a "sin bin rule".

"If you stage dive once you have to stand up near the back next to a security guard for 10 minutes, so you can still actually see the band.

"If you do it again you have to stay there for half an hour. If you do it again you get kicked out. So they're pretty fair about it."

As well as keeping the punters safe, banning stage diving and crowd surfing meant bands had more venues to play.

"Apart from people's safety, it (the ban) is also keeping venues open," he said.

"It's pretty hard to keep a venue running when they're being sued for thousands of dollars by angry parents."

Whalley believes there's a certain amount of camaraderie in the moshpit and sees it as a "really good energy outlet, it's better than going out and bashing someone". Still, he thinks it's an unusual thing to do.

"It's interesting in a way, because it's a pretty bizarre thing to do," he said.

"I'm sure, if you came from another planet and saw people moshing, you'd think there was a war going on or something."

The danger entered the moshpit, Whalley said, when people didn't know how to mosh properly.

"Some people just don't know how to do it properly, like some people don't know how to waltz," he said.

"(They) think it's all about getting in there, slamming into someone and seeing who can hurt the most amount of people, whereas others are into it for the release of the proximity of other people and being able to jump up and down as one."

There had been some "hideous" injuries at Frenzal Rhomb gigs, though Whalley said that's the exception rather than the rule.

"We've done more shows with incident-free moshes than we have

Friday Night at the Oxford

where people were injured, by far," he said.

"Those gigs with injuries are very small compared to those gigs with no injuries."

Tough demands
September 11, 1997

Despite being an experienced songwriter, Illawarra performer David Beniuk has found writing doesn't get any easier.

Beniuk, a member of much-missed local bands like The Culprits and the Merry Widows, released his first solo CD, *Port*, in January.

There were 12 tracks on that independently released CD, a small sampling of the many songs Beniuk has written over the years.

Even with that background, it can be difficult to come up with new songs.

"I'm finding it harder because, with all the promotion I have to do with the CD, that takes up a lot of time. And there's work as well," he said.

"When I do get time to do music stuff, a lot of it's to do with promotions.

"It's harder, not only because of time. You've covered a lot of bases when you've written a lot of songs, and you've got to keep dreaming up new subjects."

Some of Beniuk's songs are about events that have struck a strong emotional chord. Where once he would sit down immediately and write, now he takes his time.

"I guess, getting older, it's not such an immediate emotional reaction to everything," he said.

"You start thinking about things a bit more, letting things go round in your head, rather than an immediate emotional reaction to something that happens to you."

Despite having a strong back catalogue of songs, Beniuk mainly plays his newer material – for several reasons.

"A lot of what I wrote before was for the band (the Merry Widows) and sounded better with the band," he said.

"There were a lot of pop songs in there, and pop songs played acoustically sound like pathetic folk songs. I like to play the most appropriate set I can each night."

Another reason for playing newer material is to promote his CD. Beniuk released *Port* himself and estimated he has to sell about seven more CDs to break even. More importantly, the CD makes it easier for him to get gigs.

"Someone once said to me 'you don't exist as an artist until you have an album out'," Beniuk said. "I guess that's true.

"People have a reason to come to see you ... they've heard the songs on the album and they want to hear them live."

David Beniuk is at the Oxford Tavern tomorrow night, supported by Mustard.

Diverse Shifter goes vinyl
September 11, 1997

Local four-piece group Shifter cites a broad range of influences, from The Rolling Stones to The Melvins, and that diversity shows in its music.

"Some of our songs, you could class as full-on punk and then other songs are easy-going rock, or something in between," said Jamie Cleaves, Shifter's bass player.

"We all like The Melvins and we grew up on bands like AC/DC, Rolling Stones, Radio Birdman and others in our fathers' record collections."

Those influences do come out in Shifter's music, but it's not a conscious thing. They don't sit down and say "let's write a punk song", or "let's write a rock song".

"When we write songs, we don't aim to write a particular type of song," Cleaves said.

"One of us will come up with a riff and we'll build on it from there.

Friday Night at the Oxford

We're not actually trying to write to a particular style."

Aside from Cleaves, Shifter comprises guitarist Dave Kettley, vocalist Karl Weber and drummer Steve Krkovski. Those three started in a band at Corrimal High School and Cleaves joined later, replacing the original bassist.

They had been playing around town as covers band Dawn Patrol, before making the shift to Shifter about five years ago. The change happened basically because they were sick of playing someone else's songs.

"Every single covers band you see plays the same covers," Cleaves said.

"We were just getting really bored with it all and started getting keen on writing our own music."

Since then, the band has played gigs at places as far afield as Newcastle and Canberra and filled support slots for the likes of Fugazi, Tumbleweed, Toe To Toe and the Celibate Rifles.

Shifter is using those gigs to get enough money together to put out their debut release, a four-track vinyl EP. Cleaves said the band had recorded the tracks for the EP and the sound met members' high standards.

"We've done heaps of recording but we've never been happy with them," he said.

"We learn each time we do them and we get better at it."

In this day and age of CDs, a young band putting out a vinyl EP stands out as something different. And the band hopes their EP will stand out when it crosses the desks of promoters and record company execs.

"We're great vinyl lovers," he said.

"Also, there's a lot of bands putting out CDs. We know when people get all these CDs, they hardly look at them. If something comes in different, they might pick it up and have a look at it."

Shifter is at the North Gong Hotel on Saturday night with local band Second and Canberra metal band C.O.D Peace.

Glen Humphries

Rock or new punk ... it comes down to fun
September 18, 1997

Compressed Heads are one of those bands that set out to enjoy themselves a bit.

"We don't follow any sort of style, we just like to get in the garage and jam," said bassplayer and singer Michael Flanagan.

"All of us are into that, not taking it too seriously, just making it fun."

The Illawarra band has had plenty of time for fun; Flanagan, guitarist Mark Crawford and drummer Josh Kelly have been together for six years. "We've had heaps and heaps of line-up changes over the years," Flanagan said. "We were up to a five-piece and a six-piece at one stage."

Flanagan describes the band's style as a meeting of early '80s rock and the new California punk sound.

This can be heard on their new demo, *Say Mould Thing*, to be launched at their North Gong gig tomorrow night. Recorded in July, it's the band's second demo. *Say Mould Thing* has eight tracks, a lot for a demo tape.

Flanagan said the band wanted to keep costs down and offer value for money.

"We were going to try and do a CD or put it out on vinyl but thought, 'no'," he said.

"A lot of other bands around here, their CDs aren't selling, so we thought, instead of having CDs lying around our bedrooms, we'll do it cheaply ... if we can sell them for $5 or $6 for eight songs, that's a bit of a bargain."

Compressed Heads are at North Gong tomorrow night with Emmitt and Butane.

Friday Night at the Oxford

More Fugg fun for CD launch
Oct 23 1997

Nate, the drummer with Illawarra band Fugg, was the only member who didn't turn up for this interview.

That's because he's been kidnapped. At least that's what guitarist and singer Adam told me. But I think he's just mucking around. That's what Fugg does; they muck around.

They play gigs dressed up as priests, Elvis and whatever else they find in the op shop. They play songs like *(Ode To My) Erection* and *Vegetarian Nightmare*. They don't take themselves too seriously.

As far as the weird stage costume thing goes, Adam said it started kind of by accident.

"A while ago, we had shirts with 'Fugg' on them, each with one letter," he said.

"We wore them on stage a few times. People saw them and told us how whacky we were.

"I guess it just went on from there."

Adam and two other members of Team Fugg (Grant on guitars and vocals and Ronny on bass and vocals) are gathered together, not to worry about their drummer's kidnapping, but to talk about their debut CD.

After putting out a couple of demo tapes and a vinyl single with Sydney jokesters Nancy Vandal, the band has recorded a seven-track CD called *Drucked* (yes, it's a naughty word).

"We recorded something earlier this year and it wasn't up to scratch, so we saved up and did it properly," Ronny said.

"We decided to release it before Christmas, so people can buy them as presents for their parents and grandparents," Grant added.

There's plenty of reasons to get yourself a couple of *Drucked*.

Just one of these is the opening track, *Distortion Saved My Teenage Arse*, which is one of the coolest songs I've heard all year.

Other tracks like *Living With Your Mum* and *Eat Me* are pretty damned groovy too.

And pretty weird. So what inspires them to come up with this weirdness?

Ronny: "Just offbeat stuff. While everyone else is singing about love and hate, we're not."

Adam: "It's not new. Heaps of other people have done this ..."

Grant: "... but we're doing it the Fugg way!"

Any band influences?

Ronny: "We each have our own influences in the band ..."

Grant: "... and they all come together in one big influence."

Adam: "The four powers of Fugg unite!"

Any issue or topic that's just too foul for Fugg?

Ronny: "No, we're constantly delving to new depths."

Adam: "We'll pretty much take on any stupid thing."

Through the band's liaison with Nancy Vandal, Fugg has scored a number of Sydney shows.

And the shows seem to go well.

"We've never had people boo at us," Adam said.

"We've never had people walk out on us. Well, they walk out to the toilet, but they come back."

As well as playing their instruments, here's what each band member does to keep the punters coming back: Adam does guitar windmills a la Pete Townshend; Grant does the moonwalk; Ronny leaps around; and Nate sweats a lot.

For their big CD launch tomorrow night, the band were going to arrive by helicopter and play in a giant bouncing castle.

But they decided on some more conventional forms of fun.

"We're going to have after-Fugg mints that we're going to give out," Adam said.

"After each song, there's going to be a certain surprise from one of the band members."

The band won't be drawn on their planned costume for the launch, but Adam promised it would be "something the likes of which Wollongong has never seen before".

Fugg do the CD launch thing tomorrow night at the university with support bands Dinky Crash, Cult 45 and Nancy Vandal. The whole shebang kicks off at 8pm and it costs a measly $5 to get in.

Friday Night at the Oxford

Home-made, home-grown music
December 11, 1997

Steven Robinson is kinda worried about his new album, *Between the Dog and Daylight.*

See, he thinks some might find it a little depressing and that means they aren't likely to say: "a depressing CD? Wow, that'd make a great Christmas present".

Personally, I think he's being a bit hard on himself. Yes, the songs aren't sickeningly upbeat numbers, but let's face it, it can get really boring listening to Spice Girls tunes and happy pop songs about love.

Sometimes you want to hear something a little bitter, mixed in with a cynical world-view. And that's when you go searching for Steven Robinson.

Robinson is one of the best observational songwriters around and he observes his darker recesses on *Between the Dog and Daylight.*

He sees the moody feel of the album as an emotional time-capsule – it marks out where he was at that point in time.

"It was just my mood," he said.

"With me, music is a catharsis. You can't really tell people how you're feeling by saying 'I'm shitty today' but it comes out in a song.

"Once I write a song about a bad mood, I find that mood goes away."

What stops the album from being somber is Robinson's voice. He sounds like a man who knows the world is screwed but has resigned himself to working with it rather than fighting it.

Robinson admits this description is pretty close to the mark.

"Once you've beaten your head against a brick wall long enough and the brick wall hasn't shifted and your head hurts so much you have to stop, you tend to get used to the fact that the wall's there," he said.

"Having said that, at least I feel I've changed the colour of it somewhat. I've left some of my own blood on it."

Glen Humphries

The 12-track CD is Robinson's fourth effort, actually recorded over three years, in five different houses in Wollongong and Sydney, and using a four-track recorder.

"I've liked that process for these last two albums because it was good," he explained.

"I played all the instruments myself, and there's no way I could afford to record like that in a studio."

Recording at home also gives Robinson the freedom to take as much time as he needs with a song.

Asked to come up with his absolute fave on the album, he nominated *It's All In The Timing*, which takes a stab at business acumen.

"That one really does it for me, I don't know why," he said.

"It actually makes me laugh, it's very tongue-in-cheek. When I was a kid, you never had the financial report on the news.

"Ever since the '80s crash, we've had the report. We have all these financial things and it doesn't really matter."

Steven Robinson plays at the North Gong Hotel this Saturday with Scott Landers, Jordan and Andy Lawler.

Between the Dog and Daylight is available for $20 from Redback Music, Fireworks Cafe and Gallery Equinox.

Black hat gives muso The Edge
January 13, 1998

Pete Conran - sound engineer and musician

I've known Pete for at least seven years. And that whole time he was wearing this black hat, and I never knew why.

Until now.

Pete, who also is part of the way cool local band The Radio Shack Five, first wore his now-famous hat in 1989, when he was in the bushfire brigade.

Friday Night at the Oxford

As well as being "just ultimately comfortable", it was The Edge from U2 who helped Pete to wear his hat every day.

"I can remember wearing it to a party," Pete said.

"I went to the party as The Edge, wearing the hat and a black suit jacket."

Pete is now on hat number five, all of them being bought from Wollongong Bazaar for about $30.

The hatband, however, is from hat number one. The black hat is always accompanied by a dark wardrobe: black jacket, shirt, jeans etc.

Still, it's the hat that most people associate with Pete – so much so, he's been tagged "The Man With The Hat".

"It's more recognisable," he said.

"I'm also 'bloody idiot wearing black clothes in summer' but The Man With The Hat is easier to remember."

People being the way they are, Pete has been subjected to plenty of hat hassles.

"I get everything from 'nice hat' to 'nice hat'," he said.

"A fight erupted at the North Gong once after someone stole my hat and some friends tried to get it back.

"People usually try to grab it (at pubs) but I duck; because they're pissed, they can't move too quickly."

Beniuk goes UnAustralian
May 14, 1998

Inside Wollongong singer-songwriter David Beniuk's new CD *UnAustralian Folk Songs*, there's a picture of Beniuk holding an accordion. Nothing very unusual there.

What is unusual is that he's also done up in Kiss make-up; Paul Stanley's to be precise.

Now there's something unusual in that. See, Beniuk has never really expressed fondness for '70s glam metal bands. So what's the deal?

"When I was at the Wollombi Folk Festival in the Hunter last

Glen Humphries

September, it was my birthday," Beniuk said.

"I got my face painted as a birthday present. And I ended up playing my gig there with Kiss make-up. I don't think many people realised what was going on."

For the purpose of the CD, Beniuk sees the image of an accordion player with Kiss face paint as carrying the un-Australian theme of the CD, albeit in a light-hearted fashion.

The six-track CD is a little more serious, asking questions about what is happening in Australia right now: Wik and the treatment of Aborigines; the mass media's ability to shape our opinions; the continuing relevance of Anzac Day in a multicultural society; and pretty much everything the Liberal Party has done since gaining office.

While dealing with issues that affect the nation, it seems a little ironic to tag the album *UnAustralian Folk Songs*. But that's the whole point.

"The term unAustralian is being used more and more often, particularly against those who question the status quo," Beniuk said.

"Interestingly, it is used by both sides of politics, but more often by the conservative side.

"The songs on the CD question things that might make some people feel uncomfortable and they would label that kind of questioning unAustralian."

Beniuk doesn't mind that; if "Australian" means John Howard or Pauline Hanson, Beniuk's more than happy to be labelled unAustralian.

While the majority of his songs follow a political bent, there's more to the CD than that.

Australian Story, the CD's final song and probably its best, is a more intimate song, in line with his previous CD release, *Port*.

"*Australian Story* is one of the most personal songs I have ever written," he said.

"One of the reasons I put in on there was to let people know there is still a human being there; that the CD's more than just all the philosophies and ideologies."

Unlike *Port*, which was a solo effort, there's more than one human being on this CD.

Friday Night at the Oxford

Beniuk has called in plenty of people to appear on *UnAustralian Folk Songs*.

These include local band Erika's Jive, Beniuk's brothers Tim and Jonathan, the Illawarra Singers Union and pianist Peter Bull, known for his work with Paul Kelly.

Beniuk met Bull at a Weddings, Parties, Anything gig and asked if he was interested in producing the Merry Widows, a band Beniuk was in at the time. The Widows broke up but Bull didn't forget the request.

"I ran into him again years later, he said, 'I remember you. You still want me to produce that thing?'," Beniuk said.

"I got to know him a bit better and I thought I'd take a punt and ask him to play piano on the CD. He said, 'no worries,' came in and did it brilliantly."

One final thing. Keep listening at the end of the CD because there's an extra, unlisted track there called *The One*. It has been added because Beniuk wanted it out while it was still fresh.

"I've been playing it live, so it's happening for me now," he said.

"If I waited a few years to record it on another album, it might have lost its edge."

Beniuk's CD UnAustralian Folk Songs is on sale at Redback Music for $13.

Superheroes alter ego in new CD
October 29, 1998

My God, can it be? Is Fugg, the band known for cavorting onstage in superhero costumes, now throwing all that away and becoming a serious band?

Well, not exactly.

"We're still going to be jumping around with socks down our dacks," said guitarist/singer Adam.

Okay, so Fugg aren't going to give U2 a run for their money in the seriousness stakes any time soon.

But there are some changes afoot in the Fugg camp.

Glen Humphries

But first, there's a little catching up to do.

Fugg's last CD, *Drucked*, gave the guys a bit of a boost in popularity, partly through the way cool single *Distortion Saved My Teenage Arse*, written by bassist/singer Ronny.

Ronny: "JJJ played us a bit. *Rage* played our video."

Adam: "Triple M even played us. We're lucky that Jane Gazzo picked it up and played it on the Request Fest a couple of times."

Adam then chose to come clean. He admitted he was responsible for at least one of those times, when he phoned in a request as "Sean from Cronulla".

This new-found (and thoroughly deserved) popularity has helped them line up a one-week tour of Queensland and a two-week tour of Victoria.

The new improved Fugg attitude even translates to their live shows.

Ronny: "We'll still be playing the songs from the old CD, but the really old songs have been dumped."

Adam: Half the live set's still going to be the same stuff people know.

Ronny: And the new songs have the same energy, the same ...

Adam: Quirkiness.

Ronny: Yes, quirkiness.

Adam: Though we don't like calling ourselves quirky.

The new CD, *Altar Ego* (which may well see Sean from Cronulla's return) was recorded in June this year but only released now due to financial problems.

"We've borrowed heaps of money from people to bring it out," Adam said.

Hitting friends up for cash was well worth it. *Altar Ego* is great. There are a few songs that are similar to the pop-punk feel of *Drucked*, but others see Fugg trying something a little different.

The single, *Yoko O.N.O.* sounds like it's been airlifted straight from the 1960s. That track and a faster number, *Pale Edwards*, both make use of Ronny's keyboard-playing talents.

The title track sits on the fence between the old and the new Fugg. There's the old punky sound mixed with new, slightly more serious

Friday Night at the Oxford

lyrics.

Speaking of lyrics, the guys have decided to include a lyric sheet. Why?

Adam: "Well, I'm proud of my lyrics. And otherwise you can't understand what we're saying."

Whatever they're saying, it's a toss-up between Adam's *Yoko O.N.O.* and Ronny's *Pale Edwards* for best song.

Fugg release their new CD tomorrow night at the Thirroul Rex Hotel. They will be supported by Dropping Honey and Topnovil. One lucky punter will win a role in the band's new video.

It'll be a musical vote tally
March 25, 1999

Tough on rhyme – tough on the causes of rhyme.

That's the slogan of the Acoustic Tally Room, an election night party with a difference.

Illawarra musician David Beniuk is the man behind the Tally Room, an event that mixes music and politics.

Here's the facts – Beniuk, Denise Thomas from Erika's Jive, Adam Buckland from Fugg and Cicada will be sharing the stage with a big screen TV, tuned to the state election coverage.

Beniuk, who will also be the night's MC, said a close eye would be kept on the goings-on of the election.

"We don't want to miss too much of the election coverage so we'll be doing three songs in a burst, then watch the coverage, then play another three songs," he said.

"We'll be flexible enough to break it off if something interesting happens in the coverage."

The idea for the night, Beniuk admits, was lifted from British performer Billy Bragg, who does something similar on each British election.

"We're trying to bring to the election a sense of fun and comedy,"

Beniuk said.

"It's really the way an election should be treated."

This, however, does not mean raucous behaviour will be tolerated.

"We'll be taking a hardline on crime throughout the night, focusing on law and order," he said.

"We'll be having a zero tolerance stance all night ... the performers will clamp down on any bad behaviour on the night."

In an effort to beat the real election coverage to the punch, The Acoustic Tally Room will conduct an entry poll.

"Somehow I don't think the Liberals will stand much of a chance," Beniuk admitted.

"But remember to get out there and vote on the day. Unless you don't believe in the system, then stick up for your principles."

So, what's his tip for the election?

"My tip's the democratic socialists will be in government," he said.

"NSW will be the first state in Australia to have a socialist government."

We'll just see about that.

The Acoustic Tally Room is on Saturday at the Hideaway Cafe from 7pm. Dinner and show is $15 or $7 for coffee, cake and show.

Vote for a great night
November 4, 1999

No maybe about it, head to the Hideaway Cafe

This Saturday it's time to make a big decision – what do you do after you've voted in the republic referendum?

If you're smart, you'll head down to the Yes/No/Maybe Referendum Gig at the Hideaway Cafe for a night of food, music and occasional crosses to the tally room.

Musician David Beniuk will be your MC for the evening and entertainment will include We Love You Madly (featuring Denise

Friday Night at the Oxford

Thomas of Erika's Jive), Tim Ireland and Beniuk's Infotainment Lifestyle Band.

"A big-screen television will be set up and tuned into the referendum tally room," said event organiser Louisa Raft.

"That will be going all night and I'm sure we'll actually cross to some of the commentary as the results become clearer."

Raft said the idea for the referendum gig came from a similar show Beniuk organised on the night of the NSW election.

"We thought it would be great to have another night like it for the referendum," Raft said.

"Some of the discussion about the referendum has been that it's dividing the nation. We want to show that people can actually get together over the serious issues in life and have a good time doing it."

Beniuk said he would perform a song especially written for the referendum, entitled *Yes and No*. His Infotainment Lifestyle Band has been in the studio recording songs for a full-length album – due out in February – and some of those will also debut on the night.

In an effort to assist undecided voters, Beniuk and Raft offered the following advice.

Beniuk: "Find out as much as you can about it. Then, vote 'Yes' and, if you don't like the model, push for further change once it gets through."

Raft: "Look into your own heart and see how you really feel about the Queen's role in Australia. That's where the answer lies."

The Yes/No/Maybe Referendum gig is on Saturday from 7pm at the Hideaway Cafe. Appetiser, main and show costs $20. After 9pm dessert and show $12. Bookings 4229 6186.

Bound for New Zealand
December 16, 1999

Illawarra musician David Beniuk is going international with a tour of New Zealand during the New Year.

Glen Humphries

Beniuk, a guitarist and singer, will play a series of dates with his younger brother, Jonathan, on guitar and mandolin.

"Jonathan and I head to Christchurch on December 27," Beniuk said.

"Our first gig is the next night in a town called Temuka. We've got one in Oamaru the night after that, then a four-day festival over New Year's. We'll do another gig at Golden Bay on January 11."

Beniuk was first booked for the Whare Flat festival near Dunedin – the four-day festival – and then hit the phones to try to rustle up some other gigs while he and his brother were there.

"It's been an interesting and positive experiment," he said. "Of course we are trying to make the whole thing pay for itself as well."

Aside from playing a few folk songs in Edinburgh on a travelling holiday, the New Zealand shows will be the first Beniuk has played overseas. He said there was a mixture of fear and excitement about fronting up to a new audience.

"Generally I find that when you get out and about, away from the people who've seen you a hundred times before, there's an element of surprise from audiences seeing you for the first time," he said.

"You do your show as normal, but they've never seen it before or heard the songs before. The reaction is often better away from your home turf.

"In New Zealand we'll still be promoting the *UnAustralian Folk Songs* CD and the whole Australianness of it worries me a bit – I guess I'll have a lot of explanations in my song intros."

Before going across the Tasman, Beniuk will play a few gigs in Wollongong with his whole Infotainment Lifestyle Band.

As well as Jonathan on bass, the band features middle brother Tim on drums, Marco Forlano on keyboards, guitarist Pat Lyons and fiddle player Lindsay Martin.

As well as performing some old songs from Beniuk's former bands, the band will show off tracks from its forthcoming album.

Beniuk said the album should be out in late February-early March, and plans to launch it in Wollongong.

"It's finished in terms of recording," he said.

Friday Night at the Oxford

"It's been a huge project, mostly coordinated by Jonathan. I've been involved in three CDs before, but this is the first full band album I've done. It has 12 tracks. We'll mix it in late January when we get back from New Zealand."

David Beniuk and his Infotainment Lifestyle Band perform tomorrow night at the Oxford Tavern with special guest Raoul Graf, Saturday at the Excelsior in Surry Hills, and Sunday afternoon at Cooneys.

Fugg
Dragster webzine

Next time you see Fugg, you might notice something's missing. It's not the weird outfits – the guys will still be dressing up in whatever crap they dig up from the local op shops. It's not the great songs with hooks galore, they'll still be writing and playing those.

It's Adam. One of the founding members, he's decided to pull the pin and go off and do his own thing in The Dodgy World Of Adam Buckland. After five years, two cassettes, one vinyl single and two CD EPs, Adam's gone off looking for something different,

So, I guess the other guys in Fugg must be pissed off about that, huh?

'No, there's no bad feeling at all," says bassplayer Ronny. "He obviously didn't want to play with us anymore, which was fine, but the rest of us want to keep going.

"So now he's got what he wants – more creative control over what songs he's playing and who he wants to play with. We get a chance to evolve into something else."

Sure, most bands say a split is "amicable" but in this case there truly appears to be no bad blood between Adam and Fugg. Several members showed up at Adam's recent birthday party and, when Adam's first choice of bassplayer for Dodgy World fell through, Ronny agreed to take his place. And they say actions speak louder than words.

So where does this leave Fugg? After all, Adam (along with Ronny)

was one of the songwriters. What happens to those numbers? Well, Ronny says Adam's taking several tunes with him and when he leaves, the band plans to dump some of the older stuff. On top of that they're working on a bunch of new stuff. And Ronny reckons he'd be weirded out if they kept playing Adam's songs.

"It'd be harder for us to sing those songs because they're his and he's not with the band anymore." he says.

"It'd be like Gene Simmons singing all of Paul Stanley's songs."

It stands to reason the band's sound would change, what with the recent inclusion of two members – Noah on guitar and Pete on keyboards.

Ronny jokingly says the pair "wormed their way into the band". The multi-talented Noah had initially been recruited to play sax in one song but his role quickly grew. When Adam had to take some time out last year, the guys got Noah up to speed on the guitar parts so they could fulfil some upcoming gig obligations.

Pete came onboard to play the existing keyboard parts that featured in a few songs off the last CD, *Altar Ego*.

"(With those two) it definitely changes the sound for us," Ronny says.

"I haven't discussed it with Pete but I think we'll probably end up co-writing stuff. There's probably half a dozen new songs already; they all include keyboards. It'll be more of a fuller sound rather than that flat-out three-chord stuff."

So the three-chord stuff is gone forever?

"No, there's still room for three-chord stuff. And there will still be the element of fun. We're not going to get all serious and go new wave.

"It's all still light. We're not the sort of band that'll go into the doom and gloom stuff. It's always going to be happy, party-type music."

Phew. Thought for a minute they were going to go all U2 on us.

Even the kooky gear they wear onstage (including dresses, superhero costumes and revealing swimsuits) will remain a part of the band.

"When we started out, it was just a gimmick and I guess it developed from there," Ronny explains.

Friday Night at the Oxford

"Its main impact is we look like a band. You see bands around, they just don't look like they're all in the same band – they all look so different. Our costumes were a kind of unifying theme."

"And we liked doing it."

With talk of an album due out later this year, there is talk of adopting a certain costume theme for the release and sticking with it for some time, rather than changing from gig to gig.

And you can bet that outfit won't be the one they wore at Wilderfest last year.

"We had these really dense yellow plastic bags with 'contaminated waste' printed on them," Ronny remembers.

"They were really thick hot plastic, so two minutes into the first song we're all absolutely dripping with sweat. I was wearing one of the bags turned upside down over my crotch. Within a couple of minutes the bag snapped and I was standing there, freeballing."

Now, that's rock.

Pancake Day
Dragster webzine

That band of funksters known as Pancake Day has some fans in high places. That is, if you think of the band Bardot as being in a high place.

Yep, at a gig at Sydney's Hopetoun a while back, the trio was graced with the presence of a Popstar. Apparently, it's big news, says bassist and singer Amber Spence – even *Smash Hits* got a hold of the story.

So, which Popstar was it?

"It was Katie, the spunky leather-clad redhead," Spence says.

"She said she was gonna come … I didn't believe her. But, I was still as nervous as hell the whole week leading up to the gig. I even bought some new pants. I put her name on the door, but she insisted on paying.

"She is a very cool and intelligent woman, and suited the Hoey … We swapped CDs, so now I have a signed Bardot CD for my collection.

"Apparently she enjoyed the show and had a bit of a dance ... although, I haven't seen her since."

Chances are, Katie'll be back (pressing Bardot commitments notwithstanding, of course). See, Pancake Day are that sort of band – See 'em once, gotta see 'em again. It's not just their groovy funk sounds (though that's part of it, sure). It's also the fact that the guys know how to have a good time.

Live, they keep the vibe up and happy – clearly they enjoy performing and being in a band. If you need any further proof of that, try and find a photo of the band where they're not smiling or pulling a goofy face. You can't do it. Nope, there's no angsty stuff for these little campers.

The idea for the band came about during a drunken whinge in the beer garden at Wollongong's Oxford Tavern. Spence and guitarist/singer Andrew Phipps (who also goes by the nickname of Red) were bitching about not being in a band and their friends basically told them to put up or shut up.

"Both of us (were) playing guitars, we had to then go find us a singer, bass player and drummer," Spence says.

"All the singers sucked as did the bassists, the whole process being too time consuming, all we wanted to do was play music ... not run auditions. So I picked up the bass, and we both bought mics.

"The best drummer in Wollongong at the time was in a band called Ebb, we kinda nicked him. But that's okay, karma got us in the end, 'cause Tim (McAlary) is now one of the hottest drummers in Sydney (if not the country), and everyone's tryin' to nick him."

While the band formed in Wollongong, two members (Spence and McAlary) now reside in Sydney; Phipps still chooses to call the Leisure Coast home.

As far as rehearsals go, it's a very democratic system; sometimes Phipps travels north, sometimes the others travel south. Gigwise, the band has scored shows – and healthy followings – in both cities. Spence finds the two places very different, but still likeable.

"Wollongong is such an incredibly supportive and talented environment," she explains.

Friday Night at the Oxford

"I love playing the Oxford, you're always guaranteed of a good time. Sydney is a lot more unpredictable and tenacious ... which I love, it keeps you on your toes. I guess that can intimidate a lot of people."

Earlier this year, the band released the five-track EP *The Inedible Adventures of...* which showcases the band's sound well. Even the most cursory listen to that release will show up one of the band's influences – The B52s

"I love The B52s, the guys don't," Spence says.

"I've been trying to convert them, but they're just not into it. Personally, I think Red would look great with a beehive."

Okay, sure, seeing your guitarist sporting a towering beehive 'do would make for a special Pancake Day moment, but it's kinda unlikely. Besides, there are heaps of other instances that Spence considers when coming up with the favourite PD moment.

"The stacks are always memorable, we've all had many," she says.

"The Bardot experience was great for me, I don't think the boys cared too much for it though. Getting kicked in the face by psychotic stage diving kids was up there.

"But I think the best time was when I was flashed, point-blank by some drunken chick at The Oxford ... that had me laughin' for days. Oh yeah, how can we forget the Bexley. If anyone knows the Forest Inn, you'll know what I mean."

Coming up for the band are tours up the North Coast to Brisbane and later down to Melbourne and Adelaide. Also, there's the invitation to appear on a compilation CD from Aristotle's Box through Phantom. They'll be sharing CD space with the likes of Front End Loader, Muzzy Pep, george, Atticus and Smeg to name, well, five.

"We're really stoked about that," Spence says.

"I am such a fan of george, Atticus and Front End Loader, so I'm doubly stoked!!"

Before we leave the doubly stoked Spence, it's worthwhile explaining the origin of the band name. Just 'cause it's a cool story.

Spence says it comes from starving Arts student days, says Spence, where they would rely upon the graces of the Hari Krishnas for a decent meal. One day they served up pancakes instead of the usual "falafel and shit".

"It was one of the happiest moments of my life," Spence says.

Neveready
Dragster webzine

It's late and cartoon punkers Neveready are playing in Canberra.

Just about everyone, including several band members, are smashed. Girls are walking around, exposing themselves by lifting their shirts up. The band is playing the song that makes some people pull on the crankypants. But tonight, the punters love *Give Me My Ball Back You Fucking Cunt* and about 40 of them join the band onstage.

And that's when things start to get crazy. Well, crazier. The stage, made of a series of panels a metre or so off the ground, wasn't made to take the weight of 40-odd drunk moshers. Some of the panels start groaning and buckling. Then they break completely and punters start falling through the floor. But they keep moshing. And the band keeps playing. And, despite destroying the stage, the venue doesn't ban them.

Beer. Nudity. Destruction. Swearing. Fun. All the things that go into making a great Neveready show.

But it seems some people just don't get it. At least two venues have slapped bans on the Wollongong trio after hearing the aforementioned song with the infamous C-word. But the guys can't understand all the fuss over what drummer Adam describes as "an ode to backyard cricket".

"It's just a word," says guitarist Steve, who wrote the song.

"We get people coming up to us after a show going 'oh, you guys are so sexist and so offensive and you shouldn't swear so much'. If you're stupid enough to take anything we do seriously then ..." and he shakes his head.

And there's the basis of Neveready. They know what they're doing isn't brain surgery; they're just three guys out to have fun, let off a little steam and act like 12-year-olds for 45 minutes at a time.

Friday Night at the Oxford

"We're pretty fucking harmless at the end of the day ... apart from the swearing," drummer Adam explains with a smile.

Harmless or not, they can throw out some awesome songs. On their latest release, *4 + 3 = 2* (a split CD with fellow Wollongong band Topnovil), the band – which also includes bassplayer Marcus – lay down four tight, sharp, and (yes) fun tunes. *Give Me My Ball*'s there, though it goes under the title of *G.M.M.B.B.Y.F.C* and the catchy-as-all-hell *Love Song One* is there too. They even add a political tune – *Punk Rock Republic* – just to show they're about more than just dick jokes. But they still swear in that one too.

Musically, they come from the same part of town as NOFX and Blink-182. In fact, some morons have been labelling them a straight-out Blink rip-off, but the guys don't care.

"That's like telling a cricket batsman that you bat exactly like Donald Bradman," says Steve, again shaking his head.

Adam goes on to explain that Neveready sounding like those bands makes perfect sense to him.

"The way you write songs and the structure of them is definitely the way the bands you listen to would have done it. That's where you pick up a lot of ideas, about songs and chord structure."

Speaking of writing songs, one problem bands with 'funny' songs face is that, once you get the joke, there's usually stuff-all there musically to retain your interest. Neveready sidestep this problem easily – their main priority is the music.

"I never really have lyrics until the day we go to perform it live, really" Steve says.

"I'll come to rehearsal with a song, no lyrics. I'll have an idea in my head of the way the lyrics should go but no actual words or anything.

"It all comes down to necessity. You're driving the car to the gig and someone says 'you got lyrics to that song yet?'. 'Nah, hold on', and you quickly write something out."

The three guys are due to start working on a video for the song *Girlfriend's Mother* – which is about dating a girl and having her mum put the hard word on you. Clearly this song is another of those that tend to piss people off. It makes you wonder; is there anything they wouldn't sing about?

"Even if there's something a bit dodgy they're not done in an offensive way," Steve explains.

'You can tell that it's meant to be funny.

"We'd write a song about anything pretty much, if it can be funny."

"But *Punk Rock Republic*'s a serious political song," Adam interjects.

"But you wrote that," Steve replies. "I can't write political stuff. I get bored with it. I write about two lines and go 'naah, make it funny. Put some swearing in it'."

While the punters are getting into the guys' latest release, Neveready are already working on their next release.

"We've already recorded *Girlfriend's Mother* and some other songs that we're going to put on there," Steve says, "but we've got some new songs we really want to put on there."

Adam adds: "We recorded 14 tracks and then there's some others that the music's really good but the vocals are shit, so it's a matter of fixing that."

Do they hold out much hope of one day hearing their stuff on the radio?

"We're looking at a more melodic sound," Adam says, "Poppier. So we'll get played on 2DayFM."

"Or Wave FM. Wave'd be good," Steve chips in. "Wave would be as funny as. It'd be choice. Right after Phil Collins."

Lariat
Dragster webzine

There's this band in my home town of Wollongong called Lariat. And y'know, I love 'em.

I love their emopop sound – introspective moody songs mixed with rock-out numbers, all with huge hooks in 'em.

I love that they're a young band with the courage to play the occasional instrumental. I love that those instrumentals come off

Friday Night at the Oxford

brilliantly.

I love how they do that thing onstage where they move the guitars back and forth with the music. On anyone else it'd look goofy, but they make it look cool.

I love that singer/guitarist Ben wears a tie to every gig.

I love that it actually looks like they're having fun onstage.

Okay, now that I've completely blown any pretence of objectivity, here's the Lariat story.

Ben first hooked up with guitarist Grover two years ago when the pair were part of a band called Generic Bungi Cord. Never heard of 'em? That's because they only lasted one practice.

But Ben and Grover wanted to do something else. When Ben's sister Anna came to town, they signed her up on bass and then found drummer Dion through an ad ("he was the only guy that rang, and he happened to be alright," Ben says).

The foursome were aiming for the university band comp, where they finished third in their heat.

Two years later they had a bit more luck – winning the Oxford Tavern Battle of the Bands and $750 for their troubles ("that's our biggest pay cheque ever," says Anna).

"We weren't even going to go in this one, it was just a last-minute thing," Ben explains.

"There were a couple of dropouts and we decided, 'yeah alright, we'll play'. We always approach band comps like it's another way to get up onstage.

"It's hard enough to find places to get onstage. Anywhere's good."

Finding places to play should be a little easier now they're getting some notice. The *Rolling Stone Australia* website gave them a big wrap, their tracks top the indie charts at MP3.com.au and more and more people are turning up when they play live.

Much of the appeal is the band's sound, which Ben describes as "emopop"; a moody, atmospheric, sometimes sparse sound where the vocals are almost hidden inside the music instead of sitting on top of it.

"I've always been a fan of low volume vocals," Ben explains.

"It started off because I wasn't a very good singer but I've gotten a bit better.

"I've never really liked the idea of there being music and then great big vocals right over the top – like the vocals are the showcase and the music's just background stuff."

Or as Anna succinctly puts it: "vocals are just another instrument."

Much of Ben's lyrics match the emopop feel of the music too.

"It's stuff I'm thinking about, stuff that's in my mind," Ben explains.

"I think a lot of it had to do with relationships between people, and how they react to each other.

"Most of the time I like to write lyrics so the meaning is quite hidden, not really obvious at all."

A good example of that is *Bad, Evan, Good*, the opener off their CD EP *Scared of Heights*. A moody pop song with a killer chorus, it's the sort of song that makes you reach for the remote so can hear it again. And again. And again.

But nowhere in the song is a guy named Evan mentioned. So who is he?

"Well ... I get migraines and September the year before I was having all these tests done," Ben explains.

"I had to get a head scan done and they had to inject dye in me. This guy injected me in the arm and went 'oh, whoops, I'll just pull that out and put it in the vein this time'.

"I was like 'bad', 'good'," he says, pointing to the spots on his arm where the guy got it wrong, then right. "I didn't know his name. So I thought, 'what's a guy's name I like? Evan'."

But it's not actually about Evan the bad dye-injector, is it?

"What the song's about is, in the verse, repetitiveness, monotony, and the song's about trying to do something about it," Ben says.

"Then it goes into the meaningless chorus that everyone can sing," he adds with a smile.

And that CD also boasts *Kickers On*, one of the instrumentals and also the song where they do that swinging guitar thing.

"It didn't need words with it," Anna says. "We liked it as it was."

And the story behind the swinging guitar thing?

Friday Night at the Oxford

"We were just being stupid at practice and then we did it once at a gig and everyone liked it," Anna says. "But I kinda feel goofy doing it."

"I look at the other two doing it," Ben adds, "and I try and go the opposite way."

"And after the gig," Anna says, "people will come up and say 'Ben was doing it wrong'."

The band's immediate plans are to put out a new CD, either an EP or a full-length album and keep playing wherever they can.

Oh, there's one other thing I love about Lariat – they play music because they like it.

"I don't think we're ever going to make any money out of it but we're just going to keep doing it for fun," Ben says.

Dropping Honey
Dragster webzine

One of the more common adjectives used to describe Dropping Honey's music is 'dark'.

Their sound is kinda like early Cure heard through a post-Nirvana filter. Distorted guitars wash over lyrics that, at times, are hidden in the background. All up, it does create a slightly unnerving feel which suggests the band's songwriter isn't the happiest guy in the world.

And he's not – at least when he's writing songs, anyway.

"When I'm happy, I'm usually out with friends," singer/guitarist Damien Lane explains with a smile.

"The times I'm sitting down writing something are the times I'm usually not happy. If I was happy, I'd be doing something else."

But lest you think it's all doom and gloom, the band is making an effort to throw a bit of light in there too – as evidenced on their recently released EP *Underfoot*.

"People have been saying it's getting a bit poppier, and I suppose it is," he says.

"I have made a conscious effort recently to write songs that aren't

... well, there's one song on the CD that's really lighthearted. There were other songs that were better but that didn't make it (onto the CD).

"That song provides a balance and it makes me not think 'Oh God, I'm just whingeing for the whole thirty minutes'."

The band has been around – albeit in a different form – since 1997. In 1998, the line-up stabilised to Lane, Jolyon Pagett on guitar and vocals, drummer Darren Ireland and bass player David Lee.

The band's name comes from a lyric in an obscure Cure song, though the phrase apparently pops up in an Oscar Wilde poem ("that sounds more highbrow," Lane jokes).

"I just wanted something a bit more ambiguous," Lane says of the name.

"I actually came up with it for a friend. He wanted a band name, and I wasn't going to do anything to do with it, but I ended up using it myself.

"I found it a lot easier to come up with a name for someone else's band."

Taking a name from a Cure song is fairly appropriate – along with The Smiths, they're among Lane's major influences. Though he also names local musician Tim Ireland as a main influence. (Lane played drums in Ireland's band, Pounderhound, when he was just 16).

"I think that they (The Cure) influenced the songwriting and the singing more than the guitar sounds," he says.

"I got heavily into a band called My Bloody Valentine a few years ago and that's where a lot of the sound comes from."

Something else he picked up from those guys was the hard-to-hear lyrics.

"That's another thing with My Bloody Valentine, you can never hear what they're saying," he says.

"I really, really like that. It's the whole thing of leaving it open to your own interpretation, that's why we didn't print the lyrics on the CD. Also, it's a way of masking it if it's autobiographical, so you can't tell what it's about."

Partly because of that, the songs are more challenging than most. You're not going to listen to the CD and have catchy tunes jumping into

Friday Night at the Oxford

your lap. It takes a few listens, you sort of have to feel your way into the sound.

"I hope for that, I think of it as a slow burn," Lane says.

"It's good if something is immediate but I think the shelf-life is going to be too short. I just want the songs to bear repeated listening."

Also, he finds it too hard to write 'easy' songs.

"I listen to a lot of repetitive, really simple music but I don't write it," he admits.

"I think it takes a lot of talent to be able to pull repetition off. It requires more subtlety and I think I just fall back on complicated chord progressions. It's easier, in a way."

Easier or not, those chord progressions work. Their recent CD launch at the Oxford was packed and they sold a lot of CDs.

"I was astounded by how many we sold," Lane says. "I honestly expected to sell about 30."

They sold too many in fact – they pressed 100 CDs and planned to put some aside for promotional purposes. By the end of the night, all 100 were gone. But don't worry if you missed out – more are on the way. So you might have to wait a little while, big deal – the band's been waiting for the CD release since last year.

"It was strange with this release because we recorded it last September," Lane explains.

"We were really excited about it at the end of last year. Since then we've changed a lot. It's a shame we couldn't put it out earlier. Though in a way, it's good because it's been so long that I'm more objective about it."

Adam Buckland
Dragster webzine

If Adam Buckland hadn't decided to be a musician, he probably could have made a couple of bucks as a stripper.

At gigs with his new band, The Dodgy World of Adam Buckland, he makes a habit of getting his gear off during the show. He's on stage, dancing like he's getting sudden jolts of electricity delivered into the base of his spine, wearing naught but a pair of black undies. What's the deal with that? Is he a poser? Or is he trying to pull the chicks?

"I'm just trying to keep people's attention," he says, matter-of-factly.

"You need to do everything to keep people's attention. When you're at gigs, you watch maybe one or two songs and get out of there because it's too loud, or maybe you talk to a friend.

"I want people to listen to what I'm saying and to watch the whole thing and taking my clothes off is a pretty sure way of getting people's attention."

Such outlandish behaviour would probably surprise Adam's Year Five teacher who discovered his musical talent. A female classmate had just played the theme from *ET* on the school's Casiotone keyboard.

Adam, who'd never played anything up to that point, strolled up and played it note for note. That moment in the spotlight cost him dearly – his parents bought him an organ and he spent eight years chained to the damned thing.

Then, during Year 10, he found his brother's guitar in a cupboard at home.

"As soon as I picked it up I wanted to play it all the time, because it was heaps easier," he says.

"The first song I ever learned was *Blister In The Sun*. I played that through the stereo in the lounge room all night and had my mum going, 'shut up!'."

But there was a bit of a leap from playing in the lounge room at home to the stage. The first time he played live – at an Edmund Rice school talent quest – he wasn't actually playing. He didn't know the song (The Ramones' *Blitzkrieg Bop*) so his guitar wasn't plugged in. Paul, a schoolmate handled the guitar duties.

When Adam did feel comfortable enough to play the guitar for real, he pissed a few people off, namely the Brothers at Edmund Rice College. But surely he knew playing Dead Kennedys' *Kill The Poor* at a school social would create that reaction.

Friday Night at the Oxford

"They were taking photos of the whole night. One of the Brothers was the official photographer." He pauses and smiles before saying, "there wasn't one photo taken of us."

This sort of behaviour formed the basis for the confronting posture of his next two bands, Boys On Bex (for whom he wrote songs like the evocative *Shit*) and Fugg (for whom he did much of the band's initial costume shopping until being banned from op shops for trying on women's clothes).

Adam stuck with punk-popsters Fugg for five years before deciding to pull out. He says he felt the band "painted themselves into a bit of a corner" because it was difficult for them to do anything serious – the punters seemed to want the nutty Fugg, the ones who dressed up as superheroes and sung about living with your mum.

For Adam, it got to the stage where he felt uncomfortable playing his newer, more serious songs with the band. Though he sees it as a bit weird that he's the one to say 'enough'.

"Normally I'm the one taking things to the nth degree, saying 'come on, let's play, let's get going' but this time it's different," he says.

"Rather than other people saying, 'look, it's over' to me, I got sick of it, so it's good. I sort of wrung it out for as long as I could, then said 'okay, I need a break now'."

This isn't to say he wasn't happy with what he did in Fugg, far from it.

"You know how you have certain things you want to do? For me it was to play out of town, get played on radio stations, make a CD, have a film clip shown.

"We got all those things done in Fugg."

He admits to feeling "a bit weird" about the band's decision to continue without him but sees it as a chance for them to try something different, to head off in a new direction. And he'll even go see them play.

"And secretly underneath, I'll be hoping that they're crap," he says with a smile.

On his side of the fence, the plan is to get a whole bunch of his stuff recorded and put it out. And then? Well, he's not really worried.

"The way I think about it now, I don't even want to advertise it," he says.

"I just want to produce the stuff and I don't care if anyone hears it or not. If anything's worth anything, people will hear it in the end. And if it's not worth anything ... fuck, who cares? It's no big loss to music."

Somehow I think people will be listening. And watching too, especially if he keeps doing his stripping thing.

David Beniuk
Dragster webzine

David Beniuk is proof that if you've got talent and you stick it out long enough, people will notice. He's been performing his folk-rock-pop sounds for over 10 years – both as a solo performer and as a band frontman. He's played the big folk festivals like Woodford and Port Fairy and even undertaken a short New Zealand tour.

His total output is six releases (one tape, one vinyl single, two CD-EPs and two full-length CDs). They're all good, but it's his most recent one that's brought him to the attention of a lot of people.

The *Infotainment Lifestyle Album* has been drawing rave reviews all over the place, including write-ups in the *Sydney Morning Herald* (where it got four stars), *The Australian* and the Sydney stress press.

And deservedly so. The album (released on the newly formed Um & Ah label) contains a degree of the folk-rock-pop mentioned earlier, but he goes further. David takes a stab at country in *Chinese And Australian Meals* and even pulls off a low-key piano number – the achingly beautiful *A Swim In The Ocean*.

It should be mentioned he hasn't created this awesome album on his own. He's had the help of the Infotainment Lifestyle Band – Tim Beniuk on drums, Jonathan Beniuk on bass, Marco Forlano on keyboards, Lindsay Martin on fiddle and guitarist Pat Lyons.

David submitted to a *Dragster* interview to discuss what it was like having younger brother Jonathan (better known as Johnno) produce the album, how having record company support makes a difference and

Friday Night at the Oxford

why he likes working with a bunch of musicians he grew up with.

You turned over most of the responsibilities of producing the album to Johnno. Did that make much of a difference?

I think he was really up for this and really wanted to make this album. It was his first go at applying the large musical knowledge he's been developing over the past 10 years. He took the songs places I wouldn't have dreamed of without compromising them as songs, which is important to me.

On the practical side, it meant I didn't have to be there all the time and didn't have to organise the guests' times etc. On other occasions, I'd walk in and record my guitar track with a click and my vocal, go away for a few days and then hear what Jonno, Pat, Lindsay and others had done to it. What they turned *Chinese and Australian Meals* into was fantastic.

Did you find it easier to make this album after Jonno took up a lot of the musical organising and stuff, leaving you to focus on the songs?

Yes, it was definitely easier to make with all the help I got, particularly from Johnno, but also from the rest of the band. The songs were well and truly completed beforehand so it didn't really make a difference there.

I was just really lucky to receive help from a bunch of family and almost family who had kind of musically matured together, but who still worked out how to keep it sounding like one of my albums.

To me, you've always had a little trouble reconciling your pop side with your folk side, but on this album you haven't tried to be 'pop' or 'folk', you've just written the songs and not worried about what genre they are. You agree?

I think you're right about that difficulty in reconciling the two genres. We were less successful than say a Pogues or Weddings Parties Anything because we never really rocked like those bands. I put out what was basically a folk CD last time then put a six-piece band together to play it live and it always felt like we should be upping the tempo, but we didn't have the material to do so without raiding the back catalogue.

This album is probably as much a result of all that as anything else. It shows the versatility of the band but is definitely a 'band' album.

As for the genre, we didn't really care as long as it did justice to the song and we liked it. I guess it's best described as 'roots' music, maybe in a similar category to bands like Wilco. I'm expecting a few of the more traditional folk festivals to give me the brush-off, but we might score a few country festivals to make up for it.

Happy with the album?
We're really proud of this one and it's definitely the best thing we've done. There are always small things you might have done differently, but budgets (or lack of them) and unavoidable circumstances have a large hand in that.

Favourite track on the album and why?
I think *A Woman or a Gentle Man* is the best song on the album, but my favourite is *Rattus Fuscipes* because of the arrangement. It was written back in 1991 and Johnno and I have been singing it live for a long time. I think we both feel it's a special song because it features our similar sounding voices harmonising.

Johnno wrote a cello and violin backing for the album which just nails the mood. And Johnny Spillane guests on the tin whistle, and his playing always makes the hairs on the back of my neck stand up.

Any songs that were recorded but didn't make it?
Yeah, we started and even finished a few. They got canned for various reasons but might resurface in the future.

There's a diversity of styles on the album – that a conscious decision?
Not really on my part, but I think Johnno and Pat were very conscious of showing the band's diversity and keeping it interesting for

the listener. I guess the idea of infotainment and lifestyle programs is to keep flicking from story to story. The remote-control theme in the album artwork also suggests that.

Just about everyone on the album was either family or a friend. Does that make things easier?

Yes, definitely. My band have all known each other since school, apart from Lindsay. But anyone who meets Lindsay feels like they've known him since school. I can't speak for the others but, for me, making the album did feel like a kind of musical culmination to those years of playing together at various times.

Many of the songs are slightly different to their live versions (eg the violin intro in *North Shore Girls Get Off*). What was the reason for that tinkering?

Most of that happened in the mix. You can just do a hell of a lot more in the studio than you can live. You have more options for making a song sound interesting.

How'd you feel about the four-star review in the *Sydney Morning Herald*?

I'd never even been reviewed in the *Herald* before so the four stars were great. Mostly I just like honesty in reviews, rather than fence-sitting and I got that in that review.

Is it helpful to have a record company behind you, even if it's only a smallish one?

You sacrifice guaranteed income which would help you make your money back for a chance at increased sales and exposure. So you need to sell more to make your own money back. It's too early to tell whether sales will increase but the label has helped enormously with media exposure. I think the media take you more seriously when you have distribution because it means people can get hold of the albums they write about.

Glen Humphries

The band you've got is versatile, it can play electric, acoustic and even put on shows without members. How important is that to you?

It's good to be able to do a rock pub one night and a folk club the next. It gives us more options for shows and audiences. You need to be a bit flexible when you're basically a solo performer because you can't expect people to flog themselves around the countryside for your name.

Topnovil
Dragster webzine

Topnovil have got a weird thing happening in the drumming department – they've got two of them. Members Mick and DD alternate the strike – while one's playing guitar and singing, the other one's drumming. Then they swap.

Weird, huh?

No so for bassist Daim. He says the band figured everyone was getting along fine so, rather than look for a full-time drummer they brought in the Mick and DD show.

"That was the main reason, because we got along so well," he explains.

"Mick had never played drums before but we thought, well, we get along with him so it's going to work out better than getting someone in who we might not like."

"I showed him how to play a bit of drums," added DD. "He got a couple of lessons and he became a drummer."

Makes sense I guess.

Daim and DD have been in punk bands together for ages.

Topnovil started with the pair of them mucking around on guitar and drums in DD's bedroom. When Daim bought a bass they formed the band. The pair have been the nucleus of the group, watching surrounding members come and go.

The current incarnation (which includes drummer/guitarist/singer

Friday Night at the Oxford

Mick and guitarist Ray) have cranked out a split CD with punk popsters Neveready. Called *4 + 3=2* (four guys in Topnovil + three guys in Neveready = two bands. D'oh!) it includes four tracks from each band.

The idea came from the label that put the CD out – Care Factor? Zero – they're both Wollongong bands, so why not stick 'em together?

Both bands had appeared on the label's *Punk O'Clock Too* compilation but the actual link between the bands happened long before they paired up on CD.

"We met Neveready at a gig," says Daim. "Adam (Neveready's drummer) saw us play and wanted to do shows with us. We'd never seen Neveready play, he just came up to us and said 'I put on gigs, do you want to do some gigs with our band, Neveready?'. We said 'yeah'." And the connection was made.

The new release is Topnovil's second CD – the first being a self-financed effort called *Keen Like A Mule*. Both Daim and DD agree *Mule* doesn't represent the band any more.

"This new CD is more where we're heading," says DD.

"Some of the mixing and some of the songs could have been a bit better but we had to leave them, due to money and things like that. And basically, we are a punk band anyway."

Better production or not, the songs are great, especially Topnovil's opening track *Action Boy*. A frenetic tune with a killer chorus that cleverly mixes the sound of '90s punk with the late '70s version, it cries out to be played over and over again. First time I heard the album, I musta played *Action Boy* 15 times in a row.

"That one sort of came pretty quickly, actually," DD says. "Some songs take ages but that one happened pretty easily. I started the words to it and everyone wrote the music.

"It's about people always saying 'yeah, I'm gonna do this' and not doing it –just bullshitting pretty much. It's about people not getting off their arse and doing things."

Not that Topnovil have had any trouble getting off their arses. Through Care Factor and other contacts they've made, the band has been able to gig fairly regularly in Sydney and even head down to Melbourne a few times.

"The scene's a lot healthier in Melbourne." DD says.

"I don't know if there's a lot more bands down there but you see a lot more because there's a lot of venues, rather than in Wollongong or Sydney, where there's not so many."

Over the next six months, the band plan on spending a bit of time out there plugging the new CD (which sold over 200 in the first month of release) and doing one or two other things.

"Hopefully we'll be starting to record for our next release," DD says. "Maybe do a full album this time."

Clearly there's no way these guys'll be sitting on their arses.

Beniuk draws on family and friends
July 27, 2000

David Beniuk didn't look too far for people to help out on his new *Infotainment Lifestyle* album – just about everyone who appeared on the album was either a family member or a friend.

There's Beniuk's brothers Tim (drums) and Jonathan (bass), Pat Lyons (guitar), Lindsay Martin (fiddle) and Marco Forlano (keyboards). Several members had also played with Beniuk in earlier bands The Merry Widows and The Culprits.

This familiarity, far from breeding contempt, actually helped in the studio, Beniuk said.

"My band have all known each other since school, apart from Lindsay. But anyone who meets Lindsay feels like they've known him since school.

"For me, making the album did feel like a kind of musical culmination to those years of playing together at various times.

"I was just really lucky to receive help from a bunch of family and almost family who had kind of musically matured together, but who still worked out how to keep it sounding like one of my albums."

In addition to appearing on the album, younger brother Jonathan also took on the role of producer, something which made the recording

Friday Night at the Oxford

even easier.

"He took the songs places I wouldn't have dreamed of without compromising them as songs, which is important to me," Beniuk said.

"On the practical side, it meant I didn't have to be there all the time and didn't have to organise the guests' times, and so on.

"On other occasions, I'd walk in and record my guitar track and my vocal, go away for a few days and then hear what Jonno, Pat, Lindsay and others had done to it. What they turned *Chinese and Australian Meals* into was fantastic."

There's a variety of styles on the album, including country, folk, pop and even a smidge of slow funk.

"I think Johnno and Pat were very conscious of showing the band's diversity and keeping it interesting for the listener," he said.

"I guess the idea of infotainment and lifestyle programs is to keep flicking from story to story. The remote control theme in the album artwork also suggests that."

The Infotainment Lifestyle Band will launch the CD at the Oxford Tavern tomorrow night, with guests Gordo and Raoul Graf.

Jingle hell ... but it sells
February 17, 2001

Writing a jingle is a lot like writing a love song. Except with a jingle, the object of your affection is more likely to be an appliance than a person.

"We get told exactly what we have to write about, it's a challenge," Stuart Johnston from Wollongong's Advertrax said.

"Creatively, we don't have to write a song about a girl, we have to write a song about a toaster. And you've got to love that toaster, you've got to *love* it."

Johnston and his business partner Jim McCallum love a lot of things. The pair has created jingles for Marksman Homes, Warrigal Blinds, FX Larkin, Baby Zone and Tosti Cellars, to name a few.

Glen Humphries

Chances are you've probably heard at least one of their creations – McCallum estimates his voice features on about two dozen ads now on air.

And, contrary to any opinions you may have about the quality of local commercials, the pair's work is actually quite good. I'd always assumed the Marksman Homes jingle was written and recorded by a big Sydney company, so it was a surprise to discover it was recorded by these two in a Wollongong studio.

The partners have impressive pedigrees – McCallum has won a national advertising award and Johnston is a multi-instrumentalist who has toured with Tommy Emmanuel and Christine Anu.

The pair formed Advertrax two years ago but boast a combined 25 years of jingle-writing experience.

In those years, they've honed their jingle-writing to a fine art. They know there's more to a good jingle that simply loving that toaster. They know there are "rules" involved.

"You've got the first five seconds to capture a person's attention, that's all you've got," McCallum said.

"You've got to mention the client's name at least half-a-dozen times. The client likes to hear their name (and) they like to hear it in a melody and a context that appeals to the people they're trying to aim at."

"The idea of the jingle," Johnston added, "it's not about singing opera or anything, it's getting a feeling across. If the feeling and the message are there, great."

So you've got to love the toaster, grab the attention of the listener, mention the toaster-maker's name several times, have a good tune that appeals to the target market (which means a death-metal tune in a retirement home ad is a definite no-no) and ensure it has the right "feel". Oh, and there's one other very important factor. Time.

"Musically, you've got 28.4 seconds," Johnston said.

"It's like, as a writer, being told to write a story with exactly 527 words in it, but it's got to be a full story, with a beginning and an end and a context and a flow."

And how do they know when they've got all that right? When they

Friday Night at the Oxford

run into people singing the jingle.

"When somebody finds out I'm a jingle writer, they'll ask what I've done," McCallum said.

"I'll sing 'tried to tell ya' and they'll finish it – 'Tosti Cellars'.

"They know it, they know the next line. That proves to me that it works."

Leone Rogers also knows her jingles work. The Ulladulla-based writer was eating in a restaurant when the waiters discovered she'd written a certain jingle – for the rest of the evening, they came up to her, singing the tune.

Rogers' resume includes the Ice Creamery (at Kiama), Endeavour Phones, Mordek Roofing and Beechwood Homes.

She's a singing teacher fascinated by the way jingles work.

"I heard about surveys where jingles, because they're very repetitive, they are caught in your memory a lot longer than if you hear a spoken ad," Rogers said.

"I thought it was a good way to combine the musical talents that I had with the commercial world."

Her work with the Mordek commercial proved to her the effectiveness of jingles. She created the "Mordek – more for your money" tag line that's now associated with the company.

She said that, when working on a new version of the ad for the company, a TV station cut out that tag line at the end (or "tail") to make room for some extra information in the middle.

Mordek soon found that, without that tag line, people didn't "recognise" it was Mordek. The spoken information in the middle of the ad didn't register with the public the way the slogan at the end had.

"People often don't remember what they're saying," Rogers said.

"I've watched that Mordek ad for however long it's been on television, 10 years. I wouldn't know what they say in the middle, something about leaf guttering or something."

But they remember: "Mordek – more for your money."

According to Rogers, that "tail" is one of the key parts of the jingle.

"Whatever they (the clients) want to be the most prominent thing, you usually put it at the end," she said.

"With The Ice Creamery at Kiama, they said 'there's a lot of ice creameries around. We want a jingle, the other franchisees don't want a jingle. We want everyone to know that this is Kiama'. So I put at the end 'Kiama, Kiama'."

As well as being a success for the Ice Creamery, Rogers said the jingle had a flow-on effect for tourism in Kiama.

Sometimes a client may have a favourite song and want to use it, with different words, in the jingle.

Usually it's far too expensive to buy the rights to a song, so a jingle writer may be asked to create something that "alludes to that style but doesn't actually infringe on copyright".

"For instance, Merry Beach (caravan resort) wanted 'fun, fun, fun at Merry Beach'," Rogers said.

"I rang up the copyright council and said, they want 'and we'll have fun, fun, fun'.

"They said 'Stop'. Because you can't even do that because it's so easily recognisable as a Beach Boys song.

"So I put in things that were like the Beach Boys but you wouldn't think 'Oh, that's a Beach Boys song'."

Some jingles on air today sound especially designed to irritate and annoy. They make you want to stick your fingers in your ears and sing "la-la-la, I'm not listening!" Or change the channel at least.

According to Rogers, being annoying isn't the greatest sin a jingle can commit. Being forgotten is.

"If it gets annoying but they still remember it, that's fine," she said.

"As long as they remember it."

Rob Specogna from Main Street Studios agrees. Specogna has been involved in jingle-writing and production for 15 years.

He's worked on jingles for Warrigal Blinds, United Building Products, Unanderra Hardware Man and a Go Hire ad that has "been going for the best part of 15 years".

He said the "annoying jingle" tactic had worked for some businesses, including one he declined to name out of professional courtesy.

"They had an annoying voice singing but it worked very successfully

Friday Night at the Oxford

for them," he said.

"People know who they are. You've only got to look at how successful they've been. That particular jingle, as annoying as it is, must have worked.

"It sticks in people's heads and they know the name."

But being annoying doesn't figure in Specogna's three main "rules" of jingles. In his work, he aims for feel, simplicity and repetition.

"You're trying to establish a feeling about a particular place," he said.

"The music, in some ways, represents what sort of style a place might have, what sort of clientele it might hope to attract.

"Music and the way the voice sounds and the way the lyrics are worked around are trying to develop a sense of character about that particular place.

"You've only got 30 seconds, and you've got to try and capture people's attention within those 30 seconds.

"So you try and keep the message as simple as possible, so you can repeat it as many times as possible."

Specogna said there wasn't a lot of jingle-writing competition within the Illawarra, with "between two and five" companies writing in the region.

"There is stuff that gets brought in from Melbourne and Queensland," he said.

"There are two large jingle-writing companies that distribute and can arrange to give radio stations and TV stations very discounted rates for a jingle package.

"They can write a jingle, reuse the music and change the lyrics to suit a client down here or in Queensland or in Melbourne. So for one cost, they can off-load it around Australia."

Glen Humphries

Sound barrier
March 31, 2001

Okay, so it's a cliche, but there is some truth in it – it really is a long way to the top if you want to rock and roll.

"I'm sure it is," said Adam Brady, from Wollongong "cartoon punk" band Neveready, "because we're nowhere near it and we've been doing it for a while.

"When we started off we were doing shows on Tuesday nights and Wednesday nights. At least now we're doing it on Friday and Saturday nights.

"But it does take a long time and it is a long road."

And the story's pretty much the same for all Wollongong bands.

Endlessly harassing Sydney venues for a gig (where, if they pay you, it's a bonus), playing shows in front of no-one but the bar staff and the guys from the support band, boxes of unsold CDs under your bed, being in debt to your parents and friends after you borrowed the money to record that CD and trying to balance the generally heavy demands of a band with your day job.

That's right, most band members still have day jobs. For instance, all three members of Neveready work full-time; guitarist Steve Luck and bassist Marcus Taylor work as nurses in Sutherland, while drummer Brady works as a paralegal in Sydney law firm.

Which means plenty of bleary eyes in the office the day after a late-night gig and tours scheduled to coincide with holidays.

Sure, they could quit their jobs and devote all their time to the band. But then they wouldn't be able to do other important stuff, like buy food or pay rent.

"The band doesn't make any money at all," Brady explained.

"If you factor it all out, put in jamming costs and all the other costs, we'd be losing money.

"We'd lose money on every show."

Which begs the question, if you have to reach into your own pockets all the time, why do it?

Friday Night at the Oxford

"It's a lot of fun when it's good," Brady said. "It's really rewarding to see a whole lot of people jumping around and really getting into your stuff."

Ben Grounds from Wollongong's pop outfit Lariat agreed – you're not going to make money out of it, so you'd better enjoy what you're doing.

"We wouldn't be doing it if we didn't love the music," he said. "That's basically what it's all about. I've got no fantasies about making money off it."

One of the places he enjoyed playing music was the Oxford Tavern – a venue that stood out in Wollongong as being very supportive of young bands.

"The Oxford, that's why it's so great," Grounds said. "If you're a brand new band, they'll give you an early week support and you can build up from there."

Aside from The Oxford, Grounds said the only venues that booked regional bands were the University of Wollongong and Headlands Hotel.

Grounds said it had been fairly easy for the band to get a gig in Wollongong, but trying to break into Sydney is "5000 times harder", especially for an out of town band.

In the two years Lariat has been together they've played in Sydney about once a month and they lose money every time. That's because it costs the band more in petrol to get to the gig than they actually make from playing.

According to Grounds, Wollongong bands just can't guarantee they'll bring bodies through the door, and Sydney venues want a crowd. If you can't do that, then they probably won't give you enough money to make the trip a break-even proposition. And by Grounds' own admission, Lariat can't pull a crowd in Sydney just yet.

"We basically have not had a crowd when we've played in Sydney," he said.

"The last time we played in Sydney we were on with a band from the Central Coast, in a heavy metal joint on a Wednesday night at nine o'clock.

"We were literally playing to the bar staff and the other band who was on before us."

A heavy metal venue definitely doesn't suit Lariat's pop sound – but you can't knock back a gig.

One trap Wollongong bands desperate to play in Sydney can fall into is the play-for-free offer, according to Jeb Taylor of High Beam Music.

Taylor, who runs the record label/management and promotions company from his Thirroul home, said a band could be offered a gig on one condition – they don't get paid. The supposed trade-off is a chance to create some sort of profile in Sydney.

"I think there's too many bands that just agree to playing for nothing all the time, just because they want to play a show," he said.

"When you're playing for nothing there's still someone – the venue or the booker or whoever – that's taking advantage of that.

"If they're pulling a crowd, they have to make sure they are getting something out of it."

Taylor has been running High Beam Music (and getting woken up at 2am by United States promoters not aware of the time difference) for the past two years. The label has released CDs by Wollongong stoner rock act Thumlock and punk-popsters Fugg.

Taylor has found there's a good vibe out there for Wollongong bands.

"I think it shows when I've been getting some of our bands out – Thumlock have just played in Brisbane and they went down really well," he said.

"People are surprised by how good all the Wollongong bands are. Not just in a particular genre either. There's good bands across a range of music."

Like Grounds, Taylor saw The Oxford as an important part of the Wollongong scene.

"The Oxford does give money to any kind of band that plays there, when they'll go to Sydney and get nothing," he said. "The Oxford is a good breeding ground.

"It's unfortunate there's not a few more like that (because) if you

Friday Night at the Oxford

play more than once a month in the same place it gets a bit tired."

While Wollongong did have a good music scene, Taylor said it couldn't support a band forever. If a band wanted to survive, it had to get out.

"A lot of bands just get stuck in Wollongong," Taylor said. "They seem to play for a few years and then break up.

"There's been so many good bands who have done that just that, just because it is really so hard for them to get out."

One band that had a few half-chances to get out was High Beam act Fugg.

In 1997, the band's song *Distortion Saved My Teenage Arse* was getting a bit of airplay on TripleJ and one of the DJs loved the tune. So much so that she rang and left a very excited message on a band member's answering machine (that same member kept it for posterity).

The band's video was even played on the ABC's music show *Rage*.

You'd think getting airplay on a national radio station and being shown on a popular video program would make things so much easier for a Wollongong band. Well, guess again.

Being played on the radio doesn't mean a thing if you can't find the CD in the shops.

"I got pretty excited when *Distortion* got played quite a lot and I did think that was the start of bigger things," bass player Ronny Van Dyk said.

"There was a lot of things against us – we didn't have a distro (distribution) deal, for starters. So, even if people did like it from outside of Wollongong, it was really hard for them to get a disc or come to see us play, because we didn't have the infrastructure to get out and do big tours."

Van Dyk said he acknowledged that was a missed opportunity but added that it made the band – who have just released their first full-length CD – stronger.

"We're all in our late 20s or early 30s," he said. "We're all past being the excitable little boys on tour and if it doesn't go our way, we start crying and chuck it in.

"If the new album doesn't do anything, it's not the end of Fugg.

Glen Humphries

We'll keep doing it because we like doing it."

One musician who is reassessing what he does and how much time and money he spends doing it is David Beniuk.

Beniuk started out in Wollongong but moved to Sydney a few years ago for work (he's a teacher at TAFE's Contemporary Music Centre in western Sydney).

He still regularly plays in the region and has been doing so for more than 10 years; both on his own and as part of bands like The Culprits, Merry Widows and The UnAustralians.

His last CD, *The Infotainment Lifestyle Album* got great reviews from the *Sydney Morning Herald* and numerous other newspapers. But that didn't necessarily translate into big sales.

That recording was self-funded and he still hasn't got his money back yet. And it's the same story with the previous CD.

"I won't be making another album for a couple of years and the production will be nowhere near the scale of the last couple – which were relatively cheap anyway," he said.

"You get to a point where you can't keep pouring your own money into it – it has to start paying off at some point or be scaled right down.

"Last time I did it because I thought I owed it to myself to give it one last throw of the dice."

On top of his four-day-a-week music teaching job, Beniuk estimates he spends nearly two days a week working on the business side of things. Add that to the Friday and Saturday nights eaten up with gigs and that's a lot of extra hours.

"It's definitely like having two full-on jobs," he said.

"Luckily they're in the same area, but they're both full-on. Teaching isn't like working part-time in a bottle shop like I used to and being self-managed means a never-ending promo treadmill."

He also believed the Wollongong scene had changed since his days in 1990 with The Culprits.

"It was probably a bit easier (to get gigs) in those days," he said. "Bands were still the fashionable thing to do and agents actually called you."

But some things never change.

Friday Night at the Oxford

"It was always hard for Wollongong bands to break into Sydney, though," he added.

Having struggled with the music industry for more than 10 years made Beniuk well-qualified to teach the 80-odd budding musicians enrolled in the music centre. But the news isn't all bad.

"Most of them won't get signed, but that's not necessarily negative," he said.

"If they believe enough in what they're doing, I encourage them to do it themselves – that's what I did. I try to convince them that success is not about getting on a radio station too scared to play anything their advertisers don't approve of.

"Success is all about finding your place, making the music you want to make, maybe even making a living for a while."

'Dags' just out to have good time
April 19, 2001

Pancake Day does the weirdest thing onstage – its members smile.

Not for them is the moody, angst-ridden rock star pose – they're just having too much fun up there.

"Well, we're dags, we're pretty uncool," bass player and singer Amber Spence joked.

"We just have fun. There's no point going and sharing your dirty laundry with everyone.

"If you're going to have a whinge, do it at home – don't take it into the public arena.

"I just want to have a good time and I just want everyone else to have a good time. If we can do that, then that's cool."

The band's Wollongong fans will get to see their smiling faces at the Oxford Tavern tomorrow night.

With Spence and drummer Tim McAlary now living in Sydney, the band doesn't get down here as often as they'd like (guitarist and singer Andrew Phipps is still a Wollongong boy).

"We play Wollongong once every two or three months," Spence said.

"That's just the time it takes for us to get back there. We've been playing up in Sydney plenty and we're planning shows for Melbourne and up the North Coast in the next couple of months."

On top of that, the band is planning to record a follow-up to its supremely funky debut EP *The Inedible Adventures of*... later this year.

"It's just a matter of getting new songs together," she said. "We've just got to decide which ones are good."

Pancake Day plays at the Oxford Tavern tomorrow night with The Camels and 7th Freak.

Lounge music
March 14, 2002

Wollongong musician Adam Buckland has his own recording studio – it's called his lounge room.

It's where, using a 12-track recorder, he made his first CD since leaving punk-pop band Fugg.

Called *Six Distractions* and released under the name of his band The Dodgy World, Buckland has sold almost all of the small pressing run – about 120 CDs.

Now working on his follow-up CD, Buckland is happy to stay in his lounge room recording and releasing his own tunes.

"What I want to do is put out my songs as well as I can make them and just be able to afford to keep doing that every now and again," Buckland said.

"I record when the songs come to me, so they don't go stale. The first one was a test run in a way. I just made enough so hopefully I could sell them and make enough money to make another one."

Recording at home gave Buckland the freedom to experiment with songs without worrying about wasting expensive studio time.

"The next one (CD) should have been finished about five times but

Friday Night at the Oxford

it's just not ready," he said.

Buckland usually performs live with his band, The Dodgy World, which has been made up of musicians from other bands – Dropping Honey, Fugg, Gilded Kiln and The Unheard. At the moment, the line-up is; bassist Jonathan Beniuk, guitarist Pat Lyons and drummer Steve O'Brien.

Buckland is playing a show at the Hideaway Cafe in Wollongong tonight, but won't be bringing his band along – "we're just too loud".

Instead, he's playing solo, which he said allows him to do a few different things.

Adam Buckland plays at the Hideaway Cafe in Wollongong tonight.

Back with a vengeance
April 11, 2002

It's been nearly two years since Wollongong band Nabilone last appeared on stage.

One of the founding members, Nathan Burling said the band's last gig was to protest the introduction of the GST, in July 2000.

Burling did admit to a few nerves coming up to the band's gig tomorrow night but was hopeful of a big crowd.

"For this gig, I'm just going to sing," he said. "I usually play guitar as well but in the past I used to hide behind the guitar a bit and not sing as well as I should.

"It will be a bit nerve-wracking for me but it looks like a lot of our friends and a lot of people are going to come and have a look at it because they're interested in what we've been doing."

Although the band decided to take a break, Burling said it was never meant to be two years.

"I got side-tracked with building my studio," he said. "I had to delve into the technical side of things and I had to train up my computer skills and we had a lot of technical problems."

But there were musical concerns as well.

Glen Humphries

"We didn't have a drummer, so we were writing but we didn't feel we could cement anything down," he said. So we were just recording instrumental versions without drums and stockpiling them."

Now the band has a drummer: Danny Glasgow (ex of Pounderhound and the Gilded Kiln). There's also a new bass player – Naiad's Andrew Smetanin.

Together the band has been laying down demo tracks in preparation for a second CD. The band's last effort was released in 1998 but Burling has pretty much disowned that CD. To him, the way Nabilone sounds now has no relation to that 1998 release.

"It's a universe away," he said.

"It's only related in name. I would almost say we're a totally different band. We've got a really strong rhythm section now whereas before we always had bass players who were guitarists filling in on bass.

"Andrew is a solid bass player; that's his first instrument. He's really propped up our songs."

He has also added more songwriting ability to the band, on top of founders Burling and guitarist Jaylon Hall.

The new CD will feature about eight songs with plenty left over.

"Between myself, Jay and Andrew we've got a backlog of about another 15 songs," Burling said.

"That's great because in the past we may have had only eight songs in our set but now we've got a whole bunch of songs to choose from. So, at another gig we can do a totally different bunch of songs from what we're going to do this week."

Burling said songs on the CD will look at the attitude towards protest post-September 11.

He said police were breaking up peaceful environmental protests in the belief eco-terrorists were involved. As well as the music, there also will be plenty of information with the CD.

"We're going to have it chockful of a lot of really good websites and information," Burling said.

"Not just about America's foreign policy for the last 100 years but also Australia's foreign policy and how we are fitting into this whole New World Order which has come, post-September 11."

Friday Night at the Oxford

Nabilone play tomorrow night at the Oxford Tavern supported by Recliner and Hybrid Earth.

Ready for radio
April 11, 2002

For a band prone to the occasional dirty word, it's a little surprising to hear Neveready might get some commercial radio airplay.

Adam Brady, drummer of the Wollongong cartoon punk band, said i98fm was "very keen" to play their tune, *Girlfriend's Mother*.

The song is about having the mum of your girlfriend put the hard word on you (most Neveready songs tackle the tough subjects). Fortunately for the band, it's also a song with none of those nasty words radio stations hate.

But is it uncool for a punk band to be played on commercial radio?

"I've been waiting to sell out for years, so commercial radio was always the epitome of our success. The more commercial Neveready became, the better," Brady said.

"That's all a bit tongue-in-cheek but to be heard next to the Blink 182s and all that kind of stuff on the radio would be great.

"But I don't think it was ever a big focus for us."

The band also has been working on a video, but not for *Girlfriend's Mother*.

"The video is for a song called *Copper Pipe*," Brady said.

"We're going to do [*Girlfriend's Mother*] later, with someone else's money."

The band's also planning on spending some of their own money to record a few new tracks in a few weeks.

The plan is to use those songs as singles when they get around to releasing the album they recorded nearly two years ago.

Yep, two years ago. So what's the delay?

"We're still in negotiation with other people as to what's going to happen with that," Brady said.

Glen Humphries

Neveready are performing in Crown St Mall tonight as part of the Musicoz Youth project – an offshoot of Musicoz, designed to help bands find a wider audience.

"It's a matter of trying to get the young bands out to the young people," Musicoz assistant manager Rebecca Schmidt said.

Tonight's concert is a preview to the Musicoz Festival in November, which will showcase South Coast music talent.

Neveready is one of four bands performing in the Crown St Mall Amphitheatre. They are Doubled (6.45-7.10pm), Blind (7.25-7.50pm), Danielle Delaite (8.05-8.30pm) and Neveready (8.45-9.15pm). Neveready will also premiere its new video, Copper Pipe, tonight.

For more information about Musicoz, contact Rebecca Schmidt on 42271715.

Evolvers
May 16, 2002

The Cherrypickers' James Lopes is very happy with the band's latest single, *Evolution*.

"I know I've said that with the other ones but this time, I mean it," Lopes says.

His reasons for feeling proud about the single go beyond just liking the way it sounds. For him, it captures the Wollongong band as he's always wanted it to sound.

"We've gone through a few line-up changes and come close to where we wanted to be in terms of being a band but we didn't quite get there.

"Now, with the combination we have with Rob (Steffen) singing and Paul (McCarthy – guitar) doing back-up vocals and the input that they're all giving to the songs, it's pretty much where I want to be."

After several changes, the band appears to have settled on its line-up. Lopes says he believes the five-man Cherrypickers has a lot of potential.

"Usually someone comes into the band and they jell or they don't,"

Friday Night at the Oxford

he said.

"If they don't, there's no animosity, you just go, 'see you later'. But with this line-up, we're all shifting a bit to suit each other. It's great; we're all growing and changing and accommodating each other."

There's also a bonus for fans; the single includes a CD-ROM component featuring video footage of the band recording *Evolution*.

The Cherrypickers play at the Oxford Tavern on May 22.

Porcelain get their break
June 27, 2002

Wollongong band Porcelain had one of their dreams come true when two record labels starting vying for their signature.

"Yeah, that's always the aim," jokes guitarist Ben Richards, "but to have it occur is another thing altogether."

The band got the attention of several labels while performing at last year's Musicoz Challenge.

"We were chased by Sony and elected to go with an independent (Wizard Records)," he says.

"We weighed everything up in terms of what was being offered. At the end of the day we went with our gut feeling."

Since the 1970s, Wizard Records has been home to artists such as Tommy Emmanuel, Daddy Cool, Rick Springfield and Air Supply.

The band members have signed a deal with Wizard "for a couple of albums" and have been in the studio working on a debut single.

"It's been quite fantastic," Richards says.

"We went in there with the expectation of just recording a single and a few B-sides and just really got on a roll.

"Now we have almost half an album."

Richards says the likely first single will be *My Side* but no release date has been set.

"We've been in the studio every day for the last week and we'll continue to do so for a while yet," Richards says.

"When the songs are getting closer to completion then we'll be able to nail a date down."

Richards credits Wizard Records boss Robbie Porter with keeping the band relaxed and focused in the studio, and end up recording half an album's worth of tunes.

The band has released a CD before (a four-track EP) but Richards sees the work Porcelain is doing in the studio now as much more of a challenge.

"There is more on the line, it seems, because these songs will go on an album that will be put in stores everywhere and be sold," he says.

"So it's something that you're putting down for the rest of your life. There's always a little voice in the back of your head saying, 'Is this exactly how I want to put this down?'."

For one of the songs, Richards ended up recording 42 guitar tracks, due to the influence of record company boss Porter.

"When we first met Robbie, one of the first things he said was, 'I make big records'," Richards says.

"I don't think we fully understood that until we got into the studio."

Richards doesn't mind spending that long on one song. He admits he "loves it".

"I really get off on trying to achieve that level of perfection," he says.

"You just end up engrossing yourself in the music. And it inspires you to write good songs because you know you're going to hear them a hundred times in the studio."

Porcelain perform tomorrow night at Bar Broadway, Sydney. The band is organising a bus to transport Wollongong fans to and from the show. If you're interested simply email the band via their website at www.porcelainsmusic.com.

Oxford gig will honour Belinda
July 6, 2002

A group of Wollongong musicians are hoping to celebrate the life of one of their friends in music.

Friday Night at the Oxford

Belinda Deane, bass player with Wollongong band The Unheard, died on July 2 last year. To both mark the day and raise money for suicide prevention, four bands – The Unheard, Pancake Day, Bracode and Fugg – are playing at the Oxford Tavern.

The bands will be donating their fees to Centacare and Lifeline. To raise extra money, black armbands bearing the word "Hope" will be on sale for $2 and a prize pack of CDs from all the bands will be raffled off.

The night was organised by Deane's boyfriend Peter Conran – a member of Fugg.

"About two or three months ago, I thought about doing a night in memory of Belinda," Conran said.

"It'd be with all the bands she used to dance to playing. It was Rebecca Mayhew from Bracode who came up with the idea of putting together a suicide prevention fundraiser.

"There are things like Kids Helplines but there's nothing for suicide prevention for adults. Once you're over, say 23, you've either got Lifeline or the mobile treatment team."

Conran said money raised will go to Lifeline and Centacare because the organisations offer suicide prevention counselling for adults.

Despite the date of the gig falling on the first anniversary of Belinda's funeral, Conran is hoping the night is one of celebration.

"You get to the point where, rather than mourning that someone's dead, you want to celebrate that they've been alive in the first place," he said.

"If Belinda has been there, she would have had a drink and a dance. In fact, she would have danced until her joints were sore, because she had arthritis."

"She still would have had a good time."

The suicide prevention fundraiser is on at the Oxford Tavern tonight and features The Unheard, Pancake Day, Bracode and Fugg.

Glen Humphries

Hot metal
July 11, 2002

There's a reason why the fourth album from Wollongong heavy music exponents Segression is self-titled – it's where they want to be.

The first album for most bands is a self-titled effort but Segression waited until it had recorded something that represented the band.

"It takes a little while before you come up with an album you think is where you've truly started to find yourself," vocalist Chris Rand said.

"These are the building blocks for any future Segression albums. Our other albums were great and they've done really well for us; put us in a really good position.

"This album lays the foundations of what the band is all about."

While working on material for the release, the guys spent four months living in Grand Rapids, Michigan. The aim was to open their music up to new stimuli.

"It's a learning process," Rand said.

"You've got to go over there, see other parts of the world and be influenced by them.

"We had a management deal over there that enabled us to get over to the US, get acclimatised to their scene and work with some of their producers to see where we can better ourselves."

It was a smart choice – as Rand points out, the heavy music scene is much bigger in the US than in Australia.

"Over here what we get is a filtered-down version of what's over there," he said.

"You get Korn, Limp Bizkit and Linkin Park here. There's a million of them that are just as big over there. A band like Disturbed has sold between two and three million albums; over here people don't know who they are."

The Australian scene is a lot smaller – as are the sales for local bands – but it's a scene that likes what it hears on the *Segression* CD released last month.

"We haven't got exact figures but we sold close to 1000 in the first week," Rand said.

Friday Night at the Oxford

"For a metal band in this country, that's groundbreaking."

It's also pretty good for a band that releases its own CDs. The guys have had interest from record labels but said there was nothing there that interested them.

"We're not trying to make any major financial gain out of it," Rand said.

"No-one could seem to justify to me why a band should be paid $2 a CD when you can create your own label, license the CD and get $10 a CD – and you're not doing anything different."

Segression returns to Wollongong for the first time since November. The delay has been partly because they've been busy writing songs but also because they want to stay fresh.

"We wait until we're different enough so that when they come they get a whole new show."

Segression performs at the Wollongong Youth Centre tomorrow night.

'Dodgy' bit of history
July 11, 2002

The songs on The Dodgy World's new CD are a mix of the old and the new.

Some of the tunes have been kicking around for nearly a decade while others were written only last week.

Adam Buckland, the man behind The Dodgy World, wrote all five tracks on the CD, called *Stereophonic Sound* – named after the EP's title track.

"I wrote *Stereophonic Sound* about nine years ago when I was in Boys On Bex," Buckland says.

"The other two old songs on the CD would have been written about the same time as well.

"There's also two new songs on there that no-one's heard yet. It's sort of showing what The Dodgy World was to start with and exactly where it is now."

The older songs have long been live favourites, with people often asking if he was going to record them.

"I've always told them, 'no, I don't want to'," he explains.

"Now, I'm really happy with the recording of the songs. So it's like, 'okay, there's the songs. Listen to them as much as you want'."

When the older tracks were recorded in the drummer's basement a year ago, Buckland says there weren't any plans to release the recordings at the time.

"We recorded four songs on the day, just so we could have something to show for what we've done, just for ourselves," he says.

But, after spending time tinkering with the songs in his home studio, Buckland changed his mind.

"These songs were recorded a while ago and they're really good songs so it'd be a shame if nothing happened to them," he says.

"I never wanted to release *Stereophonic Sound* until it sounded really good. It's gotten to the stage now where it's as good as I can do it."

Using a home studio to work on the CD also allowed Buckland to add two fresh songs.

One of those songs was written last week and has never been played live by the band.

It's the same studio he's been using to work up a full-length album.

In fact, he had planned to release that CD next but decided to hold it back in favour of the more "accessible" *Stereophonic Sound* EP.

"I've got the full-length album ready to go but I think it would be just too much to dump down on everyone," he says.

"So I thought I'd do a five-song EP first and people who wouldn't normally listen to us might listen to it, might give us a chance.

"Then they might give the album a chance. If I laid down the album straight off people might get scared by it, because it's very complex and emotional."

Buckland is taking a hands-on approach to the EP, doing most of the work himself.

As well as recording the EP, he mixed and produced it and transferred it to CD. He's even drawn the cover artwork.

"I wanted to use the EP as a demo to make sure I can do it all

Friday Night at the Oxford

before my full album comes out," he says.

"So when I do that, it won't be such a stretch, it'll all be second nature."

Something else that isn't a stretch is the band's approach to performing.

"The guys I'm playing with now, we don't even need to practise," he admits with a little amazement.

"We've had three practices altogether and it's the best-sounding band I've been in. It's freaky, it's like playing in a band that's been around for a long time when it's only been around for the past six months."

The Dodgy World will launch its EP tomorrow night at the Oxford Tavern. The CD costs $10, will come with a poetry book called Love, Terror and Other Abstracts. There will only be a limited number of CDs available.

Band creATEs a legend
August 1, 2002

Lenard Fret and Blind Lemon are the members of ATE, but no-one has seen them play.

At least that's the story the band's Steven Robinson puts forward.

"They are real people and they're so legendary that they don't necessarily have to turn up," Steven says.

"Just the rumour that they may play is enough to draw a crowd. They have played a gig here and there. Unfortunately, the crowd missed them."

Okay, Steven it's time to come clean. Lenard and Lemon are just the creation of bored musicians trying to have a bit of fun, aren't they?

"Yeah, basically," he admits.

"I think we were bored at the professionalism of the industry. The music gets really serious but all we want to do is have a bit of fun with it."

Robinson started the band several years ago with saxophonist Harry Blatterer.

"He's still in the band, it's just that I can't find him," Robinson admits.

"He went over to Austria and played with some big American act on tour where he got paid a lot of money.

"I call him up but he doesn't return my phone calls."

To replace the absent Blatterer, Robinson has called on several friends, including Ed Lee.

"Ed and I were working on stuff years ago in a band called Jawbox in the early '90s," he says.

"So it's sort of evolved from that and we're actually doing a lot of the same stuff."

He's enjoying playing music he describes as "lounge, with a bit of soul and a bit of rhythm".

And the band's flexible line-up is in keeping with Steven's desire to keep things easy. After several years in other bands, he knows how hard it can be to get things done.

"It's just too hard to get everyone signed up to a band and to say 'these are the members and you've got to commit to this and all the money we make goes straight into the band and we'll cut an album and one day we'll be famous'.

"It doesn't seem likely at the moment that I'm going to be famous. So I'm not going to get people signing their life away and committing their whole world to something I'm just doing for fun for now."

He's having so much fun, he's even considering playing his first ever gig wearing shoes. Robinson traditionally performs barefoot, largely because he claims he always trips over guitar leads when he wears shoes.

"But I'm teaching myself to play with shoes now," he says.

"I did a rehearsal with shoes on and I managed it. I only pulled the leads out a few times.

"If I do it on Saturday, that will be my first shoe gig. I'm going for the image change – I'm going for the upmarket lounge feel."

ATE play at the Oxford Tavern on Saturday night supported by Frank's Plastic Monkey and Noah Hampson.

Friday Night at the Oxford

A new look Fugg get their act together
September 27, 2002

After taking things easy for a while, Wollongong band Fugg are going back to work.

Bass player Ronny says the five-piece act recently played their first show in Sydney in almost a year and were well-received.

Ronny says the band lost some momentum for a while; the reason why the guys hadn't much ventured out of Wollongong.

"We did have a few things in the works, gigs planned for Melbourne and other shows in Sydney that, for one reason or another, just fell through," Ronny explains.

"We kept getting excited and then disappointed and it got to the point where we weren't trying for a little while."

But things have changed – the band is now very much on the front foot.

"Over the last few months we've got some new material for a record so we're excited again," he says.

"Pete's (keyboardist Peter Conran) on the net actively pursuing shows. Noah (Hampson – guitarist) lives in Sydney most of the time and is doing some things up there to try and spread the name around a little bit and hook up some things."

The band has enough new material to record an album, though Ronny says it won't be as long as their last effort, *Art Brut*. At 14 tracks, Ronny felt that CD was a little too long.

There's also a different approach to the songs that are planned for the new CD.

"It's a different sound," he says.

"The style has changed a little bit. The last album we put out was going off on a pop tangent, getting into a bit more radio-friendly stuff.

"Most of the newer stuff has retained the melody elements but it's going to have a bit more of a rock sound, it's going to sound a bit more primitive."

But Ronny agrees the last CD did get the band's name out there and also received some good reviews.

"We got a couple of pretty good reviews in Melbourne," he says.

"Even though we did get compared to a whole range of other bands. Anything from Blur – which was a real surprise – to comments that we were somewhere between Tumbleweed and the Dead Kennedys."

Fugg perform at the Oxford Tavern tonight with SixFtHick.

Working together
October 24, 2002

Wollongong band the Flying Colours have an embarrassment of riches in the songwriting department.

All four members of the band are songwriters – they also perform their work in solo projects.

So, when a new song turns up, they all get a chance to shape it.

"So far, it's been me coming up with the main structure of most of the songs," singer and guitarist John Bowker says.

"Basically, the rest of the band bring forth an idea when we're practising. By the end of it, the song will be totally different from what I intended it to be."

Rather than feeling over-protective about his songs, Bowker is happy to have the other members of the Flying Colours finetuning his songs.

"That's the great thing about it because I've come from a band where it was me solely making all the decisions," he says.

"I was frustrated with that, having to ask for input. This is a totally mutual creative process.

"It works out for the best for everyone is really good at what they do.

"A decision can be made and it can be experimented with, tried out, used or not used. It's a very democratic process."

Nor does Bowker simply reuse the songs he wrote while in his old

Friday Night at the Oxford

band, Larynex.

"Songs I've written before with previous bands, I've just kept with the band," he says.

"We've broken up and the songs have gone with the band – they haven't carried over. So this is a totally fresh new start."

Bowker isn't the only member of the Flying Colours who has been around the traps.

Bass player Dylan Edwards was in Empty Bed while drummer Gordon Watt and guitarist Ben Waters were in Origami Paradise.

While all have solo projects as well, Watt's is worth mentioning simply because he calls himself Stud-Lee Muffin.

Bowker says the band formed last September with the aim of having a bit of fun with music.

That aim has led to the four piece recording their first CD – a three-track single.

"It's kind of raw but it captures the feel of the Flying Colours," Bowker says.

"It catches the sound quite well."

Flying Colours launches their CD at Klub 53 (formerly Chequers) tonight. The door charge is $5 and an extra fiver will get you a copy of their CD. Also performing tonight are Generic and Adam Buckland.

Music haven on High Beam
October 31, 2002

Wombarra's not the sort of place you'd think of if you were looking for a record label.

But there's one there – has been since 1999. That's when Jeb Taylor got together with Wollongong rock band Thumlock to release their debut EP, *Lunar Mountain Sunrise* on a label called High Beam Music.

Since then, the label has put out 24 releases – including several singles and EPs.

Taylor, who's been forced to adopt the title of "general manager", says he looks after most of the day-to-day business of the label himself.

He has an employee who helps with publicity and a business partner based in Sydney who tends to look after their bands while in the studio.

Starting up High Beam Music was a gradual thing. From the front office in his Wombarra home, with a nice view of the ocean, Taylor explains that the label sprang from a webzine he started up. Unemployed and having discovered the internet not too long before, Taylor started his online zine, High Beam, featuring band interviews and reviews.

From contacts he made overseas, he started acting as the Australian distributor for several smaller labels.

The next big step was taken in July 1999 when he released that Thumlock EP.

"There was no real intention to start (the label)," Taylor says.

"It was just something I decided to do on the spur of the moment.

"I kind of realised that kind of sound could sell a decent amount, especially overseas."

That sound is something that could be tagged Stoner Rock. Taylor simply refers to the bands on his label as "rock" and the range of bands has diversified since the early days.

High Beam has released, or is about to release, CDs from a number of Wollongong acts – Thumlock, Fugg, Monstrous Blues, El Sanchez, Hee-Haw and Shifter.

On top of that, Taylor's label has put out CDs by bands from Canberra, Melbourne, London, California and Buenos Aires.

The label's most recent release is *High Beam...Volume 1*, a compilation CD featuring tracks from bands that have recorded for the label.

Even though it's the newest release, it still bears a catalogue number of HBM002 – implying it was the label's second release.

Taylor has an explanation for this apparent piece of time travel.

"When we first started the label, we were going to do a compilation with a few bands but it never eventuated," he says.

"That was the catalogue number it had and that number was never filled.

"So we went back and filled it up, because there was this gap and

Friday Night at the Oxford

people kept asking us what it was."

Like any other record company, High Beam has signed contracts with each band, but the deals are only ever for one release at a time. The reason for that is simple – if a major label shows interest in a band, he doesn't want to get in their way.

"It's really hard to compete with the big label's money," Taylor says.

"I don't want to be holding a band to a contract where they're getting a few thousand dollars to record when there's a big label wanting to give them hundreds of thousands."

When he started out, Taylor says he never had to work hard to convince a band to release an album with High Beam.

"There was always heaps of them queuing up," he admits.

"There wasn't a lot of independent labels around at that time. It came out of that time in the early '90s where they all got bought out and disappeared for a while."

Taylor admits that, as a teenager he used to read liner notes on albums, check the inner grooves near the record label to see if any messages had been scrawled in the wax before it set (a fairly common practice with independent bands in the vinyl era).

The teenaged Taylor also knew most of those independent labels and, while he wanted to work in the music industry, he didn't even consider creating his own label.

"I always wanted to work in the music industry but when I was at school I was thinking of doing sound or that kind of thing," he says.

"Somehow it kind of changed to this side of things. I suppose, when you're younger, you don't realise there's this side of the music industry – people writing reviews, people running record labels.

"All you see is the musician onstage and maybe the sound guy. Once you actually get into it a bit, it all opens up, and you see exactly what's there."

One of the things he knew before he started High Beam Music was that there was a segment of the marketplace who wanted some rock but actually had to go out and look for it. And that included himself.

"At that time the sound was pretty underground," he says.

"There was still a lot of people and it was easy to find.

"There was a market there for a certain kind of sound. At that time the rock thing was pretty dead – it's coming back a bit now – but at that point the charts were full of really bad disco techno and novelty songs.

"I think that's why rock's back now - people are sick of hearing Bob The Builder."

This doesn't mean to suggest that High Beam releases ship as many units as the infamous Bob The Builder. Taylor says the label's biggest seller was Thumlock's first album *Emerald Liquid Odyssey*.

That sold around 3000 copies – sure it doesn't sound like much but, for an independent label without bucket loads of cash to spend on promotion, it's an impressive amount.

Even more so when you consider the label only needs to sell about 800 copies to break even.

Still, those sales aren't enough for Taylor to make a living out of the record label and any money it does make goes straight back into the label.

Financially speaking, he makes most of his money from the online store that runs on the same website as the label (www.highbeammusic.com). As well as selling High Beam releases, Taylor is still acting as the Australian distributor for a number of overseas labels.

"It's like having a record shop really," he says.

For a lot of stuff, the online store is pretty much the only place here you'll find it. There's probably two or three other shops around the place that'll sell it.

"With the online store, the interest comes through the record label. Without the record label, just trying to run the mail order thing just wouldn't work.

"But (the label) is pretty much for enjoyment – with the hours I have to put in, I could probably go and make a lot of money elsewhere – but it does excite me and it's something I like doing."

Taylor's a quiet guy and, when asked if he thinks his label changed the Wollongong music scene, he pauses for a short while.

Then he decides on the label's greatest achievement – it showed bands what was possible.

Friday Night at the Oxford

"I think there's a lot of bands that wouldn't still be going," he says.

"The shows did pick up when the label started, maybe not so much because of the label but because of some of the bands like Thumlock getting out and touring around and getting overseas recognition.

"From there a lot of other bands decided 'oh, we can still do it' and started playing again, taking it a bit more seriously."

Lone arranger
November 7, 2002

For a brief while it sounded like activist rock band Nabilone had softened up.

Singer Nathan Burling was running through the themes that will be covered on the band's new CD – due out early next year.

There's veganism ("our favourite one," Burling jokes), the technology of genetic modification and social change.

"There might even be one on personal relationships on this album," he says.

What, like a love song?

"Well, I don't know if I'd go that far," Burling says with a laugh.

That song (which isn't a love song) will be one of the tunes the band is working up for the next CD, due to be recorded in December.

"We've got six songs at the moment – they're the only ones we're playing at gigs," Burling says.

"We've got newer songs that aren't as well developed, so we decided to focus on those six songs."

Burling says there is too much cost and expectation involved in a full-length CD, which is why the band has opted to release an EP.

"We decided to stay analog (rather than recording digitally), so we've got the additional cost of having to buy the reels," he says.

"That means we've only got 45 minutes of reel time. Our songs are a fair bit longer than most, so for us, six songs are about 45 minutes anyway.

"It's sort of like a mini-album but we'll be marketing it as an EP."

The band played its first gig in April this year after nearly two years off the scene. Most of the songs that will appear on the CD have been part of the band's repertoire since its return.

But it might end up with a different sound on CD.

"There's been a bit of finetuning – we're looking at the beginnings and endings of songs," he says.

"We're basically deconstructing them, so when we get in the studio, we know what we're doing.

"We've recorded these songs a fair bit just on my computer, so we have been listening to those recordings and finding the versions that we like and focusing on those.

"With some of these songs in the past, we have probably had a few different ways that we would play them.

"Now we're just trying to consolidate them."

Something else Burling is doing is getting used to just singing. Previously he was playing guitar and singing but has decided to limit himself to microphone duties.

"It's pretty much stabilised now – I think we'll just have the one guitar, the bass and drums and me singing," he says.

"It makes things a lot less stressful for me.

"I'm feeling a bit more comfortable with it. In the past I'd be playing guitar half as well as I should and singing half as well as I should be."

Now that he's singing for the band, he realises just how difficult long instrumental bits can be for a frontman.

"Well, I feel I have to sing a bit more, otherwise I'm just standing up there looking like an idiot," he says.

Nabilone play at the Oxford Tavern tomorrow with the Hard-Ons.

Friday Night at the Oxford

Lucky for some
December 12, 2002

It's fortunate that Hee Haw frontman Lax Charisma doesn't have a problem with the number 13.

The band's song, *Famous Last Words*, was track 13 on a recent compilation put out by High Beam Music, their record label.

Their debut EP, *How to Pay Your Debts When You're a Genius*, bears the catalogue number of 013.

Finally, the band's CD launch is tomorrow night – Friday the 13th.

"It's like a cheesy superstitious fear," Charisma says.

"It's funny because it's always been considered an unlucky number but, as long as I can remember, it's brought me good luck.

"I tend to find certain things seem to line up for me around the 13th. It's unexplainable. I stopped wondering about it a while ago and just accepted it."

Hee Haw formed last year and have gone on to support acts like The Zoobombs and Nunchukka Superfly. Their first single, *Famous Last Words*, has already received airplay on Triple J and the accompanying video will soon be seen on *Rage*.

Filmed at Wollongong's Regent Cinema, Charisma says it's largely a performance video with "all sorts of strange things in it".

Charisma says he found the title of the EP while doing a creative writing course at Wollongong University.

Fascinated with the works of 19th century French poet Charles Baudelaire, he discovered an essay he'd written called 'How to Pay Your Debts When You're a Genius' and thought it'd make a fantastic title.

"These were guys who were writing incredible work but they all ended up dying young and quite tragically," he says.

"The same thing could be applied to people I was musically inspired by, like Ian Curtis from Joy Division and Kurt Cobain.

"All these guys created this brilliant art and then died."

Joy Division and Nirvana are two of the bands mentioned when describing Hee Haw's music. The Birthday Party and Big Black are also up there.

Glen Humphries

It's music with a dark, moody feel, laid under vocals that suggest the songwriter isn't feeling too happy.

Charisma, the band's lyricist, agrees with that assessment.

"I guess there's a fair amount of that sort of feeling about the songs," he says.

"I guess if I was happier about things, the songs wouldn't be so dark but at this point in time, that's what's going through my head, that's how I feel.

"Once it's committed to paper, CD or whatever, it's not in my head anymore. I don't have to deal with it."

And there's another upside to writing dark lyrics.

"People seem to like listening to it and that becomes the fun thing – playing it live and seeing people thinking, 'this is fantastic'," he says.

Hee Haw launch their CD How to Pay Your Debts When You're a Genius at Klub 53 (rooftop Piccadilly) tomorrow night. Support bands are Obsidian and Sh'Mantra. Entry is $5.

Pumping up the volume
December 19, 2002

The next release from Wollongong band Dropping Honey is going to be loud.

That's the word from singer-guitarist Damien Lane.

The band's last release, a mini-LP called *Snakes and Ladders*, has almost sold its entire pressing of 1000 copies since its release in November 2001.

Not a bad effort for an independently released CD. But Lane is planning to refine the *Snakes and Ladders* sound for the new EP, planned to be out in March or April.

"I think concentrating on four or five songs and knowing exactly how we're going to do them, rather than experimenting with eight will result in a more succinct statement," Lane says.

Friday Night at the Oxford

As well as succinct, it seems the new release will have a harder sound than the band's previous efforts.

"It's going to be a lot crazier sounding," he says.

"The more mellow moments will still be there, but there will be more full-on loud guitars happening. That's just the way the songs came out. There are some pretty blistering parts in them."

Lane says he wants to focus on the rockier side of their sound, to try and transfer the live feel onto CD.

"I just wanted to be able to translate the way we can get them to sound live onto disc, which I don't think we've done particularly well before," he says.

"I think the quieter stuff we've done in the past has come out pretty well but some of the rockier stuff doesn't have quite the impact recorded as it does live."

Early next year, they'll be taking that live sound on the road, playing a show in Brisbane with Giants of Science.

It's the second time they've played in the Queensland capital and Lane is looking forward to returning.

"We were astounded by the reception we got in Brisbane last time," he says.

"The scene seems to be a lot healthier there than it is in Sydney. There are still a lot of punters there who are still excited about seeing live music."

There's a plus for Lane as well. Most of the band's shows are in Wollongong or Sydney where a lot of the people in the crowd know him.

In Brisbane, however, there's a degree of anonymity which agrees with him.

"It's more relaxing and easier to perform in front of a group of people I've never seen before and am not likely to meet again," he says.

Dropping Honey play at Klub 53 (rooftop car park at Piccadilly) tonight supported by Generic and The Peppertones.

Glen Humphries

Illawarra musos band together for Christmas
December 19, 2002

Wollongong bands have found the festive spirit on a limited-edition CD.

Called *Bah Humbug*, the CD features Christmas-related tunes from 11 Illawarra acts, including Ludo, Stud Lee Muffin, The Dodgy World and Golgotha Method.

The idea for the project came from Oxford Tavern booking agent Alby Fares and Headjam Music's Wez Smith.

"It was only about two months ago – in the last week of October," Fares says.

"Wez and I were having a meeting. We had a date (in December) and didn't have anything for it. So we were trying to work out something to do.

"I thought, why don't we put together a compilation of local acts? It'll be a bit of fun and so we went for it.

"Basically in the space of six weeks, we put the whole thing together. We recorded half the bands and half the bands did it on their own."

Half of the bands recorded their Christmas tune downstairs in Fares' house over an eight-hour period.

So there was a line-up of bands hanging around waiting to record.

"The bands were sitting around the pool having a chat," he says.

"It was interesting because we had folky artists hanging out with the metal guys.

"It was bringing all the bands together around the barbecue having a few beers.

"It was interesting to see the different groups and musicians that don't usually hang together, all in one place and having a good time."

All-up, Fares says around 20 bands and artists were approached to contribute a song and every one that was submitted made the CD.

"The brief was to come up with a song about the festive Christmas summer season in Australia," Fares says.

"We were looking for something that was summery, something you

Friday Night at the Oxford

can put on and sit by the pool and have a beer.

"Most of the stuff we get on Christmas albums are songs like *White Christmas* – it's very northern-hemisphere oriented.

"This one is Australian – and it's Wollongong."

The CD is limited to 200 copies and will be available at the CD launch, or from project sponsors the Oxford Tavern and CD Revolution in Crown St.

The Bah Humbug Christmas CD will be launched at the Oxford Tavern this Saturday from 7.30pm. Performers on the night are Brackish, Patrick Arnold, Stud Lee Muffin, Lady, Doubled and Tania Nichamin.

Out of the blue
February 13, 2003

The Monstrous Blues play a lot of different styles of music.

But blues isn't one of them.

"We did think that when we chose that name that we'd have all these people rocking up to gigs coming to see a blues band," says drummer Steve O'Brien.

"We did have one guy turn up – he was a bit disappointed – but he hung around."

The name was inspired by The Beatles film *Yellow Submarine*. The animated film includes characters called the Blue Meanies – their original name was to be the Monstrous Blues but it was deemed too scary and they changed it.

The styles the band *does* play – and which are evident on their new 14-track CD *Colourblind* – include punk, garage, pop, metal and psychedelia.

O'Brien says the band doesn't bother to rigidly adhere to one style of music, figuring there's much to be learnt from different styles.

"We're over trying to be a certain type of music," he says.

"We listen to anything and everything these days.

"Years ago I was in a '60s garage band. We had to play '60s garage and nothing else. We wouldn't even go as far as the '60s psychedelic side of it.

"Now I've opened my ears a bit more and learnt there are a lot more types of music. Of all the bands that I wanted to see at the Big Day Out this year, Wilco was the highlight for me – and they're like a country-pop band."

For The Monstrous Blues, there's no conscious decision to write songs in a certain style – it just works out that way.

"The way the songs come together, they're not planned out," he says.

"We usually jam on things and something comes out of it. Sometimes we're making a mockery of ourselves, literally, and something comes out and we think 'oh, that's not bad. We should use that'."

As far as the new CD goes, O'Brien's only wish is that it had come out sooner.

"We actually started recording it about a year ago and our bass player went to America for a bit, which didn't help," he says.

"Then we just had a few problems with [the] finances of it, things like that. We were just sitting around for four or five months not being able to do anything with it.

"It was all recorded, apart from the vocals, and it was just sitting there for a long time."

While the wait might have been a bit long for Monstrous Blues fans, they're actually getting a little more than the band first planned.

"We originally had the idea that it was just going to be a strong EP, then because it was so long it changed into an album," O'Brien says.

"We recorded the drums in one day and realised there was already nearly 40 minutes worth on there.

"Then we went back in the next day and put down a few more songs and thought we might as well just make it an album."

The Monstrous Blues launch the Colourblind CD at the Oxford Tavern on February 22.

Friday Night at the Oxford

Live and kicking
April 10, 2003

Music is a contact sport for Wollongong band Rockafella.

The flat-out rock and roll band regularly breaks equipment during their raucous live shows.

On at least one occasion the damage extended to the lead singer – who goes by the moniker of The Reverend.

"My brother clashed with the guitar, right across the top of his nose and split it open," bassplayer Andy Simpson says.

Considering their no-holds-barred approach to live shows, it's a little surprising that there haven't been more injuries.

"With our shows they're fairly insane," he says.

The band's sound is loud and dirty garage rock – a similar sound to the likes of the Datsuns and the D4.

But Simpson says it was never a conscious decision on the band's part to copy that sound.

"It's a total coincidence," he says.

"The two guitarists, Jake (Dignam) and Luke (Nolan), write most of the music and they've been into that stuff from day one. A lot of the songs had been written four or five years ago when the boys were in other bands.

"We started playing that stuff and all of a sudden all these bands start coming out. We were like, 'far out. We didn't see this coming'."

Despite being together for close to two years, the band has just released its first CD, a four-track self-titled EP.

They had been in the studio before but weren't happy with the results. "We had a crappy eight-track recording that we did in a rehearsal studio really early on," Simpson says.

"The recording's crap but the energy on it was just explosive. After we did our first recording, we were like, 'man, I'd rather release this crappy eight-track recording than this polished studio recording'.

"So I thought we had to try and capture that in a proper studio environment."

Which is why they ditched the idea of recording each instrument separately in favour of just playing live.

"We went into the studio and said, 'let's just play. Let's just do what we do onstage and see how it comes out on tape'," Simpson says.

Rockafella launch their EP at Woonona Bowls Club on Thursday, April 17.

Fugg goes mental
April 17, 2003

Wollongong's Fugg had a big break on a quiet Thursday night at the Bat and Ball Hotel in Sydney last November.

They were playing to about 40 people. Five of those people were Mental As Anything, who'd stopped off for a beer.

"It was just a fun show," bassplayer Ronny Van Dyk says.

"We felt no need to put on an extra-good show because famous people were there. If we knew they were there, we probably would have been stressed."

It wasn't long before the band found out about its famous audience.

"Just a couple of days after the gig, we just got this phone call out of the blue," Van Dyk says.

"They said, 'we all really loved your band and can we do something together'."

That something ended up being a chance to record at the Mentals' Annandale studio and a whole bunch of support slots with the band.

Fugg has been in the studio since early February working on a 14-track album to be called *No Left Turn Unstoned*.

"It's a whole new level of recording for us," Van Dyk says.

"They spent more time recording just the drums than we've ever spent recording a whole album.

"Because there's no time constraints due to financial reasons like 'you have to be out of here by six', we're taking as long as it takes until everyone's happy."

Van Dyk admits the band's last album, *Art Brut* wasn't as good as

Friday Night at the Oxford

he would have liked but feels the upcoming release will be much better.

"I think possibly last time the problem was that a lot of the songs we had were new and hadn't had a chance to mature," he says.

"With that album, while I still like the songs that are on it, I think we were in a rush to get something out at that time."

The album includes 11 new songs, one song each from their last three releases (*Distortion Saved My Teenage Arse*, *Pale Edwards* and *Lost a Friend*) and a cover of the Go-Go's *We Got The Beat*.

All this sprang from that one phone call – but even if nothing had happened, Van Dyk would have still been happy.

"If they made the call and said all those things but nothing ever really came of it, I still would have been pretty happy that they bothered calling," he says.

"When they made the offer, I thought, great but I wasn't getting too excited because we've had plenty of opportunities in the past that have fallen through for one reason or another."

But not this time – the band's new album is likely to be released by June.

Fugg perform at the Oxford Tavern on Easter Sunday supported by Laura Imbruglia (yes, she's Natalie's little sister), Abe and Richie and The Creeps. Fugg also supports Mental As Anything at the Palm Court Hotel on May 3.

Monstrous summer
September 19, 2003

It's shaping up to be a great summer for The Monstrous Blues.

As guitarist Paul Hausmeister puts it, "there's a tonne of stuff coming out over summer".

Firstly, the Wollongong band is releasing a single from its *Colourblind* album. Perhaps unsurprisingly, that single is *This is the Summer*.

As well as the title track, Hausmeister says the plan is to also have

Glen Humphries

a few live tracks and two video clips on the single.

Next, there's a bunch of videos and DVDs due for a summer release, including some with Monstrous Blues' tracks.

"There's the surf videos and a few extreme videos as well, like FMX – freestyle motocross – and extreme skate videos."

There are a few surfers in the band, but motocross riders and extreme skaters are very thin on the ground.

The band got this opportunity because all the videos and DVDs are put together by one guy.

"As far as I know, he's sponsored by Billabong and a few of the other skate companies," Hausmeister says.

"They ask him to go out and put together videos of all the different extreme stuff.

"It's his call as to what he wants to put in these films, as far as footage is concerned, and it's his decision with the music.

"We were lucky enough for him to get a hold of the album and he just ended up emailing us and said, 'Dig the album. I'd like to use a bunch of stuff off the album for the DVDs. How about it?'

"We just said, 'Let's do it'."

But wait, there's more. The Blues' sounds will also appear on *Kore TV*, an extreme surf and skate show, on SC Ten over summer.

With all that coming up, it's easy to forget that the band did a live set on Triple J's *Home and Hosed* a few weeks ago.

The guys travelled up and recorded five live tracks, then waited a week or two to hear themselves on the radio.

"My stereo blew up about two weeks before it was on," Hausmeister says.

"All I had was a little trannie radio to listen to, so I didn't really get much in the way of a decent sound.

"By all accounts, it ended up sounding pretty cool. I've run into quite a few people who heard it; nobody's said anything bad about it."

The Monstrous Blues play at the Oxford Tavern on Friday and Bulli PCYC on Saturday.

Friday Night at the Oxford

Happy move
April 24, 2003

Wollongong can take a little credit for the success of Machine Translations' *Happy* album. It was recorded here.

Machine Translations – which is the work of one J Walker – features sounds from computers, animals, sound loops and traditional instruments.

Walker recorded the last album in a tiny house in Wombarra and tracks have been played regularly on Triple J.

He's since moved to Melbourne because it has probably the best live scene in Australia. But he doesn't want you to think leaving the South Coast behind was easy.

"I'd had it in my mind to move to Melbourne for a long time but it took about five years to bite the bullet and do it," Walker says.

"Part of me still would really like to be up there and be surfing and swimming and doing all that kind of stuff.

"My strategy is to be down here for a year or two and just try to establish myself a bit more in the music industry and then hopefully come back."

There are also the sounds of the Illawarra on *Happy*. Walker stuck a microphone out the window at night and recorded bird and insect noises, cut them up and used them on the album.

After recording albums at home since 1997, Walker is happy he's cracked it with *Happy*.

"I feel like I've kind of earned the extra airplay and stuff just because I've been plugging away at it for so long."

The success is also is a form of justification for the path he has chosen.

"When you're at home doing your thing, you feel like you're in this tiny little bubble," he says.

"After all of that time you start to question your own sanity a bit.

"So, when it does get a good response, you kind of think, 'I wasn't going completely mad'. Maybe I was, but I was going mad in the right way."

Walker covers a wide range of territory on his albums including traditional Chinese poetry, slow '80's Oz rock, and Latin-American rhythms. It's an eclectic mix that pleases Walker.

"A lot of records made have that uniform sound to them, but I find that a bit boring in my own stuff," he says. "I like records that have a fair bit of variety in them, that take you on a real journey, and that's what I try to do on my stuff."

Machine Translations performs on Saturday at the Oxford Tavern, Wollongong.

Sound of the street
April 24, 2003

A new magazine aims to fill the gap in the Illawarra street press scene.

In the past, the region has been well served by the likes of *Bulb* magazine, but when that disappeared some years ago there was a bit of a void.

Now *Illawarra Sound(s)* has rolled off the presses – a creation of the Thirroul Youth Project.

Including band interviews, CD reviews and a little history of the Wollongong music scene the magazine is looked after by a committee of young people led by Thirroul Neighbourhood Centre youth worker Rob Carr.

Carr has played in a few Wollongong bands – at the moment he is part of Phial.

Considering many of the bands in the Wollongong music scene include young people, Carr saw the magazine as a way to help both them and the scene.

"The guys (on the committee) wanted something so we could promote gigs and local bands, particularly all-ages gigs and young bands," Carr says.

Friday Night at the Oxford

He believes there was a need for such a magazine in the music scene.

"I've been in the music scene for a while down here," Carr says.

"Some people that I know reckon that, after *Bulb* magazine died out a few years ago, there hasn't been anything like this come out.

"Of late there's only been a newsletter called *Omusic* and that came out about the same time we put out our first edition.

"I think a press is essential to any music scene. Newcastle's got its own, so has Melbourne. Sydney's got *The Drum* and I think Wollongong deserves its own magazine. A magazine that provides a view or a spin on a particular regional sound and attitude," Carr says.

Banding together
May 1, 2003

There's a new voice in the South Coast music scene – and it's on the internet.

Nathaniel Sullivan started up wollongongmusicscene.com a month ago.

The site includes a gig guide and reviews, band profiles and a history of the music scene in the area. There's also the chance to hear some mp3s from Wollongong bands.

Sullivan created and runs the site himself – though he has someone helping out with reviews.

He started the site after talking to several Illawarra bands.

"I know most of the local bands around here," Sullivan says.

"They were all saying, 'we need more promotion', so I decided to start this website, seeing as how I know most of the bands.

"I thought I'd get it up and running and see what happens.

"I'd thought about it for a few months. I thought we just need all the Wollongong bands to get together. There was just heaps of Wollongong bands hating each other's guts instead of trying to help each other out."

Sullivan figures that maybe these bands will get to know each other with the help of the website and actually talk to each other – even if they play different styles of music.

Sullivan is in several bands himself, including Golgutha Method and Undertow, so he knows how difficult it can be for a small band to get noticed.

He says the only criteria a band has to fill to appear on the site is they have to be from the Illawarra.

It doesn't matter whether it's a new band or an established act or even whether or not Sullivan himself likes them.

Even though it's only early days for the site, it's already proving popular.

"We've had over 5000 hits in the first three weeks," he says.

"The message board gets about five or six new members every day."

Some of them are even out-of-towners.

"We've got a few people from Newcastle," he says.

"That's the only people from out of the area because I haven't done much promotion out of the area yet.

"I thought it'd just be local bands who were interested but there's also a lot of people who aren't in bands but just like local music."

Rockin' for a cause
May 15, 2003

Wollongong bands are doing their bit to help keep 2VOX FM on the air.

Four bands – Cikim, Red Star Studios, Countersunk and Faded Underground – are performing at the Oxford Tavern as a fundraiser for the community radio station.

Show organiser Tristram Baumber said the bands were donating their payment for the night to the station.

Entry on the night is free but people can support 2VOX by buying a ticket which gives them a chance to win a range of prizes.

Baumber said the bands were always keen to help the station that

Friday Night at the Oxford

has helped them.

"As soon as we mentioned it was for 2VOX, they all were happy to do it," Baumber says.

"I'd go so far as to say every band in Wollongong is connected to VOX in some way. They all come in and talk to the different shows and there are a few shows that do that.

"The biggest one would be the Australian Independent Music Show. I do the show before that one and I always see the bands coming in."

Baumber's show is *Sleeping At Grandma's* – on Monday nights – so he's quite aware of the constant difficulties in which VOX finds itself.

"It always gets by on the skin of its teeth," he said.

"There's almost no government funding for it, so almost all the money that it has is raised by the fundraising committee through different initiatives, and this is just one of them.

"We're always trying to get out there and promote the station and raise money."

The main fundraisers are a radiothon where listeners pledge donations and a massive garage sale.

This is the second time there's been a benefit night at the Oxford – the first one in July 2001 went gangbusters.

"We just thought, 'let's put on some bands at the Oxford and they can pay us rather than pay the bands and we'll run a raffle as well'," Baumber says.

"It ended up being really successful so we decided to do it again."

The 2VOX FM (106.9 FM) benefit show is on at the Oxford Tavern tomorrow night. Admission is free.

Ripe for the picking
May 29, 2003

Next month, Wollongong band the Cherrypickers will perform in three countries in little over a week.

Glen Humphries

The band starts off with two shows in London on June 1 and 2 before jetting to Toronto, Canada, for the North by Northeast music festival.

Then it's down to the US for a gig in New York and the final show in Los Angeles on June 11.

James Lopes, the band's guitarist, says the tour came together after they'd been accepted to perform at the North by Northeast festival – which features more than 400 bands.

"When we enquired about plane tickets, the manager found out it would actually be a lot cheaper for a round-the-world ticket as opposed to a ticket straight to Toronto," Lopes says.

"So, via some connections that he had in London, New York and LA, we've managed to fill out the whole thing with gigs."

The Toronto festival is the biggest in Canada and Lopes says he didn't really rate the band's chances of being accepted.

"When you boil it all down, who the hell are we?", he says.

"We're some relatively unknown band in obscure Wollongong, in obscure Australia as far as those people are concerned. It was just bizarre how it all came together."

To add to that, the band has managed to score an excellent spot during the festival. They play at 10pm on a Saturday night.

"We're very excited about that," he says. "I fully expected that we'd be on a Monday at 7pm or something. To get the spot that we've got, we are just ecstatic."

Lopes says the band is taking a realistic approach to what they hope to achieve with the tour. That means not having any expectations about picking up a record deal and the like.

"It's unrealistic to head over there with an expectation," he says.

"It'd be nice, but with the industry the way it is, unfortunately, the potential is we come back with nothing.

"Obviously it'd be very, very nice if someone was to sign us up or take us on. The danger in expecting too much is to come back completely crushed when it doesn't happen.

"We believe in ourselves and there are others that believe in us and, while that continues to happen, we'll continue to do it."

Friday Night at the Oxford

The five band members believe in themselves so much they've put their money where their mouth is. The trip is almost entirely self-funded.

"I'm doing without a house for this tour," Lopes says. "I was on the verge of buying my own unit, so that's now been put back indefinitely. One other guy is going without a car and the other guys are making similar sacrifices."

So, they're paying for the whole shebang themselves and aren't really expecting it to further their careers. What's in it for them?

"At the very worst, it's a trip away," Lopes says. "We get to see some great things, we get to play to audiences a lot of people won't ever play to. Chalk it up as a life experience and say, 'well, this is what we got to do'."

Sic'em with plenty of attitude
July 17, 2003

If Cikim's guitarist Johnny Mitrevski has shoes on, it's going to be a bad gig.

For him anyway – unless he's barefoot, Mitrevski is likely to lose his balance.

"I just feel like I'm unbalanced, like I'm going to fall over every time I play when I've got shoes on," Mitrevski says.

"I feel like I'm going to twist my ankle. I guess it's sort of become my thing, but there's a reason for it."

The three-piece band started three years ago when Mitrevski, who was driving taxis at the time, met bassist and singer Richard Mikic after he hopped in the front seat of his cab and asked to be taken home.

Eighteen months ago they were joined by drummer Ricky Ward.

Inspired by the in-your-face attitude of the words "sic'em", they chose them as their band name. The spelling is also Mikic's name spelt backwards.

"We thought they were two good reasons to turn it into a band name," Mitrevski says.

The trio is about to release their first recording, an eight-track CD called *RSL*.

According to Mitrevski, the wait between the band's formation and their first release can be put down to two things: money and songs.

"I think it's to do with money and it just takes a long time to get songs that you're comfortable with," he says.

"It costs about four grand to put it all together and we wanted to be sure that what we were going to do was going to be good.

"Originally we were thinking of ourselves as a heavy band. We ended up writing songs that weren't so heavy and a little bit more musical, and I think it works out in our favour to do it that way."

The album features a number of those songs and Cikim do a good job covering a range of styles including heavy rock, pop, hip-hop and stoner rock.

"We deliberately wanted to do something that was diverse to have a broader range of people listening to it," he says.

"In our back catalogue, we've got 30-odd songs and, if we wanted to, we could have had a heavier album or a poppier album or a few more hip-hop tracks on the album.

"We just chose the best of each of the styles that we can do. We wanted to have this production of the band as a whole."

Cikim launch their CD at the Oxford Tavern tomorrow night. Also playing on the night are Traces of Nut and Miner's Elbow.

Sights set on success
July 24, 2003

Wollongong band Optic Nerve had success with the first song they wrote.

"When we wrote our first song, we actually recorded it at school," singer and keyboard player Amy Ranftl says.

"We heard there was a battle of the bands for unsigned bands on 2Day FM, so we recorded the song on a crappy tape recorder and we

Friday Night at the Oxford

sent it in. We were the youngest ones to enter and we ended up winning it."

That first taste of success encouraged the band to keep going and they've released two albums since they formed in 1998.

"That gave us the encouragement to write more of our own stuff and record it," she says.

"We had a lot of originals and we'd play them live in between the other songs. We got a lot of good response from the audience for our own music. We loved it and we kept writing."

Optic Nerve also decided to try their hand at other band competitions, ending up as either winners or finalists in events like the Garage Days contest or the Future Rock show at the Hard Rock Cafe.

It's not just the lure of winning recording time or instruments that appeals to the band either.

"It's good experience because we get to meet other bands and get to meet people in the industry," she says.

"It helps with venues too – the Hard Rock Cafe was a great venue to play at. It was a good experience for us to play in the Sydney scene because now we're starting to get a lot more gigs in Sydney, so it's helped us out in that way too."

The band formed when Ranftl's brother Mark met bassist Mark Ablott when they both had the same guitar teacher.

Ranftl signed on because they were looking for a singer, and drummer Matt Brien was a friend who decided to try out.

Ranftl, who toured Europe as a soloist at the end of Year 12, is also the natural leader of the band.

"I am the oldest too and because I'm the frontperson onstage I tend to keep everyone in line that way," she jokes.

Optic Nerve plays at the Palm Court Hotel on Saturday night.

Glen Humphries

Gong music scene needs a shot
July 24, 2003

A Wollongong group has the dream that the region could experience something similar to the grunge explosion of the early 1990s.

That group is called the Wollongong Music Round Table (WMRT) and member Rob Carr is thinking big.

"We've got a passion to get local subcultures up and happening," Carr says.

"We've been talking for ages about how good would it be to have Wollongong as the next Seattle."

Sure, that's the best-case scenario, but if Carr and the other members can help to improve the Wollongong music scene, they'll be happy.

In fact, they've already mapped out ways of giving the scene a shot in the arm.

"We want to see industry links develop so that we have major conferences down here," he says.

"When those people come to town, then our bands are able to network directly with them. Musicoz brought a lot of big people to town last year and they were all back at the Oxford afterward, so, indirectly, a few bands get a few more contacts.

"Also, we want to try and draw in industry and council and state government funding bodies to try and get us to have more of those big things.

"Not just functions but big shows, maybe a festival, like a mini Big Day Out."

Carr feels the time is right for such an organisation as the scene is in need of a long overdue boost.

"In the early '90s Tumbleweed was huge and things were happening, right up until the mid-to-late '90s," he says.

"Then, about five years ago, things just stopped and it's been in a bit of a slump ever since.

"Now, five years down the track, people are starting to get sick of it. We've got over 100 members on our email group who are keen to get

Friday Night at the Oxford

involved."

Not all those members are in bands either – many just have an interest in fostering a strong music culture.

Unlike previous organisations, which focused on the bands themselves, Carr says the aim of WMRT is to "get the scene in general going, not just provide more gigs for bands".

"(The bands) are rightly concerned with their own projects, we're just a support base from which they can draw resources," he says.

"One of those resources is, we're in the process of publishing brochures on how to get gigs, how to put a promotional pack together, how to approach record companies, get management, what kind of legal services there are.

"So we're kind of like a support base for bands to do their own thing.

"We're not trying to say, if you're not part of the movement, then we'll just exclude you from our activities."

The next meeting of the Wollongong Music Round Table is July 30, 7pm, in the beer garden of the Oxford Tavern. For more information contact Rob Carr at thirroulyouthproject@yahoo.com.au

Phial's false start
August 7, 2003

After nearly a two-year break, Wollongong band Phial are returning.

The heavy groove-oriented four-piece achieved some notoriety from airplay on Triple J and inclusion on that station's first *Full Metal Racket* CD, as well as video play on several networks.

But 18 months ago they decided on a hiatus.

"We just wanted to come up with more of a niche sound," vocalist Rob Carr explains.

"We found what we had been doing was becoming a bit monotonous and not really giving us any sense of fulfillment. We just wanted to come up with something that made us feel a bit more excited and original about what we were doing."

During that break, the band picked up a new bass player, wrote nearly two sets of new material and recorded plenty of demos.

"We've got heaps and heaps of demos and we're just going to sort through them and see what we want to take with us and what we want to leave behind," Carr says.

That doesn't mean the pre-break Phial has been completely forgotten.

"You always distance yourself from what you've done in the past but, then again, there's always a sense of continuity as well," he says.

"You always want to build on what you've done.

"For a while there was talk about whether we should change the name and stuff like that.

"We decided to continue because we'd already established a basis ... so we thought, let's just go on with it, let's just build on that."

Carr says the band wasn't worried about having to start all over again.

"We kind of opted for a fresh start but, with the announcement that we've got fresh shows coming up, we've already been getting emails from people," he says.

"The fan base that we did have is still there. There's a lot of good feedback and a lot of people are going to come to the shows."

Those long-term fans don't need to worry about the band's sound changing too much. Carr says it's still the same big sound, but more thought has gone into it.

"We found what we were doing before was more for shock value – big riffs and that kind of thing," he says.

"Big riffs can only get you so far. I think there's a lot more emotional depth in what we're doing now."

Phial perform at the Oxford Tavern tomorrow night.

Friday Night at the Oxford

Double the bass
August 7, 2003

There are two bassplayers in Wollongong band Impasse.

But it's not some arty, bass-oriented deal – only one of them actually plays.

That would be Calvin.

The other guy would be Beezy, best known for his time as bassist in Naiad. His role in Impasse is purely vocal but Calvin says it's handy having another bassist hanging around.

"Yeah, it keeps me on my toes," he jokes.

"It's hard to find good bassplayers. When you've got another good bassplayer in the same band it's good for me, it gives me ideas.

"It's good to get some feedback too."

The five-piece formed late last year.

"It actually came together through myself and the guitarist (Tony), who were in a band called Awakening two years ago," he says.

"We started jamming again and writing songs. Then we located a drummer (John from Gravitron) and from there we found Beezy and (keyboardist) Dave at the end of last year."

Calvin describes the band's sound as "heavy rock with a few twists and turns" and says they're finishing up a demo recording.

"We're just starting to pick up speed now," he says.

"Our first gig was two months ago so that was just sort of testing the water for us, seeing how we were going to pull things off live and that seemed to go well."

Even though Calvin's been in a number of bands, he admitted to a bit of stage fright before that first gig with Impasse.

"I found that there was a bit (of nerves), especially with something like this," he says.

"We'd been working on it for a pretty long time and it's always a bit nervous to see how people are going to react to it.

"You're kind of putting yourself on the line a bit."

Impasse plays the Oxford Tavern on Saturday night.

Greenhouse effect
September 4, 2003

Paul Greene's shows in New Zealand after Christmas last year weren't his first outside Australia.

"I did perform once in England when I was doing athletics," Greene says.

"I also got drunk in a pub in Switzerland and got up and did a set."

They were both impromptu efforts during his time as a professional athlete, but he also played a bit in the United States last year.

During his jaunt to New Zealand he appeared in the Whare Flat Festival and, by his account, things went quite well.

"It had all that intrigue because I didn't really know what was going to happen," he says.

"The festival that I was playing at was fantastic and the people were so friendly that I thought they were trying to sell me something to start with.

"But I ended up getting into it. I was really well-looked-after by the locals and sold heaps of CDs. The trip paid for itself, so that's always good."

Since returning from New Zealand, Greene has spent some time doing residencies both in Wollongong and Sydney, as well as playing around the country.

Since the middle of this year, Greene has played in Noosa, Canberra, Melbourne, Adelaide, Perth and a bunch of places in between.

In fact, for this interview, he was calling from Darwin where he was preparing for another show.

Even with all those gigs, he still found time to start working on his third album.

"During the time I was doing the residencies, I actually sat down and set aside some time to write and came up with an album's worth of songs," he says.

"I'm going into the studio the week after the folk festival. It's early stages at the moment but I'm hoping to have something out in February or March next year."

He says he'll still be taking a do-it-yourself approach towards much of the album but he's thinking about getting some help in a few other areas.

"It will be an independent album, released through Whirl Records (the label he owns with his wife)," he says.

"But I think, this time, I'll get someone to help with distribution and I've also had a couple of offers from publishing companies.

"I'm thinking of going down those roads. It'll still be our music, we'll still own it – it's our record label. And I'll still be touring full-time, getting out there pub by pub."

Sweat, masks and rock'n'roll
September 9, 2003

If you're a band and you want to wear masks onstage, Log's B-Rad has a little advice: you sweat like a madman under them.

"Yes, they get very, very hot," B-Rad says.

"It's very unpleasant under those masks. But that's cool, it's worth the pain."

There must be a logical explanation as to why the band would put up with the facial sweat to wear the masks.

"We wanted to go with a bit of an image so it wasn't just five guys standing onstage," he says.

"We experimented with a few masks and came up with those ones. People thought they were scary and funny at the same time."

Scary and funny?

That pretty much describes Log. On a first listen, their loud, sludge-metal sounds seem vaguely frightening – until you realise they're probably playing it with a smile on their faces.

B-Rad says the guys don't believe in the inherent anger in so many similar-sounding groups.

"I think that's the image they try and portray," he says of those other bands.

"Log's definitely more fun than other bands I've jammed in. We get together and play the music we want to play rather than work."

Playing together is a bit trickier than it sounds. While most of the band live in Canberra, singer Karl and bassist Jamie (whose nickname is Amos) are Wollongong boys who also perform in Riffter.

Needless to say, that means a slightly different approach to rehearsals.

"We jam without Amos and Karl, and for the gigs they come up and have a jam," B-Rad says.

"The songs are fairly easy, they're not really technical. Once you've got the CD, you can't really forget the song. Every time we play it seems to be really fresh because we haven't seen them for a couple of months or whatever."

If you were ever in any doubt about the band's sense of fun, their second album is called *Log's Second Album.*

"We just didn't want to come up with a big fancy-pants name," he explains.

"We didn't really have a concept for the album, they were just songs that we'd been jamming on for ages. The first album was called *10 Songs of Log*, which was kind of funny and ridiculous.

"So we basically called our second album, *Log's Second Album*. I don't know what the next one's going to be called."

Log play at the Woonona Bowls Club tomorrow night.

Sweet taste of Honey
September 25, 2003

Working on a new CD hasn't been fun for Dropping Honey's Damien Lane.

But it never is.

Friday Night at the Oxford

"I can't stand recording because there's always this sense that it's not as good as it could be or that it's not as good as it is in your head," Lane, the band's singer, guitarist and songwriter says.

"It's just very tedious having to do things over and over again. Mixing really does my head in because you mix for four hours and you've forgotten what it sounded like at the start and you can't work out whether you've made it sound better or worse."

The band has been working on the CD – due to be eight tracks – in spurts since the first half of this year.

The plan is to have it out by the end of the year, once they re-record several tunes.

"Some of the songs would benefit from having more of a live sound rather than these laboured studio productions," he says.

"So we might try and do that with a couple of tracks and try and capture the energy that the live shows have."

The CD has been recorded in spurts because it was a matter of finding the time in the members' schedules.

But Lane says it's been a positive experience.

"That's the good thing about doing it in dribs and drabs because you get some kind of perspective," he says.

"You come back to it after not listening to it for a week or so and you'll notice what's wrong with it or what needs to come out more."

Lane says the CD may be called *Dreams of Broken Teeth* – if the other guys in the band agree to it.

"At this stage I haven't really discussed that with the rest of the band but I like to give things working titles even if they don't end up being called that," he says.

"It is a song of mine that the band hasn't learned yet that I want to be the last song we do (on the EP)."

It's an unusual title – but it doesn't express a fear of going to the dentist.

"I think a lot of people have dreams about broken teeth," he says.

"I certainly do, particularly in times of distress and, as distress is what most of my songs tend to be about, I thought it was kind of fitting."

Glen Humphries

Dropping Honey perform at the Oxford Tavern tomorrow night.

Band issues a Waik up call
September 25, 2003

There might be messages in Waik's songs but the Wollongong band isn't one to preach.

The nu-metal band has a motto of sorts – "not the answer, just the question" – which refers to the desire to open up debate on issues, not provide a solution.

"We don't get up and spout a lot of stuff about what we think," the band's guitarist, Simon Schroeder, says.

"We try and put the question out – what is it that you want, what is important to you. It's like 'here's the question, you should come up with whatever you think the answer is'.

"The worst thing I've seen is when people, like politicians, get up and start talking about what they believe and try to push it onto other people."

Schroeder says the band's message is simple – it's all about getting people to figure out what's really important to them.

The band's name is a corruption of "wake" – pushing the idea of people waking up to find what they really want.

It seems a lot of people want Waik. The four-piece, who have been together since 2001, have had their songs played around the world.

"We've got both internet and Californian radio stations playing some of the older stuff and stuff from the new EP," he says.

"Overseas has been a lot more open to the music, mainly because there's obviously more of a market over there. It's a lot harder to get on Triple J than people think.

"Germany's the same deal. We've got a lot of fans over there."

That new EP Schroeder mentions should be due out by the end of the year. The plan is to add another few tracks to the three they've already recorded for a demo.

Friday Night at the Oxford

"The 26th is the gig with The Butterfly Effect," he says.

"The 27th, we're heading back up to Brisbane to record the next three songs for the EP, which will be for sale and probably out through MGM distribution. It's also got distribution in the States."

Waik perform at the Wollongong Youth Centre tomorrow night with headline act The Butterfly Effect.

Mind is larger than life
October 16, 2003

It seems Beezy, from Mind at Large, is a very busy guy.

The band is only one of four the bass player is a part of – there's also Nabilone, Impasse and Phial.

"I'm just very passionately involved in them all, which keeps the energy going," Beezy says.

He also keeps fit having to lug the heavy bass amp to all those rehearsals and gigs.

But he's not the only one doing the multiple band thing. Mind at Large's guitarist Calvin Houlison is also a member of Impasse, and singer Andrew Bennett does the mic duties with Ludo.

Drummer Chris Ireland is the only one-band guy here. Beezy says it was Ireland who was instrumental in starting Mind at Large.

The pair played together in Decode and, when that band went "pffft" about 18 months ago, the guys decided to start work on what would become Mind at Large.

"Chris and I thought, we've obviously got this much time in a week to be doing music, why don't we do it with each other and start our own thing – and that turned into Mind at Large," Beezy says.

"Mind at Large was an avenue to write a lot of songs that I didn't get the opportunity to write with a lot of the other bands because of the other songwriters that were involved.

"Chris really opened up a door for me to just create as much music as I wanted to and he was really enthusiastic about it.

"He really supported that environment and the next thing we knew, we had a lot of songs which we needed other members for."

Beezy and Chris started working on the songs about 18 months ago, with the band starting in earnest about six months back. That's when they began looking for other members.

The gig at the Oxford Tavern this Saturday is the band's debut performance.

Beezy says it was good to have a date set for the first gig because it gave the band a deadline to work to, rather than just waiting until they thought they were ready and then looking for gigs.

So they've spent the last few weeks before the show finetuning their songs and their sound, which Beezy says has changed a bit since he and Chris first got together.

"When we first started the group we just wanted to have a straight-out rock and roll band, but it's atmospheric rock and roll (now)," he says.

"Some of it's cliched at times, some of it's completely not. Sometimes it touches on a little bit of avant garde but, really, it's just an interesting bundle of rock and roll."

Mind at Large perform at the Oxford Tavern on Saturday.

Well-oiled machine
December 11, 2003

Drummer Jeb Taylor feels a little guilty about the success of How Machines Work.

The Thirroul three-piece have only been together for six months but they've already had Triple J airplay for their song *Pilot Error* and seen the track added to that station's compilation CD.

Simon Dalla Pozza, the band's bassplayer, simply sent the demo CD to Triple J, with no bio or any other information attached and Robbie Buck started playing it on his *Home and Hosed* program.

Obviously it was a bit of a shock for the guys.

Friday Night at the Oxford

"You've got so many bands who push so much and put so much work into stuff and to have it happen for us with absolutely no effort is kind of weird. I suppose it's the luck of the draw," Taylor says.

"Basically we didn't have a full set when that started getting played. So we started getting offered shows without having a full set."

Because people were hearing the song and then wanting to buy the CD, the band ended up self-releasing a three-track EP, with *Pilot Error* as the title track.

It's an interesting reaction to a song that's been around since 1999. Taylor was in a band with Dalla Pozza and guitarist and singer Justin Roberts in school but they broke up.

The trio had kept in touch and earlier this year they decided to get back together.

Pilot Error was written by Roberts during the last days of that old band.

"It's actually an old song of ours – it was written a fair while back," Taylor says.

"When we played it then it sounded pretty good so we thought we'd do it again.

"I know some people have this thing where they think it's about September 11. We're trying to get away from that because the song was written before that."

The indie rock trio has been fielding some interest from several labels which might surprise those who know Taylor as the guy who runs the High Beam Music record label.

Taylor says it's his preference not to sign the band to his label.

"We've had a couple of major labels show some interest," he says.

"... It's weird to have this band that's barely together sitting in the offices of BMG and talking to them about putting out a record."

How Machines Work are one of the bands performing at this Sunday's Kemblastock festival at Mt Kembla Oval. Other bands on the bill include Rockafella, Monstrous Blues, Turbo Degenerate and The Alohas. The festival is a fundraiser for the American Creek Regeneration Group – it's free but gold coin donations would be appreciated.

Glen Humphries

Gong band plays tribute
December 31, 2003

On New Year's Eve, a Wollongong band will bring to mind a number of old acquaintances.

The Gong Tribute Band (GTB) plans to play covers of songs from Wollongong acts of the past 10 years.

Rob Carr, one of two guitarists in the GTB, says the bands covered include Tumbleweed, Scalene, Naiad, Pancake Day and Eezee (who later turned into Segression).

"It's more of a rock style," Carr says.

"There's heaps of other bands out there in the acoustic scene that we could do. We wanted to make it an upbeat show so we're just going to focus on the rock bands."

The GTB is made up of two guitarists, a drummer, three bassists and seven singers.

The guitarists and drummer stay onstage while the bass players and singers share performing duties.

The 13 members come from current Wollongong acts like Dropping Honey, Phial, Side Effect X, Nabilone, Mejane, The Chargers, Mind At Large, Nether, Tears Turn Flood, Happy Noodle Boy and Faded Underground.

Carr says he suggested the idea at a meeting of the Wollongong Music Round Table at the Oxford Tavern.

The tavern's band booker Alby Fares thought it was a great idea.

So did a lot of other people participating in the discussion.

"We had the Christmas party at the round table and I think half the people there thought they were playing," he says.

"They were going to rock up with a guitar and play a song.

"I guess I took on the coordinator role and tried to keep things in perspective because it was becoming quite a nightmare for a while with everyone trying to play.

"I think we managed to cut it down to 13 or 14 people."

Friday Night at the Oxford

In the past few days, all the members have been getting together to rehearse for the GTB's debut tonight but, as Carr says, it wasn't always easy.

"I started off with a timetable but that pretty much fell to pieces when the first person couldn't actually make it at that time," he says.

"But we've had a couple of practices the last few weeks."

The GTB is playing one set before midnight and one after. If they're a bit rusty due to lack of rehearsal, the audience will probably be too drunk to notice anyway.

The Gong Tribute Band plays tonight at the Oxford Tavern. Support acts are The Figurines (which includes singer-songwriter Tim Ireland and members of Dropping Honey) and Sharon Babaro.

Smash hits
January 29, 2004

For Rockafella, fame means the chance to smash guitars – someone else's.

Bassist Andy Simpson says the band's rocking live show does result in occasional breakage – either to instruments or band members – but he's drawn the line at smashing his guitar into the stage.

He wants to – it's just that he has strong attachments to his guitars. If the band became big enough to get a freebie, then things might be different.

"I've accidentally broken one, but I wouldn't (smash one) – no way," Simpson says.

"I like my guitars too much. Maybe if it was just some nameless faceless one a guy from the Fender factory just handed to me, I think I'd be able to smash it.

"There's definitely potential. I do like the idea of smashing things."

Rockafella are the headline act at this weekend's *Summer Blast!* at Bulli. Also on the bill are local acts Ohana, Revilo, MFS, Self-Titled, Agent Pecan and Me Jane.

Summer Blast! also includes a bodyboard competition ($10 entry) at Woonona Beach and a graffiti wall with spray can hire.

After releasing their debut EP in March last year, Rockafella are planning the long-awaited follow-up.

Simpson says the plan is to head into the studio in March to record a full-length album.

Taking the step up from an EP to an album isn't a worry for the band. Finding enough songs won't be a problem.

"We're already writing enough material for a second album," Simpson says.

Simpson says the band has no idea when the album will see the light of day, but they're not worried about trying to release it while rock is still the flavour of the month.

"We figure, everyone loves rock; there's just a fad at the moment and I think that's going to fall away and some bands are just going to fade away.

"So, if we're good enough, and I think we are, hopefully it won't be a problem."

Rockafella perform at Summer Blast at the Bulli PCYC, Saturday, 2pm-8pm. Tickets $5 at the door.

Side Effect X go live 'n' local
February 5, 2004

What was supposed to be a side project for Wollongong metal band Segression has developed a life of its own.

The four guys in Segression added bassplayer Michael Caruana and became Side Effect X.

Singer of both bands Chris Rand says Segression was "just having a little rest" but is still a going concern.

"I needed a break from doing all the heavy stuff. The boys still wanted to put out more albums as Segression," Rand says.

"I just wanted to be fresh and I wasn't coming up with ideas that

Friday Night at the Oxford

were fresh and new."

Side Effect X is taking a more melodic approach to hard rock. It's a new sound that Rand says is sure to appeal to some, but not all, Segression fans.

It's an issue Rand is not worried about.

"If God and Jesus Christ couldn't get everyone in the world to love them, I don't think we've got much chance of doing it," he says.

"You're always going to get people liking you and people hating you. It doesn't matter if you're a bricklayer or a musician."

Side Effect X has released a single, *Turn the Page*, ahead of their forthcoming album. The 14-track CD is due for release in March or April.

Rand says the band's sound is diverse, which probably reflects the range of music he listens to.

"I haven't ever really listened to that much heavy stuff," he says.

"It's not what dominates my CD player. I listen to everything from Massive Attack to Lenny Kravitz to Coldplay to U2. I listen to all sorts of stuff."

The band is one of eight finalists in the Coca-Cola Live 'n' Local Tour 2004 competition.

All eight finalists perform on TV tomorrow night and the viewers get to vote for their favourites via SMS.

The top-four bands then get to join the Live 'n' Local tour with 28 Days, Jebediah, Machine Gun Fellatio, Magic Dirt and Betchadupa. That tour hits the WIN Entertainment Centre on April 4.

Rand says their manager entered the band as a bit of fun. "We're not taking anything too seriously," he says. "It's not the end of the world if we come last."

Side Effect X met the other seven finalists when they all played a showcase in Melbourne's Crown Casino. And the guys got tagged as "the naughty band".

"That's what they call us," Rand says.

"When we came on, even though we are a bit more melodic (than Segression) it was, 'Hang on a second, this is the naughty band. They've got tattoos and piercings, they look really mean.'

"It was really good fun. There were girls at the front of the stage when we walked on and they came up to our bassplayer before we started and said, 'You're our favourite band.'

"We hadn't even played anything yet!"

Video Hits Live 'n' Local Tour special, SC Ten, tomorrow, 11.35pm.

Changing their tune
March 6, 2004

If there's ever a bad time for a band to change its name, it would be right after releasing an EP.

That's what happened to Wollongong's Riffter (previously known as Shifter).

The guys released a loud, driving, five-track EP on the High Beam Music label last month under the name of Shifter.

Then they happened to find out they weren't the only Shifter – a desire to avoid confusion prompting the change.

"We did a band search and there's a Shifter in Australia and there's some Shifters in America," said drummer Tom Risorto.

"There's a Shifter in Japan and there's one in England, so we just thought we'd save the dramas and do it now – just after we released our EP, which is a bit ridiculous.

"I think if we were a bit more on the ball before we recorded our EP we probably would have done (the search) then."

But you can bet they did a search on the name Riffter before adopting it.

It's actually the second name change in the band's 10-year history.

"We've had Shifter since about '94," Risorto says.

"Before that we were called Dawn Patrol, so we've actually had two name changes. Lucky we don't take ourselves too seriously."

Risorto says it's that casual approach that explains why the band has only released two EPs in their time together.

"Yeah, we're just slack," he admits.

Friday Night at the Oxford

"When we rehearse we're more likely to sit around telling jokes, drinking beer and talking about the footy rather than playing.

"That sums up how we go in the studio. It's not our favourite place. We're more of a live, rather than a studio, band."

That might change when they head in to record their debut album in April, when they'll be working with Rob Younger of Radio Birdman fame.

"He's actually been calling us up and he's pretty keen," Risorto says. "He's a bit of a hero to us and we're still getting over the fact that he's really keen to work with us."

They've also been getting plenty of praise for the EP, which is called *Shifter* (even though the band isn't anymore).

A standout is the first tune, *Frosty Lectro Litic*, which sounds like the guys were listening to a bit of Motorhead before recording the song.

"That song has the Motorhead influence because we're all influenced by Motorhead," he says.

"We've had reviews saying we sound like AC/DC, Motorhead and early Rose Tattoo.

"That's just too big a compliment for us. We're just rapt."

Riffter perform at the Towradgi Beach Hotel on Saturday night with Monstrous Blues and Rockafella.

Greene cooks up a storm
March 11, 2004

It can be a little scary meeting someone you've always admired.

That's what Paul Greene discovered when he and former Midnight Oil drummer Rob Hirst supported US folk singer Ani DiFranco on her recent Australian tour.

Greene says DiFranco's music and independent attitude (she runs her own record label for starters) has been the model for what he does.

So finally meeting someone who's been such an influence on you can be a little nerve-wracking.

"It was incredibly intimidating," Greene admits.

"We got on really well with her. I didn't know what to expect but she really included us and she'd come and have dinner with us.

"I talked to her a fair bit. I'd always feel weird. I'd be talking to her, having a conversation and I'd go 'damn, I'm talking to Ani DiFranco'. I know it's very uncool, but I couldn't help it."

He was able to impress her a bit too – both with his music and his talents in the kitchen.

"I got to cook her dinner, that was pretty cool," he says.

"She loved it. I did go out of my way to impress her. I bought mudcrabs and did my famous Hong Kong steamed fish."

With that tour over (though there is talk of Greene and Hirst supporting DiFranco on some US dates), Green has turned his attention to his third album.

A live effort, it's due for release in May. It features 12 new songs recorded during a gig at Sydney's Excelsior Hotel, as well as four bonus live versions of tunes from his other albums.

The release date for the album's been pushed back a few times, mainly because the project became a bit trickier than Greene had anticipated.

"As with everything, I dived into this totally unprepared and inexperienced," he says.

"I've never made a live album before and had no idea what it took. I just thought you played the gig, recorded it and banged it on a CD."

Instead, the tracks also need mixing and mastering – and it's Greene who's doing all that.

Thus he gets to hear the songs over and over again, discovering every little mistake and trying to fix them.

"I like mistakes in things, but there's a fine line between something that gives it character and a balls-up," he says.

"The more you listen to it, the more you put a microscope on these things, the more you see the imperfections.

"I don't want to release something on a CD unless I know I'll be proud of it in 20 years' time. I don't want to release anything that's not ... good, basically."

Friday Night at the Oxford

One thing he's not tinkering with is the background noise – that's essential to creating a live mood in his eyes.

"I'm going to put it together as it was, with people yelling out," he says.

"There's doors opening and closing and the post-mix machine in the background. I really like the idea of creating a whole audio landscape, if you like. You can hear the room, you can hear the people, you can feel what's going on."

Paul Greene plays tonight at the Wollongong Unibar.

ROADS show
March 25, 2004

Some people might read a bit of arrogance into ROADS' name – but the Wollongong band says there's nothing in it.

The band – which is basically three members of stoner rock act Thumlock plus a new drummer – was formed about 18 months ago.

The name is an acronym for Remnants Of A Dead Star, which could imply the band members felt they were stars in Thumlock.

But when bass player Wayne Stokes is asked about this, he laughs, so we can assume there wasn't any arrogant intent there.

"Yeah, you could probably look at it that way, I suppose," Stokes says.

"Everyone's going to interpret it a different way, but it doesn't really have any major significance to us except it's a wicked little term that sounded good.

"Ben (Lough), our singer, just picked up on it and it stuck in his head. Every day we were going through names, we were throwing all these names around and no-one really liked them.

"That was one that stuck to the wall."

While the band personnel is just Thumlock with a new drummer, Stokes says they felt they couldn't continue under that band's name.

"With the line-up change we agreed to let the band go with it because we all had an equal input in the songwriting," he says.

"So we've gone into this band as a whole new band. There's some similar sounds in there, but we think we're writing different music.

"We were happy playing what we were before, but wanted to try different sounds, different amps and guitars. We're still keeping the rock-and-roll feel, but we're trying to do something different."

The sound is a few steps away from the stoner rock of Thumlock – it's less stoner and more rock.

"Instead of getting lumped in with that genre of music, we wanted to leave that to the rest of them and do something different," he says.

"We were labelled as that style of music, as stoner rock, but it you look at any of our record collections that was just a small fraction of what we're really into."

The reaction of Thumlock fans to the new sound has been varied, says Stokes.

Some like it, some think it's "crap".

The negative comments don't bother Stokes.

"It's a progression for us," he says.

"We're not sitting there wanting to write something that will appeal to this person or that person.

"We've got our day jobs and stuff and music's just a hobby for us – it's our own self-expression.

"If people like it, it's a bonus."

ROADS CD launch is on Saturday, March 27, at the Oxford Tavern. Supports are Stone Ox and Strangers.

A dark side debut
April 15, 2004

There's a disclaimer on Wollongong band RPM's EP ...*Of Earth & Sin*.

Basically it says, "The lyrics are just our opinion. Don't take this

Friday Night at the Oxford

stuff, seriously, okay?"

The disclaimer is the work of singer and guitarist Tome Jovanouski, according to drummer Daniel Hutt.

Tome is an insurance broker and he was just playing it safe.

While the songs are dark – with subject matter like war, racism and environmental destruction – Hutt says the four band members aren't miserable people.

"We don't mean for it to be dark. We just don't want to write songs about losing a lover or anything generic like that," he says.

"They are dark lyrics but none of us are dark people.

"Instead of singing about some lollipop kind of song, we are politically conscious about what's going on. We thought we'd rather sing about things that affect everyone rather than just ourselves."

But there's a hidden track on the EP that proves the guys like a bit of fun. It's a series of snippets of the band goofing around in the studio.

"The guys love clowning around," Hutt says.

"It's a pretty serious EP but there was a lot of good times we had and we wanted to share it with everyone else.

"We all love CDs that have hidden tracks, so we thought, 'Let's put all the stuff-ups we've done on CD'."

Hutt describes the band as metal – for want of a better word. He says they just take all their influences, combine them, and the sound that comes out is RPM.

Their sound is a collective approach because the band is a democracy when it comes to songwriting.

Hutt explains that approach is the reason why the first track on the CD runs for nine minutes.

"We're all writing the songs together – it's not one person going, 'Here's a riff, let's play it'," he says.

"We've got a big whiteboard where we practice and we write down our ideas, and we put it together like that.

"For that song, each member of the band picked something they wanted to play.

"For example, I wanted to play a thrashy song, someone else wanted to play a serene song, so we got to pick the song apart and everyone got to have their own little section."

RPM has been together for four years but ... *Of Earth & Sin* is their first release. Hutt attributes that to all the obstacles that got in their way.

First they had to find a new bassplayer after the old one left the band, then they had to play plenty of shows to save up the money for the studio.

Then problems with the studio's availability pushed the recording back.

Finally, some of the band members work in Sydney, and one has a weekend job, so finding a time all four of the guys could make it to the studio was tricky.

"There were lots of things that got in our way along the road, but we finally got through," he says.

"It's a big relief that it's out. We thought it'd never come out because of the obstacles that got in our way."

ATE DVD an Illawarra first
May 6, 2004

Steve Robinson looks likely to complete another first for a Wollongong musician – releasing a DVD.

In 1991, Robinson's band A Comedy of Errors released what he believes was the first CD for a Wollongong band. Now, 13 years later, he's aiming to put out a DVD with his new band ATE and acoustic duo Erika's Jive.

To the best of his knowledge, Robinson believes it will be the first DVD in the Wollongong music scene.

"When I did a CD, it was the first CD in Wollongong and everyone thought it was incredibly ambitious," he says.

"Back then the cost of doing a CD was prohibitive. It was as hard getting that out as doing a DVD now."

But he's still keen to give it a go.

The project, dubbed *On The Lounge*, includes footage from a live

Friday Night at the Oxford

show.

Both bands are playing a gig at the Bulli Hotel next Wednesday that will be filmed. So if you want to be in a DVD, Robinson suggests you head to Bulli.

On The Lounge is a combination of a few ideas Robinson has had brewing.

"It was initially a show I did at the Oxford (Tavern). The view was to do it as a TV pilot and do a TV series like a chat/variety show," he says.

"Guests come onto a show and they usually just talk. What I wanted to do was have them talk and do what they do.

"From there it's just turned into the fact that I've wanted to get something recorded with my old mate Ed Lee (who plays with Robinson in ATE).

"We've been playing together for about 20 years and we've never actually recorded anything as a release together."

Robinson says the footage shot at the Bulli Hotel will only be part of the DVD.

"It's going to be like a documentary of what we're doing and of life as a regional musician," he says.

"It's going to have a bit of that in it. And part of it will also be a short film that I want to send off to some festivals. It can be edited in a couple of ways and one of those ways is a short film."

ATE and Erika's Jive's Live DVD project is on Wednesday, May 12, 8pm at the Bulli Hotel.

Reliving Beatlemania
June 10, 2004

Johnny Devlin didn't exactly jump at the chance to support The Beatles on their 1964 Australian tour.

He had to think about it before deciding to join the tour, which started 40 years ago tomorrow.

"I was trying to get someone else on the tour," says Devlin, who lives in Wollongong's northern suburbs.

"Then they turned around and asked me if I'd like to do it. I had a very serious think about it because I knew it would be difficult singing in a show with The Beatles – they were the hottest act in the world at the time.

"So I told them I'd do it on two conditions. Number one, that I went on first because I wanted to get on and off as quick as possible and, number two, they double the money they offered me, which was peanuts.

"I think they thought I'd do the show for nothing."

Devlin was a rock star in his native New Zealand. He got the first gold record in that country, for his debut single *Lawdy Miss Clawdy*.

Nicknamed the Satin Satan, Devlin decided to try his luck in Australia. Not long after the move, he ended up on the bill for The Beatles' only Australian tour.

Devlin had had a small dose of what Beatlemania was like in his home country, but what he experienced on that 1964 tour was something else.

"It was very, very exciting – the whole atmosphere was electric," he says. "You were wondering what was going to happen next.

"If George slipped on a step or something like that, it'd be written up in the press. There was press everywhere and it didn't matter what they did, it made the headlines."

There were also plenty of young ladies who were keen on meeting their idols by sneaking into the band's hotel.

"Yes, that was very common," he admits. "I was approached by numbers of girls saying they'd make it worth my while if I could get them up to see The Beatles.

"There was no way they could get up unless they had a pass. We all had to have security passes."

Most of the screaming crowd was there for The Fab Four but Devlin says he had a few yelling for him as well.

"I was pretty popular here in Australia and more so in New

Friday Night at the Oxford

Zealand," he says. "I was appearing on TV every second week with *Bandstand* and *Six o'Clock Rock*, so I was an idol here.

"I went over exceptionally well, probably because I was a totally different act to The Beatles. I was a single performer doing an Elvis Presley-type act, which was in complete contrast to the Beatles – four guys singing and harmonising."

Devlin says John, Paul, George and Ringo were just "plain, average guys". They even invited him to Paul's birthday party when he turned 22 during the tour.

"I hung out with them quite a few times, went to a few of their parties," he says.

"We had a very good rapport. I think they appreciated the fact that I'd had a few years more experience than they did. As a result, they asked me a lot of questions.

"I remember they called me backstage at one stage and they were all grouped around Ringo who had a little Korg drum pad. They played a song and asked me, 'What do you think of this one?' They'd played *A Hard Day's Night* to me before it was even released.

"I said, 'It's got to go straight to number one because it's such a good song'."

Devlin counts himself very lucky to have been a part of a historical tour that, he believes, changed the country.

"The Beatles changed everything, they changed the whole culture of Australia," he says. "If a guy wore long hair back in 1964 he was regarded as a sissy, but The Beatles put an end to that.

"They changed everything. People even noticed what they wore. Entertainers like myself were running around getting suits made up with velvet collars and trying to buy Beatle boots that zipped up at the side.

"That was unheard of at the time for a bloke, a boot that zipped up at the side."

After the first show of The Beatles' 1964 tour at the Wellington Town Hall in New Zealand, John Lennon stormed backstage threatening to cancel the rest of the tour because the band couldn't hear themselves play.

Johnny Devlin spoke to the sound engineer and talked him into turning up the sound at the next show. "Lennon was that excited about it, he said, 'The sound was fantastic. Anything you want, mate, you've got it'," Devlin recalls.

"I said, 'I normally get a photograph taken with the international acts that I appear with'. But that wasn't easy with The Beatles, as manager Brian Epstein refused to allow photos to be taken with any of the support acts.

"Fortunately, he didn't go to New Zealand and that's where I had the photo taken," Devlin says.

Sea songs written by the Siberian seashore
June 17, 2004

It seems Ukrainians are a bit wary of people carrying guitar cases.

At least, that's what singer-songwriter David Beniuk discovered on a 10-month overseas jaunt with his partner.

Beniuk's guitar caused many people to curse when he'd accidentally bang it into the backs of their legs as he was racing to catch a train.

But that wasn't his only problem.

"The guitar case got opened a few times at border crossings," Beniuk admits.

"The Ukrainian border guards wanted to know what the guitar tuner was all about. They needed me to demonstrate that to be satisfied it wasn't some intelligence gathering device.

"The Bulgarians opened the guitar case, then looked at my passport, saw I was Australian and waved it away.

"It amused the Mongolian circus troupe on the trans-Mongolian railway no end. Some of them could play a bit.

"It was pretty funny hearing a Mongolian circus midget playing *Hotel California*, travelling through Mongolia on a train on the way to Beijing."

As well as finding out what The Eagles sound like in a Mongolian accent, the trip also inspired Beniuk's forthcoming album.

Friday Night at the Oxford

The Inland Sea is due out in a few months and the title track was written on the shores of Lake Baikal in Siberia.

"It's a pretty inspirational place," he says.

"Despite the fact there's a city of 500,000 people half-an-hour from the lake, it really is as close to the middle of nowhere as you can get.

"The day we got there was really clear and you could see the mountains on the other side of the lake.

"It was the end of six months through Europe where I was really trying to get in touch with the history of Europe. I'd had the feeling of 'What was the whole European experience about?'."

With the 12-track CD about to be mixed, Beniuk is taking a new band out on the road to play the new material.

The band is also called The Inland Sea, and includes bassist Steve Bull (who previously played with Icehouse and Jenny Morris), former Leonardo's Bride drummer Jon Howell and guitarist Neil Beaver.

Beniuk also had former Weddings Parties Anything frontman Mick Thomas produce five tracks on the CD.

Beniuk travelled to Melbourne to record in Thomas' home studio and Thomas also played on several of the tracks.

It was a connection that started when Weddings Parties Anything helped Beniuk's old band, Merry Widows.

"I have admired him as a songwriter, I still do," Beniuk says. "I think he's a great songwriter. In a way it's a dream come true. You want to work with people you admire.

"I guess you get to know people pretty well when you're stuck in a studio with them for several days.

"We got on really well and Mick's got so many great stories about life on the road and he can keep you constantly amused."

David Beniuk and the Inland Sea perform at the Oxford Tavern on Friday and the Tea Club at Nowra on Saturday. Support band is Women in Docs.

Glen Humphries

Voice the ticket for Cosby
June 17, 2004

Naming your band Cosby is setting yourself up to answer endless questions about any influence the US comedian has on your music.

So, let's get it out of the way early. There's no connection between the Wollongong band Cosby and the comedian Bill Cosby.

"It wasn't a defining moment, we just decided, 'Yeah that'll do'," says the band's bass player Brett Williams.

"Coming up with band names is such a frustrating thing. We finally found something that didn't make us cringe when we thought of it.

"It really means nothing, it's just a name to put to us. We don't want a name to lead to any ideas of how we sound. It's a very neutral name."

Cosby has been around for just a few months but there's a lineage that stretches back further than that.

Williams and guitarist Danyl Traynor were in a band together called Schnook in 1998. Last year, they took on a new member, guitarist Cory Parker, and changed their name to Faded Underground.

That band broke up and Williams, Traynor and Parker formed Cosby with the help of drummer Matt King and singer Tania Nichamin.

Williams says having a female singer allows the band to approach songs differently.

"The main thing we were looking for was a melodic singer," he says.

"We just assumed a guy would be interested but if a girl came along, we wouldn't pass it up.

"Tania just had a really good sense of melody and she wanted to rock out as well. Having female vocals might be limiting in one direction but it opens so many more doors in other directions.

"It makes the music more interesting."

Having Nichamin on board has helped the band. She'd been a finalist in the i98fm Musicoz Listeners' Choice awards and was asked to record a song for an upcoming CD compilation.

Instead of recording *Why I Try* herself, she brought the band with her – and they also knocked over a live recording of Cosby song *Taking Me Over*.

Friday Night at the Oxford

"We were given the opportunity and, after being in bands for a while, you realise how rare those sorts of opportunities are," he says.

There's also plans in place for Cosby to enter the recording studio to lay down some more tracks.

"We're going to record again later in the year, for a longer release," he says.

"So we'll probably include those two songs on that, make it an EP with six tracks."

Cosby are on tonight at the Wollongong Youth Centre.

Start your own record label
July 8, 2004

It's no longer only old guys with gold chains sitting in expensive offices who run record labels.

Just about anyone can do it – and you don't really need an expensive office (or a gold chain).

One small operation started out in a guy's bedroom.

You don't need a business degree or loads of cash. In fact, after speaking with a few people who've started up their own labels, you don't need much more than a love of music and a few hundred dollars.

That's pretty much how Jai Alattas co-founded Sydney's Below Par Records.

Alattas was still in high school when he and a friend decided to set up the label just over three years ago.

"We were going to local shows and just wanted to start up a record label for fun," Alattas says of the pop-punk label.

"It was just a hobby at first. We enjoyed the music that we were listening to and wanted to put our own records out, in that same style."

It started up in a bedroom with Alattas and his friend kicking in $600 each.

Neither of them had a clue about how to go about this record label caper.

"We didn't know for two years what we had to do," he says.

"We just did what we wanted to do. We put together a compilation for our first release and we didn't know how to do it and we didn't pay the bands any royalties because we just didn't know what to do.

"It was just a learn-as-you-go experience. As we started working with other artists we just started picking things up."

Learning on-the-run is a better way to go, Alattas thinks. He's aware there are now a range of music-industry courses on offer, but believes you don't really need any qualifications to run a record label – though he does wish he hadn't dropped out of business studies a month before starting the label.

"I'm glad we were ignorant and naive when we started," he says. "We didn't care about how things were done, we didn't know any better, we just did things our own way.

"Now we know so much stuff we laugh at the way we used to do things."

One potential problem about being in a certain scene and owning a label is the risk of having friends in bands badger you about signing them up.

That's not an issue for Alattas – as long as he likes the band's music.

"One of my friends wants to start a ska band," he says.

"I told him I'm never signing his band because I don't like ska. And this is one of my best mates."

Jeb Taylor started up High Beam Music, based in Wollongong's northern suburbs, five years ago.

He'd started out just helping a friend's band, Thumlock, and before he really knew it, he had a label.

Taylor believes technology, the internet in particular, makes it much easier for the cottage-industry labels.

"As a business, it's getting more and more so you can run it from home or a garage or a bedroom," Taylor says.

"You could do it with a computer and a phone really. If it's only a small label you're not going to have loads of stock cluttering up your house and if you've got distributors they look after that anyway.

"A lot of bigger labels are run out of houses, just with the web. Half the people wouldn't even know where your offices are anyway."

As far as signing bands to High Beam, the first box that needs to be checked is whether Taylor likes them.

"Then you assess how they'll go commercially," he says.

"You see them play as much as you can to see what their crowds are like.

"You try and meet up with the band and talk to them a bit to see what their attitude's like. Sometimes you can rush straight into something and too late you realise this band you've signed are a pack of dickheads."

Both Alattas and Taylor agree it would be unwise to expect to make truckloads of money from a label.

Another who agrees with that assessment is Stuart Coupe, from Sydney's Laughing Outlaw Records.

Coupe helped start the label five years ago after trying his hand at everything from band management and promotions to music journalist and magazine editor.

"As I'm fond of saying, 'somebody does win Powerball every week'," Coupe says.

"You can strike first-up with that lucky record that goes crazy. But if anyone is looking at running an independent record label as a way to get their first Lamborghini in the driveway, I can think of a lot of other ways to do it."

The label had focused on psychedelic pop music and alternative country but has recently broadened its scope to include a few rockabilly records and some rock and roll.

One tip Coupe offers is to keep quiet about which footy team you support.

In the past, Coupe's joked that showing an affection for his beloved Sydney Swans goes a long way to getting a record deal with Laughing Outlaw.

Swans fan or not, if Coupe decides to have a band on his label, contracts must be signed. The handshake deal doesn't cut it for him.

"I just say to every artist on the label, 'We have to have a contract. I'm going to make it really simple so I can understand it and therefore you can probably understand it'," he says.

"The five important things in a record contract are: what is it for; how long is it for; where is it for; when is the money going to be paid and how much; and what happens if we end up hating each other?"

Coupe admits there are different ways of running a label. Not everyone wants or needs to be as big as Laughing Outlaw – which has its own retail shop in Lewisham.

"Some people have an income from another source and want to just have a hobby record label – which is what the majority of independent record labels are," he says.

"If someone is going into it thinking, 'This band is fantastic, all I've got to do is bring out the record, send it to Triple J and wait for the money to come in', they're going to learn really quickly it doesn't work that way."

Coupe's label is at the bigger end of the independent spectrum, which means it's pretty busy in the Lewisham office.

Part of that workload is dealing with any problem their artist has and, when you've released more than 70 albums, there's a lot of artists to have problems.

"Every artist has a problem of unbelievably major importance on a daily basis," he says.

" 'My boyfriend/girlfriend has left me, rent hasn't been paid, car registration's due, how do I get to Kalgoorlie next Wednesday for the show that I've booked myself into? Why aren't I on the cover of *Rolling Stone*?' Etc, etc.

"There are many days where I think I'm 85 per cent psychologist and 15 per cent person who runs a record label.

"There's probably not a day goes by when I don't learn some new tip or trick about this caper, from talking to other labels, other people in the music industry, reading magazines watching how people do campaigns, how they handle artists," he says.

"Yes, after all these years in the music industry I know a lot but I'm not arrogant or stupid enough to think that I know everything."

Friday Night at the Oxford

Match of music makers
July 17, 2004

The two musicians in Single Note Theory knew they were onto a good thing right from their first meeting.

Singer Rob Steffen (the former vocalist from The Cherrypickers) met up with Cikim guitarist Johnny Mitrevski in January this year for a jam.

"When we got together for the first time and started to jam, songs just started coming left, right and centre," Steffen says.

"Every session we were writing and recording up to three songs and we're still doing that.

"The creativity is just awesome. We both came into this with no expectations. We thought we'd just have a bit of fun and see where it leads.

"I think we knew from the first jam sessions we did, this was going to be something a little bit special."

Steffen says the band name is an indication of their desire to keep things simple, to strip the music back.

It's an interesting change in direction from two guys with rock and roll backgrounds.

"It was the desire to do something different," he says.

"I think you get stale if you don't challenge yourself or try something a little different. This is our opportunity to grow as musicians."

Steffen says they are looking for a few young and talented musicians to expand the band, but there's no time frame for when they'll go beyond the duo.

"We're happy with what we're doing at the moment so we're in no hurry," he says.

"When we do expand the band, it'll sound the same because we want our music to be song-based rather than noise-based."

The comfort Steffen has in the duo format is partially the freedom it allows. In previous bands, he says, everyone was locked into playing a song a certain way so everyone knows where they should come in. If the guitarist suddenly decides to do some fancy noodling, it can really throw off the rest of the band.

That's not a problem when there's just two guys.

"We can play a song and feel free to improvise," he says.

"Maybe in previous bands we were locked into playing a song the same way.

"Now it's just the two of us, if one of us wants to go off on a tangent, the other will realise and adapt. So we can be more creative that way."

Local lads mix dance and rock
August 5, 2004

The Fists of Righteous Harmony are one of the few acts to cross the divide between rock and dance.

The awesome two-piece Wollongong band features live drums and percussion mixed with electronic dance music.

Kane Goodwin plays the drums while Michael Lawler provides the "technical wizardry".

Both were in 1990s Wollongong band Dettol, a rock band that included sampling, but the Fists take things a lot further.

"We had a break and I moved away for four years," Goodwin says.

"In that time dance music came on the scene and everyone got right into it. We both really liked dance music so it was a matter of just playing the music we liked to listen to."

They got their name from a book Lawler was reading that included a band who knew karate and would kick people's butts when they weren't playing. It's also the name of the organisation involved in the Boxer Rebellion in China during the late 19th century.

But Goodwin and Lawler are more into beats than boxers.

While playing dance music, the pair inject a bit of their rock background into the live performance.

Friday Night at the Oxford

"We come from a background of pure energy onstage, playing instruments really loud," Lawler says.

"It's not just the production of it, you have to feel the music. That's where we come from and, when we entered the dance arena that's what we still wanted to do."

The Fists' live show is an unusual hybrid. They're playing dance music but with a rock band's attitude to performance.

"I really love electronic music but you go along and watch a DJ and there's nothing really to watch," Goodwin says.

"I was always waiting for someone to come out and do some crazy drum solo or something to give it that musicianship vibe.

"We wanted to do that – where people come along to watch us and there are actually people playing instruments and there's real live energy."

"You get some people who aren't the type to go to a nightclub and dance for six hours," Lawler adds. "They want to come along and see something, so they get a lot out of us."

The band has been trying to get a CD out for a while now. The problem they have is knowing when to stop tinkering with a song.

"We did a demo last year and we've got another five or six songs we're working on now," Lawler says.

"Our stuff changes week to week, because it's all on computer we're continually playing with it, fine-tuning things."

"We procrastinate too much. I think that's been a bit of an obstacle in getting things out. We should get something out by the end of the year," Goodwin says.

CD comes to the party
August 26, 2004

This time around, Fugg will actually have a CD to launch at their CD launch.

A few months ago, the Wollongong five-piece had organised a launch, expecting copies of their new album *No Left Turn Unstoned* to be ready in time.

They weren't – so the band went through with a CD launch without actually having a CD.

But they've got the album now so CD launch part two is a goer.

According to the band's keyboard player Pete Conran, it almost seems a miracle the CD came out at all.

As well as problems with their label and the pressing of the CD, there was also some toing-and-froing at the mixing stage, then the artwork was knocked back at the last minute and had to be changed and, once it was revised, the computer it was saved on died.

There were also hurdles to jump regarding the interactive component of the CD – some bugs needed to be removed for the thing to work.

But finally a CD the band recorded in February and May last year is out. And you can hear the band's sighs of relief from here.

While everything else seemed to be a bit of a nightmare, by all accounts the recording process itself went very smoothly.

The band laid down the 13 tracks (plus a few extras) at the home studio of Mental As Anything. Seems the guys saw Fugg one night and liked them so offered their studio.

And their instruments too, it seems. Conran played Greedy Smith's keyboards on a number of tracks.

As well as getting to look at the Mentals' gold albums hanging on the walls, Fugg also got to save a bundle of cash without skimping on quality.

"Because it was done as a home recording job, but a very professional one, it was very easy to keep costs down," Conran says.

"Because there were no studio fees you could do it whenever you wanted.

"Once you don't have the money thing hanging over your head it's really easy to sit down and get a better product.

"It means you can spend a whole day working on one song just doing a guitar part alone and not having to worry about paying $50 or $100 per hour."

The end result is a high-quality product for a Wollongong band. As

Friday Night at the Oxford

well as the 13 tracks, there's a colour insert and a huge interactive section that includes photos, videos, images and an incredible 40 mp3s of unreleased songs from throughout the band's history.

"It's getting close to the Fugg 10-year anniversary," he says.

"I had the idea ages ago of doing the interactive thing because there really hadn't been that in this city. No-one's really done that, certainly not of this magnitude.

"Maybe we've just raised the benchmark for independent CDs down here."

While he admits this is a career retrospective, it doesn't mean Fugg is planning on pulling the pin.

"No, not at all. At a certain point it's nice to just go 'Look, this is what we've done. Come and see us and give us your cash'."

Live sound a winner
September 2, 2004

Winning was never in the minds of state campus band comp finalists The Dawn Collective.

The five-piece won the University of Wollongong final last month and tonight head to Macquarie University to battle with other NSW campus winners.

The band's cello player Simeon Johnson says the band didn't enter the UOW comp to win.

"We thought with the band comp at uni, it was a good chance to get some exposure and play to some new people," Johnson says.

The band started out as a side project for a few of the guys from Wollongong act Doubled, but now they're a fully-fledged band in their own right.

As a band, they're after the emotional experience of playing music.

"It's something that engages all the senses rather than just your ears," he says.

"That's why we feel it's our live performances where the true feeling of our music comes through. A recording can't capture the expression on your face as you're playing a song and that's why, as a live experience, we're very engaging."

With Johnson playing cello, it's clear The Dawn Collective are a bit different to most other bands. Johnson believes that difference is effective.

"We do have a very original sound compared to what else is happening, so it does help you stand out," he says.

As for their chances in tonight's final, Johnson says the band's not worried about winning or losing.

"We're always really quite comfortable onstage, whether it's a competition or just a gig, it doesn't faze us that much.

"We just get up there and enjoy it. If you can get up there and have a good show and enjoy yourself then chances are the audience will enjoy it too."

Vocal chemistry the start for touring duo
September 9, 2004

The name of Rob Hirst's new band suggests he wasn't being too inventive.

The Midnight Oil drummer has formed a duo with the South Coast's Paul Greene and called it Hirst & Greene.

"It does come with a folky-pop tradition of Seals and Croft or Simon and Garfunkel," he says.

"I wasn't that keen on it. I thought we could come up with a name."

American members of their road crew started suggesting variations of the pair's first names – which in a United States accent sounded like "Rubbing Pole".

In the end, Hirst capitulated and went with the safety of surnames.

And he gets his name first because it's "age before talent".

Hirst and Greene have known each other since they collaborated on the *Olympic Record* CD, which brought together athletes and musicians

Friday Night at the Oxford

(Greene was a former Olympic sprinter).

Hirst decided to ask Greene to join his band, The Ghostwriters.

"When I stopped touring the Ghosties a couple of years ago, Paul and I kept on singing," he says.

"We'd discovered that, lo-and-behold, we had this great vocal chemistry. Also we got on really well and had fun.

"That led us to record a dozen songs, facing each other in a little recording studio in Sydney. Over the space of a couple of years we pieced together this album."

The album is unreleased – Hirst expects it to hit the racks later this year, coinciding with one of the upcoming support slots the duo has lined up.

But there is a single out – *Best Impression* – which Hirst says shows the harmony-based style of the album.

It's also the first song the pair collaborated on – even if it took a long while to finish.

"It's a couple of years in the development stage," he says.

"Mainly because of the upheavals of the whole Midnight Oil camp, there were a lot of distractions there. Plus I was touring pretty heavily with (Hirst's other band) The Backsliders.

"And Paul's got an incredible itinerary, which involves getting in his bread van, as we call it, with his wife Kate and the new baby and touring all around Australia for months on end.

"So we just took the time that we could to get to see each other."

Spending nearly three years working on an album was a relaxing way to go about things for Hirst.

"You can certainly revisit stuff, which is not always the luxury you have when you're doing an album and there's pressure to finish," he says. "We could come back to it and go 'Well, this part didn't work' and 'Maybe we can cut that part out altogether'.

"I'm kind of glad we had the extra time. After lots of years working to deadlines, it was actually really nice not to."

Hirst & Greene play at the Heritage Hotel, Bulli, this Friday.

Glen Humphries

A new political passage
September 9, 2004

The line-up of The Passenger Corridor might seem similar to that of the hard rock outfit Phial, but it's a completely different band.

The Passenger Corridor's singer Rob Carr, drummer Phil Burke and guitarist Warren Keelan were all in Phial.

The only new member is bassist Andrew Smetanin.

When Smetanin joined the trio they began writing music together.

When the music they were writing became less hard-edged and more melodic they decided what they had was a different entity.

"For the other guys it didn't feel like Phial and there was a suggestion to change the name, largely for that reason and because the music has started changing as well," Smetanin says.

"The change (in music) wasn't a conscious change, but it was something we became conscious of. It just started changing by itself and then we started going, 'Look at this, this is different'.

"I guess we're less aggro but, in saying that, we're a lot more critical about what we are aggro about.

That fine-tuning of their aggro leads them to focus on social and political issues – highlighted by Carr in his lyrics.

"Rob's quite politically charged and he has a lot of clarity as to why he's motivated in that direction and we all feel it's quite justified," Smetanin says.

"We can comment and change has occurred like that. Largely we're all quite in agreeance. That's why the group really clicks because we do have common interests.

"There's not huge personality clashes going on and what's coming out of each other's mouths is something we all agree with."

The band name also has socio-political connotations – being an oblique reference to people being channelled or controlled by others.

The Passenger Corridor is recording at the moment and the first 100 people to their youth centre gig next week will score themselves a free sample of those sessions.

Friday Night at the Oxford

The band will be handing out CD copies of the track *One Road* on the night.

As for when the rest of the songs will be heard, Smetanin says no date has been set for the release.

"No there's not and I think the reason for that is we really just want to take as long as it takes," he says.

"We will set a deadline, but probably a fairly indulgent one to make sure the product is exactly what we want it to be."

Split Machine goes on
September 16, 2004

How Machines Work aren't that big on rehearsals. And that's a good thing considering two members live in Wollongong and one in Melbourne.

Last year singer and guitarist Justin Roberts inherited a house in the Victorian capital. He could live there for free or stay in Wollongong and pay rent. So he went.

Drummer Jeb Taylor says the tyranny of distance makes weekly practices impossible.

But having members separated by 600 or more kilometres isn't as much of a headache as you'd think.

"It's good in a lot of ways because it means people don't get sick of us playing a lot of shows," Taylor says.

"Sometimes it works out better because you're not on top of each other all the time. You're not jamming every week, getting sick of the songs."

The band has just released five more of those songs on the new EP *Address in White*.

It follows on from last year's EP *Pilot Error*, which garnered them a bit of attention and Triple J airplay.

Taylor, who along with Roberts and bassist Simon Dalla Pozza, were in late '90s band Ventolin, says the new EP is a stronger effort.

"These songs were written as this band," he says. "The other songs were a hangover from the Ventolin days.

"The *Pilot Error* stuff was really intended to be just demos, it was never intended to be an EP. It was more to get some shows and some interest to do the next record."

The *Pilot Error* EP did get some interest for the next record. After it was released, several large record companies started courting the band.

How Machines Work danced around with them for a while before starting up their own label with a friend, Trans Electric Records, and releasing the new EP.

"We had a few [record companies interested] but it ended up going around in circles a lot of the time," Taylor says.

"We could have kept going at it and kept giving them demos, but it was getting close to a year since the *Pilot Error* stuff got some interest.

"We decided we wanted to keep going and thought it was time we did something ourselves and see what happened from that."

How Machines Work launch their EP at the Oxford Tavern tomorrow night.

Infused with creativity
September 30, 2004

Electronic act Infusion play huge shows like the Glastonbury Festival in Britain – but they started right here in Wollongong.

The trio – Jamie Stevens, Frank Xavier and Manuel Sharrad – were based in Wollongong until 1997.

That's when they moved to Sydney and then to Melbourne – where they now live when they're not travelling the world playing shows.

In fact Sharrad is in a London hotel for this interview, preparing for the Creamfields dance festival.

"When we started as Infusion we were still in Wollongong but had to travel to Sydney to play at clubs or dodgy warehouse parties out in the western suburbs," Sharrad says.

"It was the mid '90s so the whole dance culture was very new in

Friday Night at the Oxford

Australia. A lot of the parties were frowned upon in the press. It's not like you could stay in Wollongong forever, put it that way. There were very limited resources there.

"When we started everyone was still into Nirvana and grunge and all that and it was like, 'We're not. See ya later'."

And off they went – eventually finding themselves at Glastonbury and the Roskilde Festival in Denmark sharing stages with the likes of The Chemical Brothers and Paul Oakenfold.

They've also covered a lot of ground in Europe, Canada, Mexico and Argentina (where they recently played to 15,000 people).

So the trio are doing pretty well for themselves.

They've also released their new CD *Six Feet Above Yesterday*. Sharrad says it's a different feel on the CD to their live show, which is more of a "clubby" vibe.

"It's not really a dance album," he explains. "There is some dance stuff on it, but there's also some rocky stuff and some atmospheric stuff. There's a bit of everything.

"We don't just listen to dance music, we listen to all kinds of stuff, so we really wanted to make a proper album, rather than a mix CD, which quite frankly we get bored of.

"Listening to 70 minutes of the same kind of beats, jeez, you want to slit your wrists after that.

"We like Radiohead, The Cure, Depeche Mode, Interpol, Franz Ferdinand. There's no end to the stuff we listen to, so why not be influenced by that stuff?"

Those bands also had an influence on Infusion's creativity as well. Unlike a lot of electronic music, many of Infusion's tunes have lyrics that the band have written themselves.

"What we listen to is bands who write their own stuff, do their own thing, so we very much wanted to do that ourselves," Sharrad says.

"It does feel a bit cheap if you're just sampling someone else's work, just whacking out a cheap dance remix of some old '80s track or whatever.

"It's more adventurous to try and do it yourself and see what you can come up with."

The band are in the middle of their biggest Australian tour to date. While Sharrad says they're well-known within the dance scene because they've been around for ages, the tour will give them a good chance to gauge their popularity, see whether things have changed since they were last here.

"There are certain cities we've played at where we're guaranteed a really good time no matter what happens," he says.

"Then there are places like Adelaide and Brisbane that have taken a lot longer to get into the groove of it all. That's purely because they're into a different kind of music. They're much more into their high-energy sort of stuff and we don't really play that sort of stuff.

"But it's all catching on now, which is really cool."

They've also scheduled a Wollongong show on the tour – a gig at Cooneys. The show will be the band's first in Wollongong for at least two years.

But Sharrad doesn't think it'll be weird going from playing huge festivals to a pub in Wollongong.

"We just played to a 400-capacity club in Puerto Rico," he says.

"That wasn't big at all but we still had a really good time. It's not the size that counts, it's what you do with it that matters. It doesn't matter if the crowd is 15,000 or 150 people, it's whether they get into it or not that matters.

"We've had some really good times playing to 200 - 300 people and we've had some really bad times playing to 6000 people."

Infusion play at Cooneys Tavern on Friday.

New singer and songs, new sound for Cherrypickers
November 4, 2004

The Cherrypickers spent more than a year looking for a new lead vocalist – only to find their guitarist could sing.

In June last year, the band got on a plane to play gigs in New York, Los Angeles, Toronto and London.

Friday Night at the Oxford

A month or so after they returned, the band parted ways with lead singer Rob Steffen and started the search for a replacement.

That led to what band member James Lopes says was months of frustration – until they realised the answer was right under their noses the whole time in the form of guitarist John Greer.

Lopes says the band knew he could sing – just not so well.

"Funnily enough, Dave our bassist mentioned it early on, asking 'Why aren't we using John?'," Lopes says.

"We said no, because John plays guitar really well and that his forte was backing vocals. Plus I hadn't really heard him sing before, in terms of a lead vocal.

"Finally we had a jam with him singing and it was like, 'Jesus!' It became very apparent that he could sing. He always could, but it wasn't apparent to us at that point."

Lopes says Greer did mention to the band he could sing, but didn't really speak up because he was the new guy, having only joined a short while beforehand.

Lopes says they felt the loss of momentum after coming back from their overseas tour on a high. Now, they're keen to get things back on track.

That includes a slight change to the band's sound.

"With John came a bit of a harder edge to the lead vocal," Lopes says.

"I think we were pop-rock before, there was a poppier edge to our sound. Now it is more rock-oriented.

"But I don't think we alienate the old fans. People have commented on a couple of gigs that we've done, that it is a progression.

"Definitely it is all pretty much new material. There are one or two songs we call old because we've had them for a while but people who mightn't have seen us in a while would think they were new."

The next step in their plan is to record an EP featuring some of those new tunes.

"We've recorded three, we'll do at least another one, hopefully two," he says.

"It'll depend on when we can find the time. One of us works in

Sydney, three of us work here and getting together for a jam is difficult enough – getting together for a studio session tends to be even harder."

The Cherrypickers play the Palm Court Hotel tonight and Collegians Leagues Club on November 17.

Ending year on high note
December 23, 2004

HyTest are playing a New Year's Eve gig at the Oxford – but they're making sure they're offstage well before midnight.

Fortunately for them, they're not headlining. That fate falls to Rockafella, with The Chargers opening the night.

As HyTest bassist Luke Armstrong says, finishing your set before midnight means you can go and have a celebratory drink, or five.

They might still be called upon to play again but not in any serious capacity.

"We're thinking about having a big all-star jam at the end, at midnight," Armstrong says.

"So we've just got to find something we can all play together. We haven't worked it out yet, it'll probably be a last-minute thing.

"When we go back onstage for the jam it doesn't really matter because everyone knows you've been offstage and drinking anyway."

Then, once the show's over the plan is for the three bands to take home their pre-purchased keg of Cooper's and attack it.

So you can expect to see members of HyTest with sore heads for the first few days of 2005.

But they have earned it. They've been touring up and down the coast this year, playing gigs in Queensland and Victoria. They were one of the finalists in the NSW leg of Triple J's Unearthed contest.

And they also released their debut EP which is going well – it's almost sold out of its first pressing of 500.

Friday Night at the Oxford

"When we first started recording our EP, we were doing home demo jobs that we were going to give away at shows," Armstrong says.

"We'd never assume people would want to pay $10 for one of our CDs. It's getting reviewed in *Drum Media* ... and it's been reviewed on a lot of websites. It's getting heaps of good reviews."

HyTest play the Oxford Tavern on New Year's Eve with Rockafella and The Chargers.

Debut creeping along
January 27, 2005

Richie and the Creeps should have their debut album out within a matter of months. Richie, formerly from Wollongong icons Tumbleweed, says they've been working on the album for the last few months.

The 12-track release is coming out on Reverberation Records (maybe in April), the label owned by You Am I drummer Russell "Rusty" Hopkinson. The Richie and Rusty connection comes from the former's Weed days.

"When I was in Tumbleweed we did heaps of shows with You Am I and became good friends with them," Richie says.

"You Am I gave us [The Creeps] a show in Melbourne about a year ago. We were talking about it then and [Rusty] said, 'When you record it, send it to me'. We have very similar musical tastes. A lot of stuff that's on that label is stuff that I like."

Their last release, the EP *Subterranean Sounds*, was released on Richie's own label, Lucky Charm. While the release on Reverberation will continue the indie theme, Richie has nothing against the bigger labels.

"If bigger opportunities come up, I'll definitely consider them," he says.

"It's not a matter of not liking major labels because they can promote pretty good things. The good thing with releasing independently is you have the freedom to do what you want to do and your own time frame to do it."

Subterranean Sounds was recorded at Richie's Thirroul home. They've taken a step up for the album, recording it in the state-of-the-art studios at 313 Entertainment Media and Arts in Coniston. The result, says Richie, is a great improvement in quality.

"It's a lot more slick," he says.

"It's trying to do more different things. There's a poppier edge to it and more folky tunes."

Richie and the Creeps play the Heritage Hotel tomorrow night with The Intercontinental Playboys and The Sandcasters.

Porcelain's last gig before US recording stint
February 9, 2005

Wollongong band Porcelain still have to pinch themselves every now and then to make sure they're not dreaming.

That's because they are heading to the United States next month to record their debut album with Universal – one of the biggest labels in the world.

"There's certainly moments when it's like, 'we're not in Kansas any more Toto'," guitarist and singer Ben Richards said.

"But when you're working in a band, all day, every day, there's always a hurdle to overcome. As soon as you get over that hurdle, you're focusing on the next one. There's not a lot of time to reflect."

But he still likes relaying stories of running into Bruce Willis in a Los Angeles bar or finding himself in the men's room next to Lenny Kravitz.

But while they're making headway in LA, they don't forget their home town. Whenever they're here, they always make sure to play at least one show.

"It's been the place that helped us get to where we are today," Richards said.

Friday Night at the Oxford

"There's something special about coming here and playing to the same faces you played to years ago. It reminds you of your early days and allows you to appreciate where you're coming from and where you're going."

This Saturday the band will play what is likely to be their last Australian show for the year as part of the Angels of Hope Celebrity Gala Dinner at the Fraternity Club.

Angels of Hope was founded in August to raise community awareness and funding for mental illness in the Illawarra.

"The impetus was a family that had lost their mother, their wife and wanted to do something to make a change to the way mental illness is seen, perceived and handled in the community," chairman Peter Holz said.

"In the past, family members wouldn't talk about it. It still has that stigma and that's something we need to change. We need people to realise it's like any other illness – it can be treated."

Mr Holz said tickets were still available from the Fraternity Club for Saturday night's gala dinner, hosted by Suzie Elelman.

There's also a number of celebrities attending, including *Big Brother*'s Gretel Killeen, former rugby league player Paul Sironen and boxer Kostya Tszyu.

There's a bit of a surprise for Tszyu. Wollongong band Fly Agaric will be playing a song they've written about the champ.

Cheesy rock with bite
February 24, 2005

Babymachine's rough and raw rock music is a mix of the serious and, well, cheesy.

The trio's sound is a reflection of the sort of stuff that would make them head out to a show.

"We just try and capture that cheesy rock spirit, that Australian pub rock," bassist Kristy Newton says.

"It's traditionally a really male thing, but we were always girls that were at shows and loved that kind of music and wanted to play it ourselves."

The serious side resides in the band's lyrics.

"We definitely try to incorporate our politics into our music," she says.

"We all have very strong feminist politics and that comes out in our lyrics. Also, there's just the politics of our social conscience, the issues we feel are important.

"It goes to back to punk rock, the idea of using music as a means of communication and a means of expressing your culture and identity."

Babymachine are aware, however, that when people go to gigs they want to hear rock, not a political rally.

"It's important to keep it as fun as possible as well," Newton says.

"We try and get a fine balance between getting our message out there but making sure people can dance to it and that they like to watch our shows as well."

That mix of message and music has gone as far as the US, where the band's 2003 debut *Birth Is Imminent* is released on indie label 16records. And the Americans are getting into the music too.

"I get emails from people I've never met saying 'your record's really important' and telling me how our songs are inspirational or how it speaks to them," Newton says.

"That's really encouraging. When you get that kind of feedback from someone you haven't met or who is not part of your crowd, it feels like what you're doing is a little more legitimate."

There's a new album on the cards for later this year with the band working on songs at the moment. You can hear some of those tunes when the band plays as part of the Loud and Local night at the Palm Court Hotel.

Babymachine are one of nine bands on the bill, covering punk, garage pop, metal and psychedelia. Outside of Kemblastock, it's probably the most musically diverse festival in Wollongong.

"It's a really thriving scene and it's good to showcase that and let

Friday Night at the Oxford

people know what's out there."

Babymachine play the Loud and Local night at the Palm Court Hotel on Sunday. Also on the bill are HyTest, Monstrous Blues, Cyndustry, Brazen Hearts, MFS and Stiffler.

A fresh Dawn
March 3, 2005

It's been a quiet few months for Wollongong's Dawn Collective — at least gig wise.

After their second-place finish in the NSW campus band competition and being named in *The Brag* magazine as one of Sydney's top 10 unsigned acts last year, the band went on hiatus for a few months.

"It was a good break because last year we had about two or three months of two gigs a week," says the band's singer and guitarist Andrew Bennett.

"It got to a point where we needed a break to have a chance to work on some new material.

"At the same time our bass player and drummer went overseas. Our drummer went to Brazil and came back very brown and our bassplayer went to Japan."

Some of that new material they were working on has surfaced on their latest CD, *The Affirmation EP*.

The four-track EP is the band's second release and continues with the self-described "cinematic" sound for which the band is known.

"We're mad about the whole sweeping, glorious, triumphant sound," Bennett says.

"We've always been into epic-sounding music. The newer stuff we've been writing is like the first track (*Park Covered with Trees*), where there's build upon build until it reaches a really big climax.

"That's what we've always been a fan of and that's what we've tried to produce, something that even sounded like a soundtrack."

But there's a twist at the end of the EP. *The Unstoppable Missy Brown*, with its footstomps and handclaps, sounds like a different Dawn Collective.

"It came out of listening to too much Tom Waits," Bennett says.

"From that came a lot of stomping and clapping and smashing plates and pots in the hallway of my mate's house where we recorded it.

"It also makes the EP more round, more real. The first two tracks are heavy, emotionally as well as lyrically. We're not really dark and gloomy so we don't want people to think that."

Chargers to launch EP
April 14, 2005

There's a spate of bands naming themselves after cars but Wollongong's Chargers aren't one of them. But the band members don't mind if you think it is.

"I'll wear the car thing, because it'd be cool if you had people come up to the shows going 'Hey Charger' and making that peace symbol thing," says guitarist and vocalist Griffin James.

"Where the name comes from, I was thinking electronics and got to charger, as in a battery charger, then from there it was The Chargers.

"I thought, 'Someone's got to have that name'. I checked websites and all I could find was the gridiron team in America and the old Gold Coast Chargers. No band seemed to have it so I took it."

So has he gotten around to copyrighting the name to stop someone else stealing his idea? "Not yet, but it's been in the pipeline," he says.

James formed The Chargers in late 2002 and the band's about to launch its debut EP *Simple But Effective*. It's five tracks of rough-and-ready rock and roll. The rough bit mainly comes from James' vocals – sometimes it sounds like he's gargling gravel in a throat made of sandpaper.

"I've always had a gravelly kind of voice," he says.

"I've found, when we do shows with the Chargers, I try and stay away from the beer before we play.

Friday Night at the Oxford

"What I've cottoned onto is drinking a glass of Coke before we go on and that, strangely enough, loosens up my vocal chords and gives them a bit of protection.

"The last song on the CD, the *Sex in Trees* song, that's the song we always finish with because it takes the most out of my voice."

That's easy to understand; as well as the gravelly caper, there's also a fair bit of shouting going on. And with a title like *Sex in Trees* you can't help but ask what it's about.

"There's not much meaning to it," he says.

"I wrote it in about 30 seconds back in 1998. It was on the first demo tape I made of my solo stuff. When the Chargers' thing happened, I thought we'd get this one out and play with it."

The Chargers CD launch on Saturday at the Oxford Tavern. The gig is free and CDs are $10.

Greene knows his Oils trivia
April 14, 2005

Paul Greene probably knows more about Midnight Oil than the band's biggest fan.

That's because he's part of a duo called Hirst and Greene – and the other half is the Oils' drummer Rob Hirst. So it's quite hard for Greene to resist temptation and not prod Hirst for the inside goss on the band.

"I'm constantly quizzing him about things," laughs Greene.

"Getting the dirt on the Oils and all the affiliated stuff, like Wave Aid. I'm always probing to find out what was going on.

"That and other bands, because he's had a lot to do with INXS and Spy Vs Spy – a band I was a huge fan of. Also the tour van banter on Midnight Oil was quite entertaining. Yes, there's a few things there that are privileged information."

The pair met in 1999, when Hirst was working on *Olympic Record* – an album of songs that paired up musicians with athletes (Greene is a former Olympic sprinter).

Six years later, the pair has released the first Hirst and Greene album, *In the Stealth of Summer*.

Before you ask, it didn't take that long because Greene was too busy pestering Hirst about Midnight Oil to work on the album. Both guys were busy with their own projects, so it was a matter of finding blocks of free time in their schedules.

"Rob's got a fairly healthy competitive streak and I was worried he was going to put out this album before I got to put out my (first solo) album, and I really wanted to put out my album first," Greene says.

"I managed to do that – managed to put out three albums as it turned out."

With such a length of time between the meeting and the album, it's no surprise its content has changed over the years.

"Those first songs were pretty much all Rob's with just some embellishments from me," he says. "A year later we wrote a second batch and that was more of a collaboration.

"We were able to work on these songs and there was no pressure of a release date or what sort of songs we had to write."

Hirst and Greene play tomorrow night at the Nowra School of Arts, $15. Paul Greene also plays the UOW UniBar tonight with his band. Tickets are $5/$10.

Infusion three plus a couple
April 21, 2005

They might have been born and raised here but it took Wollongong audiences a while to get into Infusion.

The three-piece of Jamie Stevens, Frank Xavier and Manuel Sharrad started out in Wollongong before moving to Sydney and then Melbourne.

Xavier says they'd played shows in their home town for years but nobody got it.

"Because we're an electronic band and there are a lot of primarily rock kids in Wollongong, we used to have bad shows. People would go 'What the hell is this?'," Xavier says.

Friday Night at the Oxford

"So we stopped doing it for a while but kind of over the last few years electronic music in general has just shot up so much in Wollongong and now there's a demand for us to play down there."

The last time they were in town, in September 2004, the ARIA-award-winning band packed out Cooneys Tavern.

It seems Wollongong caught onto what others around the world had already figured out – Infusion can put out a great show.

But when the band plays next week, the audience will find a slightly different Infusion.

Xavier says the plan is to perform a lot more songs from their 2004 album *Six Feet Above Yesterday* than they did in September. And there will also be a few extra people onstage.

"This upcoming tour we're bringing along a bass guitarist and a guitarist to recreate some of the parts on the album," he says.

"It's an interesting experience for us playing with another two people. I've been playing with the same guys for six to eight years and we kind of know what we're going to do onstage just by looking at each other."

While the world may see them as a dance band, it's not the category Infusion prefers.

"We see ourselves as a band who happens to use electronic music as an alternative to just using guitars," he says.

"Manuel can play guitar, I can play a little and we can both sing.

"We can all play different things and, if we wanted to, we could sit in a garage, knock out tunes and play like that.

"Jamie and I are also engineers and producers in our own right and we've always been inspired by producers like Brian Eno and Flood, who would try and make something sound a little bit different.

"That's what we've been trying to do; create different sounds and not limit ourselves to just guitars.

"There are other ways of achieving a certain mood in song by using different instruments – there are other instruments in the world."

Infusion play the University of Wollongong Unibar on April 28. Tickets are $10 students/$15 others.

Glen Humphries

Fists find new sound
April 21, 2005

Part of the reason The Fists took a year to release their debut EP was the amount of time they spent arguing over the band name.

The duo of technical whiz Mick Lawler and drummer Kane Goodwin have been known for years as The Fists of Righteous Harmony. It's a great name, but not one that exactly rolls off the tongue.

"I had to argue with Kane for about three months for that, but finally he accepted it," Lawler says.

"He said Rage Against the Machine was a long name and that's fine. I counted out the syllables and we had one more than them, so I said, 'Once you go past Rage Against the Machine, that's too many'."

Truthfully, the name really didn't have that much to do with the CD delay. Lawler puts that down to the nature of digital music – it allows you to keep going back to a song and changing it.

Now they've overcome that, the pair's long-awaited debut CD is due to be launched at Cooneys Tavern tomorrow night.

The six-track EP, *Sunshine 'n' Breaks*, features the band's trade mark mixture of live drums and electronic dance music.

Tracks on the CD are more lyric-heavy than The Fists' earlier tunes. They've ducked into a bit of hip hop with the groove-laden title track and Lawler's brother Andy adds original lyrics over the slinky *Mr Strong*.

"We'd always been talking about getting rid of the vocal and dialogue samples that we traditionally used because it's easy writing lyrics and getting vocalists in to sing them," Lawler says.

"The CD is a lot different to what we have been doing, but I still think we're going to have that energy at the live shows. That's what people like – live energy onstage.

"On the CD the songs are about four minutes long, but if you're really into the groove live, sometimes the song can go for six minutes."

The Fists launch their CD on Friday at Cooneys Tavern. Tickets are $10.

Friday Night at the Oxford

Rockafella's new release
May 19, 2005

Signing to former Tumbleweed singer Richie Lewis' label is already paying off for Rockafella – and their album hasn't even been released.

Rockafella bassplayer Andy Simpson says the band members were about to release their debut album *Sinner* on their own. Then they bumped into Richie at a pub, and he suggested they join his new label, Dead Records. The guys thought, 'Why not?'.

"Richie, his wife Sharon, and the other people involved in the label, they know everyone," Simpson says.

"When they're just going out and hanging out with their friends, they're going to be telling lots of people about us.

"Just recently they were at some industry do and there were people asking about the label and about us, people from high-profile bands like Jet. So being on the label already gets the ball rolling.

"And Richie's been there before from a band perspective. He knows what it feels like to be in a band."

The new album was produced by Rob Younger of Radio Birdman fame. That was quite a blowout for Simpson and the rest of the band – they're all fans of the Australian legends. So they couldn't let the chance to hear a few Birdman tales go by.

"When we were in the studio we were doing what had to be done because time is money," Simpson says.

"But when we were sitting around having lunch or whatever it was 'Tell us about that time when you played that show in London in 1978'. He'd go 'I remember that' and he'd tell us a story and we'll all be hanging on every word."

There were rumours Younger would be getting up onstage with the band at the Oxford Tavern CD launch but Birdman is playing a private party that night.

However, you can head to the Rockafella CD launch in Sydney, at the Spectrum, where Younger will belt out a few covers.

Release-wise, it's been a long time for Rockafella. Their last release was a self-titled EP in 2003. Simpson says the new album is a lot less rough and ready than that effort.

"The first EP, we just went in and did it really, really quickly and all live," he says.

"At that point, when we were playing we were a lot more spontaneous and our shows were a lot crazier. [The new album is] more polished and having a producer simply made it that way. He wouldn't let us get out of the live room until he had that one take he'd been waiting for."

The Rockafella CD launch is on at the Oxford Tavern this Saturday with Hell City Glamours, Jed Whitey and Citizen Dog.

Ireland is back on the map
July 14, 2005

Tim Ireland knows all about the power of music – it helped him pass Year 10 geography.

The former Wollongong singer-songwriter (he now calls Sydney home) wasn't doing too well in his geography class and neither were two of his mates. When the next assignment was due, to make it less painful they chose to record a song on a small cassette player.

"We were given this assignment asking for an Aboriginal viewpoint on Kakadu National Park," Ireland says.

"None of us wanted to sing so it ended up as kind of a rap song – the lyrics escape me, which is probably a good thing.

"We played the song on a tape and the class went wild for it. The teacher loved it and took it next door to the other classroom and it ended up doing the rounds."

And they passed with the best marks any of them had ever received. So of course that meant every geography assignment from then on was completed in song.

Friday Night at the Oxford

He's recorded a few more songs since then – including a 1997 CD EP with Pounderhound, his band at the time, and a solo EP the following year, *Sojourn*. But you had to wait until this year for his next release – the excellent album *Down in the Well*. It's a time Ireland refers to as "the inconvenient seven years".

"I think I just got sidetracked," he says. "I kind of got lost in the workforce for a while there. I never stopped playing gigs but I just found myself in a difficult place, mentally."

So he went the artistic route – getting away from everything. He ended up at Bawley Point on the South Coast after a friend offered up his parents' holiday house.

"I spent three and a half weeks there alone trying to sort my head out," he says.

"I took some recording gear down and made half-hearted attempts at recording. I'd retire from music forever, then drink a lot of whisky and go bushwalking. Then I'd come back and immediately start work the next morning."

The time-out worked; Ireland says his new album was born in that Bawley Point house.

"The first two songs on the album still have guitar tracks on them that were recorded in that beach house," he says

"You can even hear the rainbow lorikeets that were outside singing in the background. I love that sort of stuff, that ambient sound creeping in."

Ireland's not bringing those rainbow lorikeets along for the Wollongong launch tomorrow night, but he is bringing a few other friends.

His band for the launch includes Felix Akurangi from Sydney popsters Peregrine and fellow singer-songwriter Paul Greene.

Ireland met these musicians in the scene around the Excelsior Hotel in the Sydney suburb of Glebe.

"About three years ago I first started playing there and met the guys from Peregrine and then Paul, then Melanie Horsnell," Ireland says.

"There were maybe about eight or 10 songwriters all playing at this pub on different nights and we all knew each other. I found it a very nurturing environment to be around people trying to do the same thing as me. It was all very encouraging and it's certainly where I learnt a lot about my craft."

Tim Ireland performs with Peregrine and Jesse Younan on July 15 at the Oxford Tavern and August 4 at the Yallah Roadhouse Shooter's Bar.

Riding out Tumbleweed roller-coaster
November 15, 2008

Former Tumbleweed guitarist Lenny Curley has an analogy to explain the rise and fall of the Wollongong band.

"From day one the band was on a really shaky roller-coaster and there was no way it was going to make it to the end," he said. "That's my analogy for Tumbleweed."

Curley and his original band mates – drummer Steve O'Brien, guitarist Paul Hausmeister and singer Richie Lewis – talk to the *Weekender* today about Tumbleweed's rise, fall and chances of a reunion.

Curley believes they had a habit of "shooting ourselves in the foot", whether it be by sacking their management, ousting band members or generally not being able to cope with their popularity.

"With the music, I feel as though I fluked it big-time," he said. "I don't consider myself a great guitar player - I was just in the right place at the right time."

For Lewis, the 10 years as part of Tumbleweed were the best days of his life.

"It was just a really, really good time," he said.

"It had its ups and downs but, in hindsight, there were more ups than downs.

"We were in the band since the time we left school basically and so a lot of things were just taken for granted.

"We could have done things a little differently.

"But all these experiences have defined me. Not only me, everybody, really. It's a very important part of my life and a very incredible experience."

The band is an important part of other lives as well.

Although the group hasn't played together for eight years, fans still ask about Tumbleweed. And there are also new fans being made – including Curley's son, who loves watching dad's videos.

"He wants to watch them on YouTube every day," Curley quipped. "I have to say 'no, no more'."

Taking a tumble
November 15, 2008

They played their last gig nearly a decade ago but it seems Tumbleweed, one of the biggest bands to come from Wollongong, hasn't been forgotten.

Offers still come in to reform for shows. Their CDs rarely turn up in secondhand stores, which is always an indicator of a band's continued popularity because it means people don't want to part with the albums. And the band members still have people asking them about the 'Weed.

"Last time I was in Melbourne," says the band's original drummer Steve O'Brien, "I don't know how he recognised me because I don't look like what I did 15 years ago, but, pissed two o'clock in the morning, this dude walks past me and then walks back and asks, 'aren't you the drummer out of Tumbleweed?'. I couldn't get rid of him for the next half-hour."

The other founding members – singer Richie Lewis and guitarists Lenny Curley and Paul Hausmeister (bassist Jay Curley was uncontactable) – all have similar stories.

Hausmeister says he feels a "little bit embarrassed" when people go on about the band, while Lenny Curley says he's moved on. "When I'm playing in my new band people will come up and want to talk to me about Tumbleweed," Curley says.

"I'm like, 'can you please just get over it? I'm over it, can you please get over it?'

Glen Humphries

"I feel as though I've moved on whereas a lot of people haven't. I don't want to go back and talk about it with people all the time."

Tumbleweed grew out of late-1980s band The Proton Energy Pills. After releasing a few singles and an EP, the Curley brothers and Lewis (who was then on drums) changed the name to Tumbleweed, and asked Hausmeister, who was in Wollongong band The Unheard, to join. When Lewis decided to switch from drums to vocals, Hausmeister drafted in his Unheard band-mate and drummer Steve O'Brien.

At the time, there was never any thought the band could become huge. This was 1990, a few years before Nirvana would come along and completely change the musical landscape.

"Back in those days there was no chance a loud band with distortion pedals was going to make it," Lewis says. "That crossover hadn't happened.

"So you were used to playing The Lansdowne, The Annandale and going down to Melbourne. There was this nice close-knit subculture of rock and roll fans in those days. It had nothing to do with making it."

When Nirvana broke through with their album *Nevermind* in 1992 suddenly there was a market for the type of music Tumbleweed was playing.

"If Nirvana hadn't existed I don't think Tumbleweed would have ever been as huge as we were," Curley says.

"That whole resurgence of grunge and punk created a situation in Australia where people said 'okay we need a band with long hair, gym boots and flannelette shirts' and we fit the bill.

"We were in the right time and the right place."

In fact, Tumbleweed saw the change first-hand, supporting Nirvana on their only Australian tour in 1992. As the tour progressed, Nirvana got bigger and bigger and the venues went from seating a few hundred to a few thousand.

"I was only 20 when that happened, I'd only been out of school for two years," Curley says.

"Thinking back on it, it was a fantastic experience. I remember those Nirvana gigs, thinking there was something in the air. This band were probably one of the sloppiest I'd ever seen but they were fantastic."

Friday Night at the Oxford

Things were pretty good for Tumbleweed as well. They'd just released their first self-titled album and switched from the indie label Waterfront to Polydor in Australia.

Most impressively, US giant Atlantic Records signed them to a deal to release their albums all over the world after a label rep walked into a record store and heard a Tumbleweed single playing. Hausmeister says that news was like "all our Christmases had come at once". And he's not alone.

"I thought I was going to be a millionaire," Curley says.

"I actually believed that. At that moment I thought we were going to be right because we'd just signed to Atlantic."

But things didn't quite turn out that way – after releasing a collection of their earlier material as *Weedseed* in the US, Atlantic didn't like the *Tumbleweed* album or its 1995 follow-up *Galactaphonic* and refused to release either in the States.

With the benefit of hindsight, Hausmeister says Atlantic were looking to jump on the grunge bandwagon by signing a band for relatively little money in the hope they'd become big.

"We would have been one out of 20 bands they signed with the same objective," Hausmeister says.

"And one of those 20 was a band called Stone Temple Pilots. All (the label) needed was one of those bands to start charting well and the others mean nothing."

He adds that the band didn't help matters by adopting a somewhat less than ideal attitude when playing in the US.

"We also didn't play well when we toured the States," he says.

"It was all an experience and we 'overindulged'. There's a level of professionalism when you get to that level, and we didn't quite have it."

Problems started to surface back home as well. The band had earlier sacked their management, despite Curley admitting "they were a big part of why we became popular initially". And cracks started to open up within the band, with the three younger members (the Curley brothers and Lewis) on one side and the older Hausmeister and O'Brien on the other.

After the release of the band's second album, *Galactaphonic* and subsequent tour, push came to shove and the younger trio agreed to shove out Hausmeister.

O'Brien says the reason was because Hausmeister wouldn't give up his day job in the engineering records department at BHP (up until that point, Hausmeister had been taking holidays and leave without pay to tour with the band).

But Hausmeister himself isn't so sure.

"Nobody has ever actually told me what the real reason is," he says. "I had no idea it was coming. When it happened we'd just finished a tour, we'd just played Perth on a Sunday and I'd flown back for work for Monday. It was either the Monday evening or the Tuesday, I get a call from Lenny 'dude, sorry man, you're out of the band'.

"So I never had an exact reason as to why. Quite a while afterwards I heard that was it, I wasn't quitting work."

It came as a shock to O'Brien as well, who left the band a short while later, angry at the way his friend had been treated and figuring the same thing could happen to him. (O'Brien and Hausmeister then joined up to form a band called Zero "cause it's a weed killer," he explains.)

Despite regretting the sense of lost opportunity after being sacked, Hausmeister harbours no ill will. "Once me and Steve left the band they had a pretty rapid decline and that was kind of satisfying and that was enough for me," Hausmeister says.

Both Curley and Lewis now think this could have been handled better. Now older, Curley can totally understand why Hausmeister would want to keep his job and not want to "commit to something that was under the sway of these younger, rebellious pot-smoking unrealistic people".

He also thinks the pair leaving the band was the beginning of the end for Tumbleweed.

"The departure of Steve and Paul had a lot to do with the demise of Tumbleweed," he says. "Certain combinations of people create better bands than others. There are just something that happens between four or five guys and you can't just get someone else in to be that other person.

"I think Tumbleweed had that thing with those five guys – we had

Friday Night at the Oxford

a chemistry. I realised that chemistry was gone as soon as we started playing live without them. But I had to stick with whatever decision had been made. I had to try and create that chemistry again. For the rest of Tumbleweed we were trying to recreate that chemistry that we had originally."

The band trundled along, releasing *Return to Earth* in 1996 and asking bassist Jay Curley to leave the band before recording what would be the band's last album, *Mumbo Jumbo* in 2000.

"It became a real test of endurance towards the end," Lewis says.

"The good days were the good days and you tend to remember that kind of stuff. But when you're playing The Entrance on a Tuesday night to nine people and you've got a gig the next night at Taree to 15 people. You're doing the same songs, you've got a sore throat and you don't want to do it but you have to do it anyway. That's a real drag."

With Curley and Lewis starting families, the pair decide to call it a day. But there was never an official "final tour" and the band never officially broke up.

"We just didn't do anything ever again," Lewis says.

Curley: "We were playing at Wollongong Uni one night, it was a great gig the place was packed. We looked up at the wall and the date on the poster. The date was 10 years to the day of our first ever gig. So we said, 'hey let's just call it quits', and we did. That was it. We didn't tell anyone. I don't think we even told the other guys in the band. It was just obvious that that was what's going to happen."

In the years since the band ended, any ill will has passed and Curley, Hausmeister, O'Brien and Lewis all get along fine.

"We don't go to BBQs together or anything like that," Hausmeister says, "but, as far as I'm concerned there's no problems. It's all cool. I don't see them a great deal anyway but when I do see them it's fine."

"Early on it was a bit rough," Curley adds, "but I feel as though we all get along pretty well now.

"Kemblastock's great. We all meet up at Kemblastock, have a chat, our kids all play with each other. There's a bit of weirdness but we're all civilised."

Musically, the members have gone on to other projects. Lewis started up Richie and the Creeps, Hausmeister and O'Brien formed Monstrous Blues and went back to The Unheard and Lenny Curley is playing in The Pink Fits.

O'Brien says there was one New Year's Eve when all four of their bands played on the same bill. Which sort of brings us to the burning question; will they every play in the same band?

There's occasional talk of Tumbleweed reforming – Curley says offers come in every now and then. Curley's all for a reunion show, though he's not too keen on playing one of their early tunes, *Stoned*.

"When we were 19 and had that big single, 'Why don't we all get stoned?' that was hilarious," he says.

"That's funny when we were 19 years old but it's not the kind of thing you want to go preaching when you're 37.

Hausmeister is also putting his hand up for a reunion gig. "I'd love to do and have wanted to do it for quite a while," he says.

"When I was kicked out it was a surprise and I went from playing really great gigs to not doing anything, overnight. So it's always been a bit difficult to deal with that. I really enjoyed the stuff we were writing and playing, it was really good stuff. I really enjoyed playing live. To be able to do that again would be really good fun."

O'Brien says a reunion almost came together a few years ago – "it was 99 per cent there" – until one member pulled out.

"In a way, I'm glad that it didn't go on," he says. "I think the chance has come and gone ... I don't think it'll happen now."

So that would mean the band member who pulled out was Lewis. Which makes sense, of all the members he seems to be the one who has put the band behind him the most, the one who decided to end the band because "it was time to get on with life".

The other members aren't sweating on him changing his mind.

"I don't want to pressure him into it," Hausmeister says. "He's probably the most important part of the deal, being the singer. If he's not comfortable with it, it's just going to be awkward anyway. As far as I know, the day he decides to get together and at least have a jam, the rest of us will probably jump at it and give it a shot."

Friday Night at the Oxford

BREAKOUT Q&A
What was your favourite time to be in the band?

Lenny Curley: The best time was before we became popular. The early Wollongong gigs before we broke big. We'd just gotten the band together, we were really enjoying it and everywhere we played, here and in Sydney, we were selling them all out.

Paul Hausmeister: We did the full tour for one of the Big Day Out years (1994), the same year as The Ramones. They had portable sheds out the back of the main stage and each shed was for a band. They put two sheds near each other and a roof between the two so there was this common area.

We rocked up to our shed on the first day and went inside. We were thinking, 'man, can't wait to see The Ramones'. We step out of the shed an hour later and who happens to be in the shed across from us? The Ramones. For the entire tour we had the Ramones sharing our common area which, for us, was just out of control.

Richie Lewis: For me the camaraderie of the earlier days was something that we've never had since. Everything seemed to be in place and everything seemed to be almost effortless. We were enjoying creating together, enjoying playing. It was on the crest, just before things really started happening. Those were the best days – the first two EPs and recording the first album.

Steve O'Brien: Playing parts of England were great, especially playing with Mudhoney. We got to play at Leeds University, where The Who recorded *Live at Leeds*. Playing with the Lemonheads at the Astoria (in London) and getting to have a beer in the Keith Moon Bar.

Tumbleweed reunite
July 24, 2009

Groundbreaking Wollongong band Tumbleweed are about to play their first shows in almost a decade.

The original line-up of the Australian grunge pioneers – singer

Richie Lewis, guitarists Lenny Curley and Paul Hausmeister, bassist Jay Curley and drummer Steve O'Brien – will perform at Homebake in Sydney on December 5.

One of the biggest bands ever to come from Wollongong, they supported US grunge heroes Nirvana on their only Australian tour, signed to a US record label when its members were barely out of high school and released indie classics like *Stoned*, *Daddy Long Legs* and *Sundial*.

But infighting and the acrimony created by the sacking of Hausmeister and O'Brien and, later, Jay Curley seemed likely to forever quash the idea of a reunion.

It appears an *Illawarra Mercury Weekender* retrospective about the band published last November may have been partially responsible for the re-formation.

It is understood that the story, which touched on previous attempts to reform the band, led to the band members to start discussing it again.

"The time is right for us right now," Lenny Curley said.

"We've dealt with all our old demons and we're all very enthusiastic about getting the band back together. There have been tensions there over the years for obvious reasons but I think we've finally reached a level where we're comfortable with one another and we really want to have another crack at it."

Curley says the band may stay together after Homebake.

For Curley, the best thing about the Homebake show is that his son – a fan who has only seen dad's band play on YouTube – can watch a live Tumbleweed gig.

Tumbleweed rollin' back
October 31, 2009

Tonight, a decade's worth of prayers from many Wollongong rock fans will be answered when legendary band Tumbleweed take the stage for a sold-out show at Waves.

While the band broke up not long after their last studio album,

Friday Night at the Oxford

2000's *Mumbo Jumbo*, this gig features the original members – who haven't shared a stage since the mid-1990s.

But the fans never forgot them and, for most of the past decade, they've pestered the five members with questions about the band getting back together.

However, infighting and the acrimony created by the sacking of guitarist Paul Hausmeister and drummer Steve O'Brien and, later, bassist Jay Curley made it seem unlikely that they'd ever be in the same room together, let alone on the same stage.

What helped get them together? The Homebake concert, an *Illawarra Mercury Weekender* feature on the band published late last year, and more than a few glasses of wine.

The band had been offered a spot at Homebake's 15th anniversary concert this year and, around the same time, the *Weekender* featured a retrospective on the band.

A week or so later singer Richie Lewis went out for dinner and, sitting at the next table, was Hausmeister. After a few wines, they got to talking about the band, the article and Homebake.

"We ended up back at his place having a few more wines and, a week or two later we were in a practice room," Lewis said.

"As soon as we plugged in and played it sounded great. It just all made sense. It was time to let go of our demons, of our past."

Not that he expected that to happen. Lewis admitted there were a lot of nerves at that first practice session.

"I got there first and watched everyone show up and they all seemed a little bit apprehensive," he said.

"Nobody wanted to bring up the past and everybody was wondering whether this practice was going to be any good.

"So we decided, look. there's no pressure, let's just plug in and see what happens.

"Once we set up it was like 'well, what now'. I suggested 'let's just do *Sundial*, see how it sounds'. It sounded great, just like the record. From that moment on there were smiles on the faces and it was really good."

It was proof that the chemistry the band used to have was still there, the very same chemistry missing from the bands they would form after Tumbleweed.

"It's a typical example of how the sum of the parts is greater than the individual," Lewis said.

"In every band I've been in since – and I've spoken to the others and they've said the same thing – it's always seemed like a lot more effort to get a sound that isn't as good.

"When we practised it was so effortless – it was just there, this amazing connection. These five individuals who are very different from each other but, when they're in the same room making music, there's a magical quality to it and I've never experienced it since."

The band has been rehearsing every Sunday for the past four months and, even though they had to refresh their memory as to how their songs went, Lewis said they were ready for their first show in nearly 15 years.

"We should be right," he said.

"It sounds fantastic. I'm still a little nervous about how it's going to sound on a big stage in front of a lot of people.

"We haven't played in front of a lot of people for a long time, so there's a few nerves about that.

"But I'm really looking forward to it.

"We've got people coming from all over the country.

"There were a lot of people who wanted to hear the songs again. And we wanted to hear them again too."

Crafty musos band together
February 27, 2010

The region's artists and musicians are joining forces for an art show that rocks.

Called *5x5x5*, the project is both an art exhibition and a gig. Five Wollongong artists will each create five posters for five South Coast bands.

Friday Night at the Oxford

Half the project will feature the posters from artists Shane Kenning, Gordon Watt, Trina Collins, Steve O'Brien and Lenny Curley in an exhibition at Project Contemporary Artspace.

The other half has those five bands on the posters – Babymachine, Ye Luddites, Bulldoze all Bowlos, Leadfinger and The Nice Folk – playing at Waves.

As well as designing five of the posters, Collins is one of the organisers of the project. She's also the drummer in Ye Luddites – so she's pretty busy.

She says *5x5x5* was the brainchild of fellow artist Kenning, who has created posters for quite a few Wollongong bands.

"We wanted to give the local talent, both musically and artistically, a showcase," Collins says.

"Venues are dying off in Wollongong and also we can't put posters up on poles or the places we used to. Even the uni, we can't put posters up there any more without paying a gigantic fee to put them on the noticeboards.

"So these artists don't have anywhere to put their work legally and bands really don't have many places left to play in the city either."

As well as that, the link between art and music makes sense because most of the artists involved are also musicians.

Watt is in Ye Luddites with Collins, and O'Brien and Curley are in Tumbleweed.

For Collins, the music is what brought her to art.

"I definitely started out as a musician who dabbled in art," she says.

"I started out trying to make artwork for the band that I was in – websites and posters. The tables have turned now and I'm more of an artist than a musician.

"I make my bread and butter being an artist, the music is more of a hobby.

"I think there has always been a really strong link between music and art for me. The two for me go hand in hand."

Something else that makes *5x5x5* unusual is the way the works of art are for sale.

There will be a limited edition of 100 high-quality A3 copies of each poster available for sale and one A1 copy of each poster will be auctioned off at the exhibition's opening night.

5x5x5 the exhibition is on at Project Contemporary Artspace from April 21 to May 4 with the official opening and poster auction on April 23. The five-band concert is on at Waves on April 24.

Site celebrates music scene
June 3, 2010

Rather than sit back and watch so much of Wollongong's rock and roll past be forgotten, Warren Wheeler decided to do something about it.

That something would be the blog Steel City Sound, which Wheeler started in March this year as an ever-growing archive of the changing Wollongong music scene since the 1960s.

Wheeler's era was the 1990s and, while he wasn't in bands, he was writing about them in *Bulb* and *Pulse of the Illawarra* – two of the street press publications around at the time.

"As I've grown older I've hit my CD collection and realised there were all these bands I loved during the '90s which are no longer around," Wheeler says.

"Indeed, a lot of their music is no longer available – they're not being re-pressed and they're not up on iTunes or anything like that. That's just from the '90s and not taking into account the scenes before I was around, dating back to the '60s.

"Some of that stuff is really difficult to get your hands on – not just the recordings but the history of the bands.

"The idea was to put all this in one central place, not only for the people who have come through the scene to reminisce but also to show people around the world that Wollongong has had and continues to have a thriving independent music scene."

As well as detailed biographies on several bands, you can download songs, videos or even flick through almost 300 band posters on the site.

It's not just Wheeler's own era he's keen on documenting – the first

Friday Night at the Oxford

entry he posted was on 1960s band The Marksmen.

"That was the earliest recording I could find from a Wollongong band – they may have even been the first rock recording," Wheeler says.

Wheeler has been using his own collection to start off the site but is keen to hear from people from past Wollongong bands and punters who are keen to share their stories and music on the site.

Steel City Sound is at steel-city-sound.blogspot.com and there is also an email address there to contact Warren Wheeler. You can also find it on Facebook by searching for "Steel City Sound".

Tumbleweed Mark II
December 16, 2010

For the first time in a long time, you can go into a music store and buy a new Tumbleweed album.

That album is the two-disc effort, *The Waterfront Years*, which contains all their early stuff, released on the indie label Waterfront.

It includes the first EP *Captain's Log* (featuring Dave Curley on vocals and current singer Richie Lewis on drums), the band's debut album and some songs that previously only appeared on ultra-limited edition vinyl singles given away at gigs.

Guitarist Paul Hausmeister says the CD – released by Melbourne label Aztec Music – came about because fans at the reunited band's shows kept asking for one.

"With the shows that we've been playing, we've been selling a bit of merchandise, T-shirts and stuff," Hausmeister says.

"The majority of people turning up to the counters have been asking for records, whether we had any available, particularly the early stuff.

"It's been difficult to get the early recordings because once they'd sold out of their initial runs, they were never re-released. Waterfront, as a label folded, and when that happened, that was it. They didn't release anything any more."

So the band put out some feelers and Aztec came back keen to release all the early stuff.

Glen Humphries

At the end of this month, the band are hitting the road to promote the CD. That tour includes a New Year's Eve show at Waves, the first in their Wollongong home town since the reformation gig in October last year.

Hausmeister says the band have had several short tours of the North Coast, Queensland and Melbourne since reforming and there are plans for a national tour in 2011.

So it's clear the members of Tumbleweed are getting along much better than they used to. Before the reunion some members hadn't talked to each other in 15 years.

"It's great. It's been great fun," Hausmeister says of Tumbleweed Mark II.

"The attitude's way different to what it was. Everyone's taking it a lot easier."

Hausmeister is even enjoying band practise in the Tumbleweed rehearsal rooms – a small, hot space behind guitarist Lenny Curley's house that is mighty cramped once all five members get inside.

"In the jam room now it's just really, really cool," he says.

"Apart from the really early days I don't remember the jam room being as comfortable as it is now. It's actually good fun to get around there and play.

"Now we enjoy getting back together, shutting the door on the joint and turning the amps on and working through stuff."

Fans will be happy to know that some of that stuff they're working through are new songs. There is a chance a few of them may appear in the New Year's Eve set-list but Hausmeister is making no promises.

But he will say that the songs will eventually see the light of day.

"At the end of the day we do want to record those songs, we do want to release them and we want people to like them," he says.

"We've got two that are pretty well complete and there's probably about another seven ideas that we're working on.

"At the moment we're not really sure whether we'll just jump in with two or three songs and record just a single to get some new stuff out there, or record something more.

"I think what it'll depend on is how quickly we can write the songs

Friday Night at the Oxford

and be happy with the final arrangements.

"If it's a bit of a slow process, we'll probably go in and record two or three and look at releasing those first and then continuing on with the album."

Tumbleweed play Waves on New Year's Eve with Spiderbait and HyTest.

Rolling out new tunes
March 29, 2012

The future of Tumbleweed was decided in November last year — and it was good news for fans.

After reforming in 2009 and playing a range of shows around Australia since then, they took a break from each other for a few months last year.

Then they all got back together and had a formal discussion to address what had only been mentioned in passing before.

"In November we sat down and it was like 'what are we going to do?," remembers Paul Hausmeister.

"Are we just going to keep going out there and play our old songs or are we actually going to get serious and write some new stuff and actually think about an album?"

The answer was "write some new stuff". From there they went into 313 Studios in Coniston to record 20-odd demos.

"All of us were starting to compile new songs," Hausmeister says.

"Over the last year I'd had stuff that was coming into my head and I was throwing it down onto a cassette recorder at home.

"It's just what happens, you tend to write stuff. I know (guitarist) Lenny (Curley) would be the same as well; he'd spend a lot of time in his jam room on his own and twanging away. So I think we were all getting pretty itchy about writing stuff, it's just that we hadn't sat down together and said, 'let's get serious about it and let's have a point in doing it as well'."

The band liked what they heard on those demos so much that

they've scheduled in 10 days in June to record tracks for a forthcoming album.

There is no release date scheduled for that album.

But fans don't have to wait for ages to get an earful of the new songs. Hausmeister says they'll be road-testing five or six of the tunes at their Unibar gig.

Those fans can rest easy too because Hausmeister says those new songs don't herald any massive change in Tumbleweed's sound.

"We're always going to sound the same," he says. "I think we have a fairly unique sound and the stuff that we're writing is pretty similar to what we were writing before.

"... The old fans should like it – there are plenty of Sabbath-sounding riffs there. And there's plenty of pop gems too."

Tumbleweed play the Wollongong Unibar with Sydney Girls Choir and Kaleidoscope on March 30.

Hidden talent on show
June 13, 2012

Wollongong's art and music scene is thriving, but the problem is many people don't even know it exists.

The organisers of the two-week festival *Unscene* aim to change that by showcasing what the city's artists and musicians are doing.

"There are always so many events happening in Wollongong but a lot of time people never know about then until after they've occurred," says Trina Collins, one of the organisers.

"So we thought, let's look at two weeks and try and advertise as many events as we can locally in that time. Some of them we've organised especially for the event, others would have happened without us.

"It's just putting the spotlight on all the creative stuff that is happening in Wollongong, especially with smaller businesses who haven't got the money to promote things. They've always got things on but they haven't got the facilities to promote them to large audiences."

Friday Night at the Oxford

Events over the 11-day festival include *I'm With the Band*, an exhibition of photographs of local bands, a display of Wollongong music memorabilia, a film night showing locally made music docos and, of course, a handful of gigs.

Unscene is the work of two websites Helter Smelter (which Collins runs) and Steel City Sound. The former details the goings on in the music and arts scene, while the latter chronicles the history of numerous Wollongong bands.

That mix of past and present is covered in the festival's events and Collins says keeping an eye on the past is important.

"There's a history of music and art in Wollongong," she says.

"There's a whole history here and people should value that and look at what people have done in the past."

Steel City Sound founder Warren Wheeler has been heavily involved in collecting music memorabilia for the *Unscene and Unheard* exhibition at Wollongong's Yours and Owls cafe. The exhibition includes posters, gig flyers and street press.

Wheeler has put items like this on his website but believes it will mean more for people to see them in person.

He says it will open people's eyes to what has been happening in Wollongong for decades – and continues to happen.

"On the face of it Wollongong often appears to be a cultural wasteland, but you scratch the surface and there is an incredibly rich diversity of art and music going on underneath that surface.

"More and more people are crying out for that stuff to be recognised so the whole *Unscene* festival is about seeing the unseen and hearing the unheard and discovering what has, until now, been lost or hidden away in archives."

Unscene opens tomorrow and runs to June 24 at various venues around Wollongong. Visit steelcitysound.net or heltersmelter.com for details.

Glen Humphries

Four-headed creature
June 29, 2012

For a band called Bruce! you might expect that at least one member actually sports that name.

But in the case of Wollongong's Bruce! (the exclamation mark means you're supposed to yell the name), that's not the case.

Bass player Luke Armstrong tried to explain the birth of Bruce!.

"We all live underneath Broker's Nose and all spent time camping in the bush when we were kids," says Armstrong.

"So we're imagining Bruce as this big four-headed creature that lives in the bush ... That question's been asked before and we don't really have a good answer for it.

"Bruce is just what we call each other, so if we call each other on the phone it's 'Hey Bruce', 'Oh Bruce, what's happening?'. It's a nickname of sorts."

Armstrong and guitarist and singer Mick Curley, who are both in Wollongong music scene stalwart HyTest, started Bruce! to fill in a gap when their drummer moved to Melbourne.

But that hasn't finished off HyTest – there are plans to release an album and the band's semi-annual HyFest is planned for later this year.

"We did think about canning it but it's been our childhood band," Armstrong says.

"Me and Mick started it when we were 15, 16 years old. I realised that sometime this year we will have been in HyTest for more than half of our lives. It's pretty hard to walk away from that.

"And we've had drummers leave before so it's just another HyTest hurdle."

The other two members of Bruce! are drummer Elwyn Brindle-Jones and guitarist Mick Brady, both from the band Life Adjustment Order.

"We actually got Elwyn in first, to audition for HyTest," Armstrong says. "We were going to have him be our local drummer. He had a friend he played in a band with, Mick, and he joined too.

"We started to write new songs together and at first we started

Friday Night at the Oxford

writing HyTest songs but because the songs were out of the vein of HyTest, we thought we'd set up something different."

The band's sound is somewhat different from HyTest, partially because of Armstrong and Curley's recent habit of listening to classic rock radio.

"Curley and I started listening to a lot of WSFM lately, a lot of classic hits," Armstrong says.

"So we've dialled it down a little bit from the screaming and stuff that HyTest does. It's still heavy rock but it's probably a bit more melodic and we're trying to do some vocal harmonisations and turning the fuzz down on the guitars.

"It's more classic rock than the punk stuff that HyTest has been doing."

The foursome has been pretty busy – just six months after forming they've recorded an album's worth of songs, with the aim of releasing it on vinyl sometime this year.

"We don't want to be one of those lazy bands – like HyTest – that only does things every now and then," says Armstrong. "We wanted to get on top of things and make sure we had something to push for all the shows we're going to do in the next year."

Bruce! play at the Palm Court Hotel tonight and The Patch, Fairy Meadow, tomorrow night.

Tough guys get hard time
July 12, 2012

Born Lion's new single *Livin' Tough* is pokes fun at those who fancy themselves as "hard" – and perhaps at the band members themselves.

The song, part of an EP the band has recorded for release later this year, has been released online and boasts a loud, aggressive sound.

"It's taking the mickey out of what it is to be quote-unquote 'tough'," says John Bowker, the band's singer and guitarist.

"It's about a fictional character that's a bit of a bogan and he thinks quite highly of himself – but it's not really that way.

"It's also a bit about us as a band which is playing this quite hard, tough music but we're not hard, tough guys."

Born Lion grew out of Bowker's old band The Watt Riot – they figured the group had changed so much that a new name was in order.

"There are still two original members from The Watt Riot, that's myself and the guitarist Red," Bowker says.

"The Riot was together for seven years and in that time we'd had four different drummers and three different bass players, so it reached a stage where it felt like a completely new band.

"Because we were recording, and with this new line-up and the sounds have changed fairly significantly, we thought it didn't feel right to release it under the name of The Watt Riot so we thought we'd conjure up a new name."

Describing the new band's sound as "more angular and more discordant" than The Watt Riot, Bowker says the members concentrated on the new style after they noticed it had changed.

"The sound had already changed organically," he says.

"There was something different that was happening, through the sort of music we were listening to. So we did then make a conscious decision to write in a particular style, to have a particular sound.

"Prior to that we had a lot of ideas, a lot of different-sounding songs and there was no uniform approach to what we were doing."

Bowker has been part of Wollongong's music scene for a while, in bands including Larynex, Karma and The Flying Colours.

It does make him a sort of elder statesman of the scene.

"I definitely know all the bands and I can see the scene in its entirety and can see all the younger bands coming through," he says.

The reason he keeps making music is simple – he loves it.

"With songwriting, when I'm writing music, it's a way for me to get into a space where I'm only focusing on that and it's relaxing. I like being able to share things I've written with other people and get feedback from them."

Bowker says getting older doesn't make it any harder to rock.

"I have children now so I've still managed to keep it afloat. Your perspective does change ... I can feel a sense of accomplishment that's come with being the age that I am. I have begun to be proud of what I'm doing ... I've got more of a grasp of what I like."

Born Lion play The Patch at Fairy Meadow tomorrow night.

Posse rides out as a unit
September 23, 2013

About a year after Tumbleweed reunited, the band reached an agreement that they weren't going to continue being a "nostalgia act".

Singer Richie Lewis said the band were backstage at a corporate show and realised that, if they were going to be a band, they had to be a "creative unit".

"I think that during those corporate shows we were really at a crossroad," Lewis said.

"We either put up or shut up. We either come up with some new stuff and start being a relevant, creative unit or we stop.

"We asked each other what we wanted to do and everyone said, 'let's give it a crack'. We felt we had some unfinished business."

The result was the 13-track album *Sounds From The Other Side*, the first album featuring the original line-up since *Galactaphonic* in 1995.

It's a release fans wanted since the band reunited in 2009.

The album includes songs recorded for *Galactaphonic* but not used, material that had been kicking around in those days and also new material brought in by Lewis, and guitarists Paul Hausmeister and Lenny Curley.

Far from being nervous about fans hearing the first Tumbleweed album in well over a decade, Lewis said he's excited about the prospect.

"I think that we're one of the very lucky Australian bands that have a really loyal fan base," Lewis said.

"They've stuck by us without us releasing anything for years. We've formed a lot of soundtracks to great moments in their lives and we're all really grateful for that.

"I think that we've been so honest with this record. We're a very honest, organic band, we don't try and do anything that's unnatural to us.

"That approach is what eliminates my fear as to how it's going to be received by those long-term fans, because I know they're on the same wavelength and I know they'll understand it."

Lewis said the new album highlighted the chemistry the five original members had. That chemistry was missing on the last two albums Tumbleweed made as they were recorded after Hausmeister and drummer Steve O'Brien left the band (bassist Jay Curley also left before the recording of the last album).

It's also a chemistry he appreciates more now than he did when he was in his early 20s.

"Not only in the other line-ups of Tumbleweed but in every other thing that we've ever done since, we've always tried to make it better than Tumbleweed and never gotten anywhere close," he said.

"It's taken so much effort to get there whereas with these five individuals it's effortless. We don't even have to try, it's just there.

"It's something that we know exists and we appreciate the difference each member brings. Since those early days, we took it for granted, we thought that was just something you could get anywhere with anyone, but it certainly isn't."

Tumbleweed's Sounds From The Other Side is released September 27.

Tragic loss of loved musician
August 27, 2014

The music of Tumbleweed blared out of record and CD players on Tuesday in tribute to the band's bassplayer, Jay Curley, who died on Monday.

The band broke the sad news to their fans via their Facebook page on Tuesday morning.

"It is with deep sadness that we inform everyone of a great loss in

Friday Night at the Oxford

the Tumbleweed family, our brother, friend and bass player Jay Curley passed away suddenly in his home yesterday," the message read.

"We are still shocked by the news of his death. We hope that people will remember him for his music, his big heart and his total dedication to rock and roll."

Curley had only moved into the Tarrawanna house a few months earlier.

Jay Curley was one of the original members of Tumbleweed, along with brothers Lenny and Dave, who left not long afterwards.

The band is the biggest rock act to come from Wollongong. They supported Nirvana on their only Australian tour and released four albums before breaking up in 2003.

They surprised fans by reforming in 2009 and released a well-received album, *Sounds From The Other Side*, last year.

Comments from devastated fans have been flooding onto the band's Facebook page.

The band is still reeling from the loss, with guitarist Paul Hausmeister calling Curley, "the face of Wollongong rock'n'roll".

"Long hair, big smile, tattoos on the outside with a warm, loving, gentle soul on the inside," Hausmeister said.

"Always had time for a chat, a beer and a laugh."

He said Curley boasted a natural talent for "killer bass riffs" and showed total commitment to his craft.

"He has inspired countless musicians over the last 30 years and will continue in the future.

"The Australian rock'n'roll community has lost a great musician and a great bloke. We have lost a great mate."

Luke Armstrong, who plays in the bands HyTest and Bruce! with Curley's brother Mick, had bass lessons with Curley.

"We went round there a couple of times and sat there with him," Armstrong said.

"He had a little room off the front of the Tumbleweed jam room and that's where we used to have the bass lessons.

"A lot of the lessons weren't even playing bass, they were just sitting around listening to him tell stories about touring with Nirvana and things like that."

Despite those lessons, Armstrong said he still can't play the Tumbleweed songs and give them the same feel that Curley did.

Armstrong said he remembers Curley as "a happy go lucky guy".

"I've known him since I was 13, 14 years old," he said.

"He was the most generous guy you could ever meet. He would give the shirt off his back to anyone who was doing it tougher than him."

Warren Wheeler, creator of the Wollongong music history website Steel City Sound, said he had only spoken to Curley a few times.

"I think that's quite indicative of his demeanour," Wheeler said.

"Even onstage he'd be the one standing further back, not wanting to take the limelight.

"His bassplaying was of a similar style, it didn't overpower what was going on. He kept it very simple and very straightforward and that was the brilliance of it.

"I think he did it so well because of who he was. He was very much someone who just didn't seek the attention."

He said Curley's death was a "big loss" and paid tribute to his band's inspirational effect on Wollongong.

Band will perform in honour of Curley
September 2, 2014

The remaining members of Tumbleweed will play a show in honour of bass player Jason "Jay" Curley, who died last week.

Curley, who had a young son named Max, died suddenly in a Tarrawanna home on August 25. He was 42.

He was believed to have been looking after the house for a friend and had moved in only a few months earlier.

Curley was one of Tumbleweed's founding members, along with

Friday Night at the Oxford

brother and guitarist Lenny, singer Richie Lewis, drummer Steve O'Brien and guitarist Paul Hausmeister.

Before Curley died, the band had been booked to headline the Young Henrys Small World Festival in Marrickville on September 20.

The future of that show was up in the air until Monday when the band posted a message on its Facebook page saying it would go ahead as a tribute to Curley.

"We will be playing Young Henrys Small World Festival in honour of Jay," the post read.

"Filling in on bass will be Jay and Lenny's older brother, Pat Curley. Hope to see you there to celebrate the life and times of Jay Curley.

"Any other future bookings will be decided at a later date."

The news was warmly received by fans on their page, with some seeing it as a fitting way to pay tribute to Curley.

Tumbleweed had agreed to play at the River Rocks Festival in Geelong on Saturday, November 15, with two other shows pencilled in before that but O'Brien said the band was unsure if they would play any of them.

He also said the band was about to release a new video, for the single *Drop in the Ocean*.

"It was intended for release anyway and was in production at the time of Jason's death, just that now the song has more meaning and will be a further tribute to him," he said.

Last week Hausmeister called the bass player "the face of Wollongong rock'n'roll".

"Long hair, big smile, tattoos on the outside with a warm, loving, gentle soul on the inside," Hausmeister said.

Lewis wrote a Facebook post, listing the good times they'd had.

"We shared a dream, a life of wild musical adventures and we did it! And we had fun," he wrote.

Curley's funeral service will be at H. Parsons Dapto Chapel on Friday, September 5, at 2pm.

Glen Humphries

Back for some more fun
October 24, 2014

Wollongong's "fun party band" of the 1980s, Svegies Vegies, are reforming for a show next month – and their fans are stoked.

Fans have been hitting social media since the show was announced, keen to see the band's first official gig since a private reunion in 1998.

Singer Mark Chester says people still recognise him from his days fronting the band in the mid to late 1980s.

"What I've discovered is people of that generation are very nostalgic about what we did," Chester says.

"They remember us and they remember feeling good. It was about having a good time.

"In one way I think the legend of Svegies Vegies has grown bigger than the reality because we were never a particularly tight outfit. We never let that bother us, we were just out there trying to entertain – and I think that rubbed off on the audience."

The band played a mix of originals and covers from the likes of Motorhead, The Smithereens, Echo and the Bunnymen and The Teardrop Explodes – bands not widely known in '80s Wollongong.

Though fans probably did recognise the theme from *The Love Boat* TV series. But they also had some originals, and released the vinyl single *Lonely Trail*.

"We had social comment songs, we had songs that were based on just having fun," Chester says.

"I think three of the songs we wrote had the word 'fun' in the title, so we were heading down that road.

"We had *Lonely Trail* backed with *Just Tell Me Lies*, and that was quite successful by Wollongong standards.

"It was on high rotation on Triple J at the time, and we did a clip for *Lonely Trail* which was being played on *Sounds Unlimited*, which was Channel 7's morning video music show.

"So we were getting some exposure but the timing of it was that all happened near the end of the band."

Chester says the band ended not long after he moved to Sydney for

Friday Night at the Oxford

work and the distance became too much to keep it going.

The idea to reform is linked to *Steel City Sound*, a forthcoming Wollongong City Gallery exhibition about 50 years of rock'n'roll in the city.

Band member Frank Marcy was approached by curator Warren Wheeler to see if he had any Svegies memorabilia.

Marcy then started talking to the other band members and soon the idea of getting together for a gig was on the cards.

Wheeler, who also runs the Steel City Sound website, says he first heard of the band about five years ago while researching a story for the site.

"I was immediately intrigued by how different they were to what else was happening in the local music scene at that time," Wheeler says.

"Where other bands were drawing strongly from the garage sounds and beat, Svegies were marching to the sound of their own off-beat drum.

"Svegies Vegies embody the celebration aspect of the exhibition. They are all about having fun and enjoying the music.

"From a personal perspective, I am looking forward to seeing the band perform, as I was born too late to have witnessed their success the first time round."

Svegies Vegies play the Heritage Hotel on November 28 with White Trash and The Gangsters.

A chronicle of rock
November 15, 2014

You may not have heard of Wollongong bands like The Marksmen or The Sunday Painters, but record collectors around the world have.

And they're willing to part with a decent wad of cash to get their hands on one of their recordings.

The Sunday Painters were a three-piece band from the 1980s and they certainly left their mark – copies of their vinyl singles have sold for well over $300.

But *Why*, the only single from 1960s surf band The Marksmen, is even more expensive. The band themselves paid for the single and only released 500 of them. A copy of the single has recently sold on eBay for more than $2000.

The chances are high that people who lived during those bands' heyday don't remember them. But Wollongong music historian Warren Wheeler has set out to change that.

About five years ago he started the website Steel City Sound, which chronicles the history of the Wollongong music scene. And on Friday, his exhibition of the same name opens at the Wollongong Art Gallery.

Through his efforts, people will remember the bands they grew up seeing on a Friday and Saturday night at places as varied as the Ironworkers, the Oxford, the Patch, Pioneer Hall and Zondrae's.

And some bands who have been forgotten through the years will get the attention they deserve. That's the driving force behind Wheeler's work, that this stuff is important and needs to be celebrated.

"There's a car museum or a war museum that preserves that important cultural things, but what we don't do very well is preserve our artistic or our musical heritage," Wheeler says.

"We've got a strong musical heritage here and it's now an opportunity for people to discover that and give it the kudos and the praise it deserves."

The exhibition arose out of a smaller one Wheeler organised a few years ago at what was then Yours and Owls. Soon afterwards, the city gallery contacted him about doing something bigger.

Then 18 months ago, Wheeler started collecting whatever Wollongong musical treasures he could find. Some came from his own collection but others came from local musicians and fans responding to Wheeler's numerous calls for help via the exhibition's Facebook page.

While people took a while to get into it, Wheeler says the response ended up being pretty strong.

"People had been keen to get involved," Wheeler said.

"All the stuff that their partners told them to throw away countless times over the years, they've finally been able to find a use for it."

Friday Night at the Oxford

Also, the delay in responding was understandable, Wheeler says, because in many cases he was asking to borrow items that are very important to people. They'd obviously want to make sure they were going to be looked after – and that the exhibition was actually going to happen.

And it is happening – all over the ground floor of the Wollongong Art Gallery, which features four smaller galleries.

Each of them has a different theme – one features a display of T-shirts with an interactive timeline.

Elsewhere, each of the five decades covered in the exhibition are written on the wall and people can grab a sticker, write a memory on it (such as a great band they saw in that decade or the show where they met their significant other) and then stick it onto the timeline.

The *Mercury* Gallery has been transformed into a venue, complete with stage, bar and sticky carpet, where videos of live shows are played.

There is also a performance list that details when each band's "set" comes up, so fans don't miss it.

And there's also a "hall of fame" that will include photos, records and other artifacts.

People can also take home their own piece of *Steel City Sound* – each copy of the exhibition catalogue comes with a 23-track compilation CD. The CD runs chronologically, starting with a track from 1961 by The Wanderers and ending with a 2014 tune from Hockey Dad.

The Wanderers' song was the earliest Wollongong rock tune Wheeler could track down. But he knows of at least one that is older still.

"Wollongong's first rock and roll recording that I'm aware of was by a group called Johnny Johnson and the Rebels," Wheeler says.

"This would have been in the late '50s, just after Little Richard toured. These guys went down to Victoria and recorded an album's worth of material. Unfortunately no known copies are still in existence. Which is a real shame."

As well as the compilation CD, over the coming months Music Farmers will be releasing a trio of split seven-inch CDs of new or rare recordings from Wollongong bands with covers designed by local musicians who are also artists.

Wheeler says the hardest part has actually been tracking down copies of the music itself.

"Tracking that stuff down has been quite a hunt at times," Wheeler says.

"Recorded music, as powerful as it is, it can also be very disposable. So people do just get rid of it, especially in the digital age.

"People say 'why do I still need CDs, why do I still need records, everything's digitised'. So they get rid of it."

Even if they don't have the vinyl any more, they still have the memories. And, as Wollongong feels like it's moving forward, Wheeler says, people want to hold on to their memories for a while longer yet.

"As we travel down that road we're not yet prepared to let go of our past," he says.

"I have found that people, their eyes light up when they talk about their youth or young adulthood and they remember the bands that they went and saw. They remember the venues and the people they met, the people they fell in love with.

"They also remember the tragedies, people that they've lost along the way, people they haven't seen for 20 or 30 years. So it's been a very beautiful experience, meeting new people and hearing their stories. And then getting them into a room together when they haven't seen each other for 20 years."

He's aware that some might not think Wollongong's music scene is deserving of such reverence. For him, that attitude is part of the city too – but something that needs to change.

"This is my home town," he says.

"As many of us do, I have a love-hate relationship with this town. We love it for everything it offers, but there is also room for improvement.

"In terms of art and culture, that's one of the areas where we can improve. Not in terms of quality, because we produce some great music, but in terms of preserving it and giving it its due and actually supporting the scene.

"We can always do better at that."

Friday Night at the Oxford

Steel City Sound – 50 Years of Rock and Roll in Wollongong opens at the Wollongong Art Gallery on Friday and runs until March 15.

Recalling echoes of the past
November 21, 2014

For the next four months Wollongong Art Gallery will have a bar inside – minus the sticky carpet.

The bar forms part of a "live" venue inside the extensive *Steel City Sound* exhibition, which opens on Friday night.

The venue is done up like a live music venue, with gig footage of various bands of the past playing on the wall.

Curator Warren Wheeler said there were 11 hours of footage, and a set-list had been posted so fans could see when their favourite band was "playing".

Wheeler said there was also a plan to remain true to a live music venue and have sticky carpet – but the gallery decided that was a step too far.

The entire ground floor has been given over to the exhibition, which chronicles 50 years of the Wollongong music scene and includes posters, music, artwork by band members and an impressive display of memorabilia.

One display is a tribute to Tumbleweed and features a huge range of memorabilia from the band's own collection – including the never-used cover the label commissioned for their first album.

"They asked a guy called Ed Fotheringham, who was from Seattle and had done work for Mudhoney and Soundgarden," Wheeler said.

"They commissioned him to do that work but they never used it. I wonder why they commissioned someone else to do it given they've got terrific artists in the band itself?"

Wheeler said the idea behind *Steel City Sound* was to celebrate the city's musical heritage.

"We want to explore what's come before us and celebrate the

success of bands from way back," he said.

"We want to acknowledge their work because popular culture can be disposable. People forget about those successes, or information might not be passed on to younger generations.

"It's also celebrating and exploring what's happening now, which is why you'll also see stuff in here from bands that are new, that are performing at the moment."

Road crew

This the only piece in this book that has never been published before. At one stage the Steel City Sound exhibition was going to include a book made up of pieces written by those involved in the scene at one time or another. Warren Wheeler asked me to write one of them – but for budgetary reasons the book was shelved. So this is what I wrote for that book.

In the first two years of the 1990s my friends formed a band called The Culprits. I went to every single gig they played but almost never saw them from the front. Instead I usually got to see them from the side or the rear – such is the life of a drum roadie.

I didn't have much knowledge of the drums beyond the fact that you hit them and they made a noise. But I did have a car – and the drummer Ty Emerson didn't. So I volunteered the services of myself and my Nissan Bluebird. In return I got to see a lot of the band's backs and sides from my vantage point behind or next to the drum kit – and to bask in their reflected glory and be able to say "I'm with the band".

The band also featured lead guitarist Pat Lyons, singer songwriter and guitarist David Beniuk and brother Tim on bass. Incidentally, no-one remembers who came up with the name, though Tim later said it was me. I have no memory of doing so – I can only recall pushing for them to call themselves Vacant Lot (in hindsight, that'd be a name more deserving of a '70s punk band).

One of their earliest gigs was in a venue that no longer exists – The Balkan Club. Located at the top end of Atchison Street right next to

Friday Night at the Oxford

what later became an adult book store, it was a small social club for old Mediterranean men that doubled as a band venue from time to time. I remember it as being poky and you could get cans of VB under the counter for $2 a pop.

As can be expected, most of the venues the band played during their run in 1990-91 no longer exist. Venues like the Ironworkers, a night club located over what is now Dicey Rileys. I remember that place because it was the only time I ever saw the band from out front after being asked to take over the light show (which was really four switches that controlled four different coloured lights). Still it was nice to have a different view for a change.

The most well-known of the defunct venues was the Oxford Tavern. At that time it was starting out as the legendary venue it became. The stage was four wooden rectangular boxes carpeted on top, joined together and shoved diagonally into the corner. That gave me some necessary drum roadie space between the stage and the wall in which to sit but it was really to provide access to the office behind the stage. It wasn't unusual to see an employee walk across the stage mid-performance to get into that office.

While gigs went on virtually every night of the week, Friday and Saturday nights were the big nights where as many as three bands would play. It speaks volumes about the strength of the music scene at that time that there were enough bands to fill all those slots without doubling up or just putting the same bands on each week. The Culprits went straight into the Friday and Saturday slots, pretty much headlining from the start and building up a fanbase that would follow them from gig to gig.

Not defunct but much changed is the North Gong Hotel. Back in the early 1990s, it was the archetypal Oz rock pub. The band room was a long rectangular space that reached back from the main entrance with the stage at the far end of the room. Much to the dismay of female punters, their toilets were right down the far end too, forcing them to push their way through a crowd of sweaty guys to get there and back. It was loud, grungy, a bit rough but I still think it looked better than it does today.

Glen Humphries

The Culprits' big moment at the North Gong was winning the Battle of the Bands, beating acts like Thousand Plane Raid and Crown the King. The guys added that to the win at the Uni Battle of the Bands, the heat of which was the band's first ever show.

They headed to Macquarie University for the state finals and came second. I've got a recording of this show someone made from the crowd and, 20 years later, I still listen to it from time to time.

There was also a contest the band didn't win. In 1991, Waves at Towradgi opened up and was, at the time, the biggest music venue in town. There was this undeclared competition to be the first Wollongong band to play there. With an impressive CV, The Culprits seemed assured to score the first gig – but that went to a band called Inscape, who I remember as an INXS-like act. As for The Culprits, they never played on that stage (David and Tim would fix that a few years later in the band Merry Widows).

Towards the end of their run The Culprits scored a residency at The Patch, which had just started booking bands again. The car park there was also the location of a somewhat heated discussion that, in some way precipitated the band breaking up.

That break-up marked the end of my drum roadie career. And my tambourine-playing career too. After seeing a Paul Kelly show where he got his roadie up to play tambourine on a song, the guys had figured it'd be funny to get me to do the same thing.

It soon became a regular thing and, funnily enough, after those gigs, I would be as recognisable to the punters as the rest of the band. Which I figured was just reward for the bruises that would appear on my playing hand the next day – I always bashed the tambourine much more violently than necessary.

As well as memories – and my Culprits Crew roadie T-shirt I probably still have at home somewhere - the band left behind a four-track cassette (yep, it was that long ago that bands recorded on cassettes) called *Remember The Birds?*. There would still copies floating around, even though most of the people who own them probably don't have a cassette player with which to play them. If you want a hint of what The Culprits sounded like, drummer Ty has posted the first song from that tape –

Friday Night at the Oxford

Insurrection – to YouTube. A search for "The Culprits Insurrection" will get you there.

Without a hint of bias, I have to say it still sounds great. Especially because I don't have to be crouching behind a drum kit to hear it.

Bringing music home
November 27, 2014

Luke Armstrong sure goes to a lot of trouble to get his band a gig.

The bass player in HyTest has organised his fourth HyFest music festival, which he says is all so his band can play their one gig a year.

"We don't get offered anything else, "Armstrong explains.

But it's not really that simple. Armstrong now plays in Bruce! and the other members of HyTest all have other bands on the go too (yes, they're all playing at HyFest).

So they're all likely too busy to play as HyTest more than once a year but, as Armstrong says, "we're not really ready to let go".

"The whole thing when we started HyTest was that we always said we wanted to be a band like The Hard-Ons," Armstrong said.

"We wanted to keep it going as long as we could. It's our teenage love, it was the way we expressed all our feelings, got out all our anger when we were young and it feels like a healthy thing for us to hang on to."

It's also a chance to encourage other Australian bands to come and play.

"A lot of national bands don't really stop in at Wollongong a lot any more, so it's a good chance to get bands that we've met to come here and play," he says.

Armstrong has been running HyFest each year since 2011. He says he got the idea while touring Europe and seeing local festivals spring up in small towns.

The timing was also appropriate, given the first festival took place not long after the Oxford Tavern shut its doors. It was a chance to offer some stability to the music scene after its home shut up shop.

"That was a huge influence on starting it up as well," he says.

"The scene seems to have fractured a lot since then. The Oxford was the place you could go to see all different genres of bands. Now there are all these little scenes that are taking off on their own instead of that big amalgamated thing.

"What I try and aim to do every year is try and get bands from all different genres together, to try and get that Oxford vibe back."

This Saturday's HyFest show at the Corrimal Hotel has 21 acts spread across two stages, kicking off at noon. And, yes, HyTest are the headliners.

It's been a big effort for Armstrong to organise this year's event, partially because the festival is so popular bands are almost fighting each other to get a gig. And it's harder to find the time to do the work, too.

"This year's been the hardest so far," he said.

"I've got a new baby boy and with Bruce! doing a lot of stuff at the moment it's been really hard to try and find the time to organise it.

"I get a bit of help from some people with the art and posters, but apart from that it's pretty much a solo effort in dealing with all the bands.

"This year has been the hardest of the lot. There were a few bands who were a bit upset that they didn't get put on.

"As hard as the effort is, it's still a great reward to have all of our friends around on the day."

HyFest is on at the Corrimal Pub on November 29.

Old bands, new vinyl
December 2, 2014

A few slices of Wollongong's music history are being released but you'll need a record player to hear them.

As part of the very popular *Steel City Sound* music exhibition at Wollongong Art Gallery, Music Farmers is releasing a split seven-inch vinyl single series with a different band on each side.

Friday Night at the Oxford

There are three singles in the series and the first – featuring The Sunday Painters and The Unheard – is released this month.

Bands on the other singles are Mojo Hands and Evol and HyTest with Thumlock.

Music Farmers owner Jeb Taylor says there will only be 100 of each single pressed.

"It's a bit of a collector thing," Taylor says of the decision to release them on vinyl.

"Also, it's probably easier to sell vinyl now than to sell a CD. The bands on the first two seven-inches were from that era where things were on vinyl. With HyTest and Thumlock they haven't been on vinyl that much, so it's just to get it out there on that format."

Taylor says the bands were chosen because they had some impact on the local scene – whether that be in terms of the band itself or members going on to form other also influential outfits.

The most influential band of the six would surely be 1980s band The Sunday Painters, whose EPs now sell for hundreds of dollars.

They're a band Taylor had heard about here and there but he'd never experienced them until *Steel City Sound* curator Warren Wheeler played him a few tracks.

"When Warren first played me their stuff, it was a big eye-opener to see that those guys came out of Wollongong," Taylor says.

"They're so ahead of their time and to actually be doing that here in Wollongong in the 1980s is actually really crazy.

"Some of that stuff is on par with a lot of stuff that's going on now.

"You can understand why, especially in Wollongong back then, it didn't really get too much traction."

Taylor saw the *Steel City Sound* exhibition on the opening night and, like many others, plans to go back several times to check it all out. He says it's great for those who lived through those times – but also for those who came afterwards.

"I think it's also really good for a lot of younger bands that are coming through now and they can see what came before them," Taylor says.

"People I know, and myself, we've been involved for a long time –

you're aware of some stuff that came before but for a lot of people, in their minds, the music scene would have started when they started.

"So it's good to be able to go back and have a good look at what was around before any of us started doing stuff in the music scene."

Trio stand test of time
December 10, 2014

It's probably not completely accurate to say the members of Dropping Honey are back together, because they never really broke up.

The Wollongong band was around in the late 1990s and early 2000s, recording two EPs and an album before singer-songwriter Damien Lane and guitarist Jolyon Pagett left for the UK in 2003.

Now the original trio of Lane, Pagett and drummer Darren Ireland have joined up to play a gig at RAD this month.

Though the band played a few gigs in recent years as a four-piece, these are their first shows as a trio – and with new material – for more than a decade.

But, despite the passage of 12 years, Lane said the band never actually called it quits.

"It was never something that was spoken about, but we just didn't know what was going to be happening," Lane says.

"From that point on, none of us lived in the same city. We got together for a one-off gig in 2010 and after that Tumbleweed asked us to go on tour with them so we did that as well.

"Without doing that I don't know that we would have gone on to do any more shows.

"It made us realise it was something we enjoy and was worth doing a bit more."

But only if they were performing some new songs. Lane says a third of the set-list for next week's show will be new material, which includes songs he wrote several years ago and one or two that are a few months old.

Friday Night at the Oxford

For Lane, it was crucial they took some new songs to the show in Wollongong and another in Sydney.

"Just to make it something we can be enthusiastic about," Lane explains.

"Some of the old songs I wrote when I was 17 so it's a bit odd to be playing them now.

"I don't mind playing them, but they need to be amongst newer songs, otherwise it feels like a nostalgia thing, which we're not really interested in doing."

Bringing the band back also gives Lane – who composes soundtracks for TV and film – an outlet for material he has written but didn't really fit anything else he was doing.

But they did fit Dropping Honey, even if age may have changed a few things here and there.

"I think we're better as players and I think I'm better at writing music now," Lane says.

"But they definitely do sound unmistakably like Dropping Honey.

"I think we're more aware of what our strengths are so I'm more likely to write things that I know we're going to be able to pull off well, rather than go off on these tangents just to prove to myself that we could do stuff."

These days, Lane says the band is "more peaceful", with everyone in it more for enjoyment and a sense of escape than any idea of becoming a big band.

"When you're younger and in a band you're constantly trying to go up whatever ladder of success you might be on," Lane says.

"But now, as long as some people rock up to our shows and they have fun, I'm pretty happy."

Dropping Honey play the RAD Bar on December 20.

Glen Humphries

Bandmates reunite to take tunes from cloud
December 26, 2014

It was never David Challenger's plan to form a band – he just wanted to record some of his songs.

Challenger was part of Wollongong bands of the 1980s, Engineer Brains and The Start, and 1990s outfit Merry Widows.

In that time, he'd written a few tunes and – with technology making things so easy – decided to record them all and post them up on Soundcloud.

"The original idea was to get down all the songs I had already written," Challenger says.

"That was about 10 of the 14 songs. The oldest one that made the cut is *Never Would Be Too Soon*, which I think might have been the first song I ever wrote, back in 1985.

"During the process, it stirred the creative juices and in between recording the older songs, every now and then I'd be sitting down with a guitar strumming a few chords and thinking 'that sounds good'. It was the catalyst to going ahead and writing some new material.

"Even though I didn't think they'd ever be played live at the time I thought, given that these ideas are there I'll just go through and record them as well."

And that's where it was supposed to end – partially because recording and posting them online is an easier way to get people to hear your songs than getting a band together and the hassles of finding time to rehearse.

But then Challenger tapped former Merry Widows bandmate Johnno Beniuk to help with some of the mixing.

"I got the last song out about a few months ago and then Johnno said 'Hey, what do you think about playing these songs live? We should play these songs live at least once'," Challenger says.

"It really started from that idea. I thought it was great because I didn't think I'd ever play live in a band again."

Getting that band together turned out to be pretty easy. Three-quarters of Merry Widows – Challenger, Beniuk and Beniuk's brother

Friday Night at the Oxford

David – signed up for The Insiders.

The rest of the band features drummer David Crowe, keyboard player Marco Forlano and bassist Malcolm Wales from Mustard, who supported the Merry Widows at a few gigs back in the 1990s.

There's another link to the Merry Widows in that the show is a fundraiser for the band's former roadie Kevin English who has Huntington's disease.

The Insiders and support acts Stephen Robinson and Patrick Lyons and the American Creek Band will be donating their fee for the evening – a percentage of the bar – to English.

Another reason to turn up is this is probably going to be The Insiders' only gig – at least for a long while.

"I think so," agrees Challenger.

"It's likely to be a one-off, but we'll see how it goes. I wouldn't say no to something again a year later, but we certainly won't be doing three or four gigs in the next few months."

David Challenger and the Insiders play the Corrimal Hotel on January 16.

Touch of seriousness
January 7, 2015

The Nice Folk have come a long way since their days as an "obnoxious" duo.

The band, now a six-piece, is marking a decade with this weekend's release of an eight-track vinyl album called *Touched*.

Founding members Lax Charisma and Dave Mutton started the band as a duo – two guitar players and a drum machine – and a side project to the other bands they were in.

"Early on we were quite obnoxious," admits Charisma.

"We'd get really drunk, we'd turn up. We weren't playing well but it was amusing. People would say 'I didn't know you could write songs that were that offensive'. But it would be a good time."

Over time, those other bands fell by the wayside and the side project became the main focus. And they started to take things a bit more seriously.

"Also, with people joining the band and the sound changing, it got to a point where it wasn't a joke anymore," he says.

"We were actually writing some good music and people really liked us."

The sound continues to change as some members leave the band and new ones join – the new album *Touched* is the result of that.

Charisma says the origins of the album can be traced back to April 2013 when their keyboardist left, prompting a rethink on how the band would do things.

"Up until then we'd been working with stuff that was more piano-based, with the other instruments taking a back seat," he says.

"When we finished playing with the keyboardist, me and Paisley Nightmare – the other guitarist – forged more of a guitar sound, more of a straightforward rock'n'roll sound.

"And there's the trumpet in there as well giving it a different flavour."

The sound is one Charisma is reluctant to describe – beyond "rock'n'roll". He is happy for others to do it and I'd say The Nice Folk are a swampy punk blues band.

Spiritually, they have ties to the bands of the 1980s Australian independent scene. Bands who did what they wanted just because they wanted to, not because they figured it would lead to a record deal.

Which is how the members approach the band.

"It is really a casual thing with us," Charisma said.

"We're not about to embark on any lengthy tours – there are just two launch shows. We do want to try and work out of state later in the year but we're older guys, we've got other commitments and do other jobs – so we have to work around that.

"We're not in any position to drop everything and disappear for however many weeks on the road. We try and do less shows but make them the best that we can."

The Nice Folk launch their CD at RAD Bar on Saturday

Friday Night at the Oxford

Ahead of their time
January 10, 2015

The Sunday Painters occupy an unusual niche in Wollongong music history.

Records from the 1980s band sell for hundreds of dollars on eBay. They have fans around the world. A label in the United States is keen to re-release all their EPs and albums.

Yet it's likely most people in Wollongong have never heard *of* them, let alone heard them.

It's not really surprising, given all six of their releases – from 1980 to 1985 – were very small runs (a cassette release totalled just 100 copies). So there were never too many albums or EPs out there to begin with.

And, if you were to buy one, well you'd have to get into a bidding war with record collectors around the world willing to pay several hundred dollars for a three-track EP.

And their music – a mix of full-on electronic noise, rock, discordant pop, classical, punk, jazz and whatever else they wanted to play – was probably too out there for Wollongong in the 1980s.

"Not even Wollongong," admits band member Peter MacKinnon.

"We would find the same when we played in Sydney or Melbourne. I remember one gig we did and at the end of the set, we tended to do a fairly full-on number that would go completely off. At the end of it there was just stunned silence from the audience.

"We were the support for what was essentially a pop band. The audience was there to see this pop band and we came out and just played this completely off the wall, almost wall of noise music and they just didn't know how to respond to it."

MacKinnon formed the band with school friend Peter Raengel in 1979 with third member Resident (born Dennis) Kennedy joining in 1982. While there was a number of other musicians who played with the band during the 1980s, this trio was the longest incarnation of the band.

Glen Humphries

MacKinnon and Raengel met in Year 5 at Wollongong Primary School and went right through Wollongong High School together.

"It was while we were in high school, we each bought a $30 Kmart guitar and just started playing in his bedroom through a little amp.

"We started playing music in high school with a friend, and then after high school, decided to form a band. A friend of ours who was at school was the one who called us the Sunday Painters.

"It was after one the Impressionists, it might have been Monet, who was sometimes called the Sunday Painter because he had a day job and that was what it was like for us.

"We had day jobs and this was something we did on the side."

While Raengel had a musical background – having learned piano as a child – MacKinnon pretty much worked out how to play guitar himself. That approach no doubt adds to the unique sound of the Sunday Painters.

"I don't really consider myself a musician as such," MacKinnon said.

"I don't think I'm good enough. We used to joke that the reason we played our own material was that we weren't good enough to be a covers band."

The band was very much influenced by the punk scene of the late 1970s – in terms of the DIY attitude, the socio-political songwriting and the embrace of creative art.

The band's songs would be recorded themselves and put out on their own Terminal Records label. The covers were works of art – one EP would come with three different covers, another featured an individually made and coloured cover for each of the 250 vinyl EPs. A cassette release featured Raengel's bloodstains on each of the 100 copies.

On top of this, every single release was hand-numbered.

For friends MacKinnon and Raengel, it was about doing what you wanted to do. About "just making sounds and seeing where it led us".

"Peter and I never had any ambitions that we were going to make a living out of music," MacKinnon says.

"We never thought we were going to be that approachable that we were going to be able to make money out of it."

Friday Night at the Oxford

But others have managed to make money out of the Sunday Painters, mainly those selling their recordings online for between $200 to $300 a pop.

"There are people who are making more money from them now than we ever made at the time we sold them originally," MacKinnon laughs.

"I've got some [copies] of the first single and a few copies of the first album that have never been sold. I haven't bothered to flog them because it's something Dennis and I need to talk about in terms of how we're going to do it.

"Should we be putting them up surreptitiously on eBay and see how much we can get for them? It'd be like 'wow, we finally made some money out of this album'."

Today, it's easy for a band to get their music heard around the world.

All they have to do is post it online.

But in the 1980s it was much harder – to listen to a band you either had to have a physical copy of their album or know someone who did. Add to that, the fact Sunday Painters never released more than 500 of any record – and in some cases just 250 – the odds of any of them winding up overseas seems slim to none.

"In terms of pressings of albums, we're only talking in the 100s that were ever pressed," MacKinnon said.

"For some of them we didn't have a distributor, but we found some of our stuff was ending up in other countries.

"Peter got contacted from Germany, the UK and the US. Some of our stuff used to get played on university radio stations in the US back in the day.

"So it was filtering out there."

Some of those vinyl releases ended up in Boston, where Michael Train was a college radio DJ. A friend named Chuck sold underground rock in the US and would put together compilation tapes of bands to introduce his buyers to bands they'd never heard of.

"Most bands as sonically inventive as they were don't have the pop smarts to get all their ideas into tight songs," Train said.

"And they had emotional range too – from tenderness to fury in a beat."

Driven by a desire for more people to hear this band from Wollongong, Train initially planned to release a double CD of the Sunday Painters himself. He eventually turned to friend Kevin Pedersen, who runs US indie label What's Your Rupture, for help.

The result will be the release of the band's first three EPs as one album early next year, along with a bonus download of a live show. The two Sunday Painters albums will follow later in 2015.

Train said it seemed apt that a US label was re-releasing the songs from an Australian band.

"Given how determined Peter Raengel and the other Painters were to get as much music as possible from the far side of the world – New York, Edinburgh, London, Manchester, Ohio – and then turning it into something new, it feels right that a New York label should now be involved," Train said.

"It reminds us that the best art freely crosses borders."

The news of the re-releases pleases MacKinnon, partially because it means he'll be able to own copies of all the band's stuff again.

"We're pretty chuffed that there's this interest from overseas," MacKinnon said.

"Again I'm certainly not expecting to make any money out of it. That never was the point of the exercise."

The band itself never really broke up but rather "petered out" (an apt descriptor for a band with two Peters) in the early 1990s. MacKinnon reckoned the last gig was at the Star Cafe in Port Kembla in 1992.

Marriage, children and work took over and, while MacKinnon never played in another band, he would go over to Raengel's house to jam. The two were such close friends that MacKinnon said there would hardly have been a week since they were 10 they didn't see each other.

"That was right up until the Wednesday before he died," MacKinnon said.

Raengel had been working in Chatswood and commuting from Wollongong, a trip MacKinnon believes contributed to his death in 2007.

Friday Night at the Oxford

"He had an aneurysm a few years before he died which he survived, but he was having seizures on the train going to or from work.

"I told him he just needed to tell work to shove it and when he did give them notice, they finally allowed him to work from home," MacKinnon said.

But by then it was too late – Raengel passed away six months later.

"There's still not a week goes by where I don't think about him and don't miss him," MacKinnon said.

He also thinks about the Sunday Painters and when the older MacKinnon looks back at what the younger MacKinnon was playing, he reckons it sounds crazy.

"But to be honest I thought we were playing some crazy stuff even then, in the sense that we didn't think we sounded like anyone else," he said.

"These days, it's probably me being a grumpy old man, but if Triple J's on in the car and a piece of music comes on, I'm going 'oh that reminds me of something that was made 30-40 years ago'. I'm doing that a lot.

"I find that when I listen to our stuff I never think 'oh that sounds like someone else'. So it's clear we were doing our own thing.

"Whether we were ahead of our time, well, that's for others to judge."

Energetic album
January 27, 2015

In the 1990s, plenty of people were watching the three teenagers of Silverchair taking their music to the world.

In the Shoalhaven, the brothers Ben and Neil Foley were among those watching. That they were only a few years younger than the guys in Silverchair gave them the inspiration to form a band themselves. So, with Ben on guitar and Neil a drummer and singer, they drafted in cousin Daniel Edge on bass and Elia was born.

"Silverchair were young guys having a go," Ben says, "If they could do it, we can give it a shot.

"We could only play a little bit when we started and thought we were rock stars then. Now we're a little bit more awake to the fact of what it takes to get ahead."

Now they're a lot more serious – they've even recorded their debut album, *New Year*, in their home studio. During the recording of the album Neil made the decision to just take the role of vocals during the live shows, so they brought in Lake Madge to play drums at their shows.

"With the new album we wrote, it's a pretty energetic album and so it's good to have someone out front interacting with the crowd rather than having a drummer-singer," Ben says. "We realised, if we were going to pull it off live, we had to go to the fourpiece."

Elia launch their album tomorrow night at Nowra's Bridge Tavern.

Working like demons
February 10, 2015

Braydon Denmeade, the singer-songwriter with the band Glab, may only be 18 but he takes his music very seriously.

He was playing his own music at The Basement when he was 11 and was touring China when he was 13, and he's aiming to make music his career.

Denmeade says his bandmates are very like-minded and taking a serious attitude to Glab.

"We've all toured internationally in one way or another," Denmeade says.

"Our bass player, he's one of the most committed people I know. He's technically signed to a 10-year contract with Warner Music Mexico and he used to tour around Central America supporting people like Pink and A Simple Plan."

The band's approach is simple: If you want something to happen, you need to take it seriously. Otherwise you miss out on opportunities.

Friday Night at the Oxford

"Yeah, that's what we've experienced," he says.

"We've only been playing for six months or so, but things don't happen by themselves. When you end up saying no to people who are trying to book you, it increases the chance of them not coming to you the next time.

"You've got to get yourself out there as much as absolutely possible.

"The only way you can do that is by playing as much as possible and that's going to make more people come to your shows and get used to your music."

Glab got a leg-up – and some money to pay the rego on their car – by winning last year's Original LP band comp judged by the likes of multiple ARIA-winning engineer Al Wright and Tumbleweed frontman Richie Lewis.

"The gig itself was really good; at the final there was a lot of people and we got a lot of attention," Denmeade says.

The show probably won them a few more fans of what Glab calls the "alternative soul rock" sound. Fans which may well buy the band's debut album *Are*, featuring eight songs and three bonus tracks.

The album is named for its title track, which isn't actually called *Are*. Confused? Let Denmeade clear things up.

"We have a song on there called *We Are The Children*, which was pretty heavily featured in our live set," he explains.

"When we first wrote it it was just called *Are* and we named the EP after that – as the title track.

"Later on we decided to change the song name to *We Are The Children* but we still had the artwork for the album cover, a painting with the word Are on it.

"So we decided to stick with that name."

In case, you've been wondering what a "Glab" is, well – it's nothing.

"It's very specifically nothing because we were kind of sick of band names having a whole lot of meaning that you're supposed to look into," Denmeade says.

"We thought it would be funny to pick a band name that meant absolutely nothing so no one could associate it with anything else when they thought of us.

"It's funny, though, some people still think it's an acronym and come up with little meanings for it. We don't usually tell them it means nothing, we just say 'well, what do you think it means?' "

Glab play at Three Chimneys on Thursday.

Homeless hub of gig
March 17, 2015

A gig at Dicey Riley's this month includes an unusual cover charge – tinned food.

To get into the four-band bill *Where Did You Sleep Last Night?*, you need to bring some tinned food to leave at the door as a donation.

You see, the show is looking to help the Wollongong Homeless Hub do its work.

Opening in 2013, the homeless hub provides food, laundry facilities and a warm shower to the region's disadvantaged, as well as other forms of assistance.

Warren Wheeler, the organiser of the fundraiser, says the idea for the donation of tinned food is it allowed the hub to continue giving the homeless food hampers.

"It also causes people to think about what they're doing," Wheeler says of the tinned good door charge.

"They're not just coming to a gig and handing over some money for a cover charge. They can grab something from their cupboard on their way out the door, but it just gets them thinking about what is it they're contributing to.

"The process of being able to donate an item like a can of baked beans is, for many people, simple but for someone who is doing it tough and sleeping rough, it is a huge thing for them."

Wheeler, who works at the Illawarra South Coast Tenants Advice and Advocacy Service, says his day job is guided by the same aims at the homeless hub. And that was what drove him to want to find another way to help out the organisation.

Friday Night at the Oxford

"In my real job I work very closely with the hub and the work I do is very much related to preventing homelessness," he says.

"Working closely with the hub I could see they were doing things in a very unique manner. I describe what they're doing as having a very punk rock ethic, it's very DIY, meaning that they are very resourceful, they don't just sit around and talk about things, they get their hands in and do it.

"Seeing how they were operating and seeing how they were struggling for ongoing funding, I thought it would be cool to promote what they do and raise a bit of money and a bit of practical assistance to combine my two worlds, the music community and my interest in housing and homelessness."

Given that Wheeler felt the hub had a punk rock ethic, it made sense to ensure the four bands on the bill shared that same vibe.

"The music's punk rock and by that I mean it's fast-paced, it's energetic, it's visual and a little bit obnoxious but all in good fun," Wheeler says.

"Babymachine have been around for the longest of those four bands. But the others are doing pretty good things too. Hoon and Kaleidoscope, they've just come back from Indonesian tours and Scumm always put on a very interesting show. You never know what to expect when those guys turn up."

The Where Did You Sleep Last Night? Punk rock fundraiser features Hoon, Babymachine, Kaleidoscope and Scumm. It's at Dicey Riley's on March 28.

Poster boy for music
March 21, 2015

Shane Kenning is happy to create posters for Illawarra bands, but one of them wants him up on stage – playing a triangle.

Kenning's work can be seen in band posters for a range of Illawarra bands, including Babymachine, Bruce!, The Nice Folk, HyTest and The Watt Riot.

"The drawing has led to getting known by everyone on the

Wollongong music scene and becoming really good friends," Kenning says.

"I've always admired people who can get up onstage and sing and play. It's not something I could do.

"Though Bruce! are trying to do it. They said 'what do you play?' As a joke I said 'triangle'."

But they didn't leave it there either – one of the members of Bruce! later went into a music shop and bought him a triangle. Which means he has one less excuse for not playing.

While Kenning does create other works, the bulk of his output is band posters or CD covers. That's fine with him because he's a big music fan and keen to help out the local scene.

"I love the Wollongong music scene," he says.

"When you listen to some of the crap that's on radio and you see all these great bands in your home town, you want to support them."

Describing his work as "Saturday morning cartoons with an evil twist", Kenning is holding an exhibition of his art at the Captain's Quarters Gallery, upstairs at Beach Burrito in Wollongong.

"There's no real theme for this exhibition – it's just going to be bits and pieces of everything," Kenning says.

Trying to pick out about 15 works for the exhibition has proven a bit tricky.

"It's a bit difficult," he says. "It's like trying to pick your favourite kid.

"I always pick my drawings to pieces after I've finished them. 'I could have done this better, I could have done that better'.

"The idea you have in your head is never going to go down on paper. It's taken me years to be OK with that. But I've come close a couple of times."

All his work is drawn freehand before being scanned into the computer, where it is coloured.

Even though it is on the computer, Kenning says he resists the urge to constantly tweak the work until it's "perfect".

"I work on the computer and I could get things exact because it's on the computer and can be very precise," Kenning says.

Friday Night at the Oxford

"But it's got to look like a person did it. There's a lot of computer work out there and you can tell straight away it's done on computer – there's no human element to it.

"So I'm very conscious of not letting the capabilities of the computer dictate how the image is going to look."

The exhibition of Shane Kenning's art opens March 27 at Captain's Quarters Gallery, upstairs at Beach Burrito, 1 Globe Lane, Wollongong. They will be on exhibition until the end of April.

Band member's shock death
June 6, 2015

One of the core members of influential Wollongong band Sunday Painters has died in Malaysia.

Dennis Kennedy was the bass player in the band which performed in Wollongong in the early 1980s.

While they remain unknown to many people in their home town, their releases sell for hundreds of dollars on eBay and music aficionados have described their sound as decades ahead of its time.

Kennedy was heavily involved in efforts to see the band's back catalogue re-issued through a US label.

The reissues hit record stores earlier this year.

In recent years, Kennedy had been living and working in Singapore and Malaysia.

According to Jon Knowles, a friend who has established a fund-raising effort for his family, Kennedy was crossing the border back into Malaysia on the Friday evening last week.

He fell ill and died later that night. No autopsy was conducted but it is believed he died of a heart attack.

Sunday Painters guitarist Peter MacKinnon took to Facebook to say Kennedy's death had come as a shock, much like the 2008 death of another band member Peter Raengel.

"If Peter was the intellectual and creative force of the band, Dennis was the driving force, the one who wanted us to make a go of it," Mr MacKinnon wrote.

"I've always felt Dennis was the member of the band who really wanted to be a rock star. I still meet Peter in my dreams and expect Dennis will now be there too."

Curator of last year's *Steel City Sound* exhibition Warren Wheeler worked with Kennedy – in person and then online – while developing the project.

"In all the crossing of emails and Facebook messages I found Dennis to be very genuine," Wheeler said.

"He wore his heart on his sleeve. He never left me guessing as to what he was thinking. That's not to say he was blunt. Rather he was a good, efficient communicator and would not waste his words on dancing around a subject.

"I am proud to be able to call Dennis a friend. Distance may have prevented me from being as close to him as others, but his openness and warmth was crucial to me taking the first steps in *Steel City Sound*."

Kennedy leaves behind Polly, his wife of four years, and an infant daughter in addition to his Australian daughter Jazz and her child.

Knowles said Polly was having trouble obtaining her husband's remains and dealing with the costs of the funeral.

"Cremation, autopsy and associated expenses, Polly's airfare to travel to Singapore from a remote province in the Philippines ... It all costs and must be paid for within a week of today!" Knowles said on Facebook on Thursday.

To help his wife with these expenses, Knowles has started a fundraising effort. See youcaring.com and search for 'Remembering Dennis Kennedy'. Or donations via PayPal can be made with the email jon@jonknowles.com.

Friday Night at the Oxford

Bands make amends
June 12, 2015

Just seven days before Anzac Day, the community was outraged when a Corrimal war memorial was vandalised.

Part of the granite monument was broken away and the words "No tears for dead soldiers" and "Scab Eater" scrawled in felt pen. Melbourne punk band Scab Eater had played at the nearby Corrimal Hotel the night before the vandalism was discovered.

The region's punk community was displeased with the actions as well, which led them to organise a benefit gig for Legacy.

One of the organisers, Warren Wheeler, says it was important for Wollongong's punk scene to distance itself from these actions.

"The show is a way of us saying that we're members of the community too and we're not happy with this kind of behaviour and we don't approve of it," Wheeler says.

"Whilst we support someone's entitlement to a point of view and to express that view, that was not an appropriate way to do so.

"We don't support it and this is a way of showing the community that we will speak out against people who come to our town and think it's appropriate to vandalise important memorials."

Fourteen bands have put their hands up to play for free at the show – including BRUCE!, Lint, Rukus, Run for Cover and Steel City Allstars – and Wheeler says the level of support is a good indication of how the majority of the music scene feels about incident in April.

"The music community is like any other community, there are dissenting voices and not everyone thinks the same," Wheeler says.

"So there are elements of the music scene who weren't necessarily behind what we were doing. But overall, the wave of support and the number of bands who contacted us asking to be put on the bill – keeping in mind they weren't going to get paid for the day – was overwhelming.

"It was unfortunate that we couldn't fit everyone in."

Several bands had to be turned away for the show, which starts at

2.30pm on Saturday.

"We could have easily started before lunch but that makes for a very long day," Wheeler says of the number of bands keen to appear.

"We had bands from out of the area contacting us. We had a lot of bands from Sydney wanting to be on the bill.

"The incident got national exposure and so people recognised it was an important issue and wanted to support it."

Wheeler says he was concerned that the incident could damage the Wollongong music scene.

"The reality is venues will only support live music, regardless of the genre, as long as people attend and ... are well behaved," he says.

"Poor behaviour will reflect poorly on the venue.

"So, yes, it was a natural concern of mine as a supporter of the live scene that venues, particularly in the Corrimal area, may think twice about putting bands on.

"By putting the show on and by having the discussion, it's about saying to venues, this is a one-off – it's not reflective of the community as a whole."

Call to Arms: A punk benefit for Legacy and the RSL university scholarships is on at the Corrimal Hotel, Saturday June 13 from 2.30pm.

New take on old songs
July 21, 2015

Tumbleweed's next tour will see the band play some songs live for the first time, even though those songs are actually 20 years old.

The reason for the tour is to mark the release of a 20th anniversary edition of their *Galactaphonic* album.

As well as the original album, it comes with an extra 21 tracks including demos, B-sides and live cuts – some of which the band had

Friday Night at the Oxford

only recently uncovered.

But it's not those 20-year-old songs the band will play live for the first time – there are some tracks on the original album that are about to get their live debut, according to singer Richie Lewis.

The format of the shows will see the band play all 13 *Galactaphonic* tracks in sequence, which includes some tracks the band hasn't played since the recording.

So Lewis and the other band members have had to pull out their old copies of *Galactaphonic* to relearn their own songs.

"It's the first time I've listened to *Galactaphonic* in a long time," Lewis says.

"We've been playing certain songs off it for years, like *Hang Around* or *Nothin' To Do With The Weather*.

"But there are other ones like *This'll Be The End of Me* or *Jupiter* or *Feed the River*, these are songs that I haven't heard for years and years and years. I'm looking forward to playing these songs the most because they're new and fresh."

Listening back to an album he recorded 20 years ago has thrown up a few "cringey moments", Lewis admits.

But it's also turned him into a fan of songs he didn't much care for at the time.

"*Feed The River* I didn't like that back in the day but now I do," he says. "It's strange how things change, how your tastes change and you can have more appreciation for elements you didn't quite understand when you were younger.

"Then there are other ones that you thought were fantastic when you were younger but that don't work for you now."

The upcoming shows will be the first new ones booked since the death of bass player Jay Curley last year, with Luke Armstrong playing bass.

After playing several shows last year that were booked before Curley's death, Lewis says there was a very real chance Tumbleweed may never perform again. But they've decided to keep going, but are taking things at their own pace.

"The band is something we've been doing our whole lives and it's difficult to just let go," Lewis says.

"At this moment we're taking it project by project and taking it easy. It's hard to know where it's going to go, it's certainly changed things a lot in terms of how we feel about it.

"When we do get back together and practise, we do enjoy seeing each other and we enjoy playing music together.

"So long as we keep it as an interesting thing to do for ourselves and something different so we're not just going through the motions, then it makes us want to do it."

Tumbleweed play at Waves on September 26. The Galactaphonic 20th anniversary edition is out August 7.

Sing 'no' to violence
August 5, 2015

A fundraising gig this weekend aims to address the issue of violence both in Illawarra music scene and the community.

The Safety Dance is an all-ages gig raising money for domestic violence services at Wollongong Women's Information Service.

It is also about raising awareness of the issue at music gigs, organiser Warren Wheeler said.

"Occasionally you might be at a show and in the crowd you might get someone who is a little bit energetic and wants to get the pit going and they start being a little bit aggressive," Wheeler says.

"I've been at shows where people have come up in my face and pushed me. I'm not going to respond to that but other people would respond in an aggressive manner and then you've got problems."

Wheeler said there have been instances of women being assaulted.

"It's not unusual for girls to complain that they might have been groped in a big mosh pit because the perpetrator thinks they're anonymous, that no one can see what they're up to," he says.

"That's just not on and if people at shows see that kind of behaviour or someone is a victim of that kind of behaviour it ought to be reported

Friday Night at the Oxford

and it ought to be dealt with."

Wheeler organised the show after being inspired on several fronts.

He spoke with Bec Machine from Babymachine about trying to promote a safer kind of environment in our music scene and he watched *The Punk Singer*, a documentary about musician Kathleen Hanna and the riot grrrl movement of the 1990s.

"It got me thinking about young people in general and what they'd be exposed to at music shows," Wheeler says.

"With my kids now at an age where they are going to shows, violence at shows was a topic of conversation around the dinner table sometimes.

"I just thought we could do something that kids could go to, that was safe and also promoted a longer-term message of keeping people safe at shows.

"People go to gigs to not have to worry about stuff – to let loose and shake off their worries," he says.

"The last thing they need is to be pushed around and bullied and harassed or in some instances sexually assaulted while they're trying to enjoy a rock show."

As well as the physical harm violence causes to the victim violence can make others and the scene itself feel unsafe.

"The music scene is a broad church, where you get people who are into it for the love of it," Wheeler says.

"You also get people who want to disrupt, who want to cause problems. That puts the whole scene at risk.

"People will be less likely to go to shows if they feel they're unsafe and venues will be less likely to put shows on if they feel that there's a history of violence at their events.

"It just undermines the whole music scene."

The Safety Dance features Topnovil, Babymachine, Love Buzz and The Night Fans. The all-ages show is on August 9 from 4pm at Rad Bar, Wollongong.

Glen Humphries

Getting the word on ARIA nod
October 12, 2015

The debut album from Wollongong band Born Lion has put them in line for a prestigious ARIA award.

The band's *Final Words* album has been nominated for the Best Hard Rock/Heavy Metal Album ARIA.

Singer and guitarist John Bowker said the nod "came out of nowhere".

"When I received a call from our manager to let me know, I was more puzzled than excited," Bowker said.

"We haven't even had a song in the ARIA charts, so it took a little while to sink it, but it now it's like 'yeah it's really cool'."

The album was released in July and Bowker said it has been getting a lot of good reviews and has even featured as the album of the week on The Music website.

The foursome are up against bands In Hearts Wake, King Parrot, Northlane and Thy Art Is Murder.

"Compared to the other artists and their followings, we're far less established," Bowker said.

"We feel like the underdogs a little bit."

Even though they only heard about the nomination last week, Bowker said it has already changed things for the band.

"It's given us a good deal of exposure," he said.

"We've had a lot of attention put on the band since it's happened and the numbers on Facebook have gone up fairly significantly."

Taco Outfit is a Smash
October 29, 2015

If you are at the Halloween party at Jane's on Saturday night, keep an eye out for a giant walking taco.

The all-ages event at the Wollongong venue has four bands – one

Friday Night at the Oxford

of which is Wollongong's Smasheddybash.

Other bands on the bill are Sydney punk trio Skinpin, Love Buzz and new two-piece My Official Failure

Smasheddybash's frontwoman Keziah Sugarat will be there on the night dressed as Vampira, while the band's drummer could well be going with some Mexican style.

"We have always liked dress-up things," Ms Sugarat said.

"We've done Day of the Dead shows and things like that. The drummer got dressed up like a taco, which is quite hilarious. It's his costume du jour – he tends to like to go as a taco to everything.

"Fingers crossed he gets the yellow foam out for this and sticks crepe paper to himself for lettuce and tomato."

Ms Sugarat said she had only gotten into Halloween recently but was taking advantage of the chance to get dressed up.

"I've got a kid so it's just starting to be a thing," she said.

"I know it's an Americanised holiday but we love dressing up and stuff like that. So me and my drummer are going to take the kids trick or treating first and then we'll be dressed up and ready for the gig."

Her five-year-old daughter – who will be dressed up as Sally from *The Nightmare Before Christmas* – will be at the all-ages show.

At least until bedtime.

"I'm looking forward to playing an all-ages gig in Wollongong and seeing some different faces," Ms Sugarat said.

"All-ages gigs are important; age shouldn't limit the amount of live music you get to see.

"It's a great atmosphere when everyone is welcome to enjoy events."

For those who turn up and have forgotten to wear their Halloween finest, Ms Sugarat will have a make-up artist ready to help out.

"My friend is doing special effects make-up so I've just asked him to bring some latex to make some scars, some fake blood and things like that," she said.

Glen Humphries

Limo ride is ARIA prize for Born Lion
November 25, 2015

Wollongong band and ARIA nominee Born Lion don't reckon they're in with a shot at taking home one of those pointy trophies.

They're just in it for the limo ride.

The band's *Final Words* CD was nominated in the Best Hard Rock or Heavy Metal Album category.

The band's lead singer and guitarist John Bowker says they're still really excited about the nomination but they're not expecting a win.

Which is really the sort of level-headed approach from a band who turned a dismissive comment on their nomination ("Who the F..k is Born Lion?") into a T-shirt.

"We feel like there's no real prospect of us actually winning, to the degree that we haven't really written a speech or anything," Bowker said.

"But we probably should do that, just in case.

"We'll get to walk down the red carpet. No one will know who we are but that's alright.

"We just found out we're going to be going in a limo. Everyone arrives in a limo but I've never been in a limo so that's exciting as well.

Merry reunion for one of Wollongong's most-loved bands
June 10, 2016

To hear bassplayer David Challenger tell it, time wasn't on the Merry Widows' side.

Perhaps one of Wollongong's most-loved bands, the pop-rock-folk band was around in the early 1990s.

Made up of Challenger and the three Beniuk brothers –David (vocals and guitar), Johnno (guitar) and Tim (drums) –they won the NSW campus band comp, came second in the national final, scored

Friday Night at the Oxford

Sydney management and drove endless hours in a Tarago up and down the coast supporting the big bands of the day.

They broke up in 1995 but three of the members (Tim has retired from performing) are reuniting for several shows next month.

While the band did achieve some success, Challenger reckons it could have been so much different if their timing was better.

"I sometimes think, we were one of the most unlucky bands in the history of popular music in terms of timing," Challenger says.

"We came out about three or four years too late. Literally a month or two after we started rehearsing, grunge exploded and we just weren't in that vibe of the music scene.

"I remember, within months, every four out of five guys at the Oxford had longhair and flannelette shirts on and were trying to look like Kurt Cobain.

"If it was 1988-89, when Crowded House was huge, it might have been different. So I think we were a little bit misaligned with the timing."

But Challenger still marks that early 1990s period as one of the best times of his life – and the Merry Widows as the best band he's been in.

"It's been the only band that I've been in that's ever really mattered," he says.

"To be able to play with those three Beniuk brothers, everything just fitted so well. From the first rehearsal I remember thinking, 'wow, this has got it'."

About 18 months ago, Challenger got a reminder of that when he formed a band called The Insiders for a one-off gig in Corrimal.

That band included Johnno and David, as well as bassist Mal Wales, drummer David Crowe and keyboard player Marco Forlano – all of whom will be performing in the reunited Merry Widows.

Challenger came off the stage after that Insiders show on a high – and then realised it was probably the last gig he would ever play,

But that show also changed the minds of the other members of the Widows, who had said no to getting back together just six months earlier.

"I remember when we got off the stage after that Insiders gig and I think David turned me and said 'oh, that was great'," Challenger says.

"It's just special for me to be playing with these guys again. It was just a special part of my life in the 1990s with the Merry Widows and I certainly didn't think it would ever happen again."

But it is, and for David Beniuk, the idea of being 40-something and playing rock and roll isn't a problem at all.

"The age thing is more about 'can we get through an hour and a half on stage without running out of puff'," Beniuk says.

"I don't subscribe to that idea that you're too old to play rock and roll and you're immature if you're still doing it.

"It's what we love doing. Even though we've got a lot of other things on our plates, there's not many things better than playing in a band when it's cooking. We're still making music and we still love making it."

Preparing for the reunion shows has been tricky because, while the rest of the band is in Wollongong, Beniuk lives in Tasmania. The full band won't play together until a few days before that first show.

And then there's crossing the divide of 20-odd years to try and remember the damn songs. Even Beniuk, who wrote almost all of them, is struggling with that.

"There are some I have not played since that last gig in 1995," he says.

"Some of them I didn't even remember that we did.

"I used to always be able to visualise something about writing each song. I could think of a song that I wrote and visualise some aspect of where I wrote it or why I wrote it.

"Some of these I've struggled to do that with."

For Beniuk, his memories of the Merry Widows are mixed – he thought the band was great but quickly tired of the grind.

"It was a very hectic few years, especially after we got signed and were playing three or four nights a week all over the state," Beniuk says.

"And we all had jobs or study too. It was a great experience but it was also a bit of a grind by the end of it to be continuing to open for other acts.

"That's why we finished, because it was a bit of a grind and we were getting sick of that. Our manager wanted to invest in a second EP and

Friday Night at the Oxford

we didn't want him to put his money into it if our hearts weren't in it.

"So I think we decided to pull the pin."

Challenger remembers a different breaking point, which is understandable – it's been more than 20 years. For him it was waiting to see if BMG, one of country's biggest labels, was going to sign them.

"I remember thinking, after this long, if we get disappointed, it will kind of kill us," he says.

"And that's what happened – they passed. That was about mid '94 and we were only together for another five or six months."

The band is only playing four shows next month – but it seems further shows down the line haven't been ruled out.

"No one's discussed anything after this," Beniuk says.

"We do like to make new music and we've found in recent years that we enjoy doing that together.

"It's probably a case of never say never, but I don't know."

It's the same story from Challenger.

"I honestly don't know – I have a feeling we'll just see how it goes. Never say never."

The Merry Widows Wollongong shows are on July 1 at The Illawarra Brewery and a double-header with '80s Wollongong legends Svegies Vegies at Dicey Riley's on July 9.

Short film that rocks
June 13, 2016

The idea was to make a short film about a band but John Bowker ended up joining them too.

Bowker, a member of Wollongong's ARIA-nominated band Born Lion, has signed on for a short stint on bass for The Rockers.

The connection with the band started when Bowker – who works at Uniting Care as an "Ability Linker" helping with people with mild to moderate disabilities or mental health issues – was thinking about entering a film contest.

"I heard about this Focus on Ability film competition focusing on people who have disabilities and making films that aim to look past the disabilities and see them as people," Bowker said.

He tossed around some ideas at work before remembering The Rockers, which includes members with an intellectual disability or autism.

"It dawned on me that there were these guys called The Rockers," Bowker said.

"We had them play at the Ability Links launch a couple of years ago. I thought those guys would make some good subject matter.

"I was thinking of a mockumentary Spinal Tap thing but then it switched to a straight doco because the subject matter was interesting enough."

Bowker brought in film-maker Brendan Blacklock to shoot the film, but that's not where his work ended.

He also joined the band, found them a drummer and got them in the studio to record their "psychedelic fuzz rock".

"The guys had never been in a recording studio before," he said.

"We recorded seven tracks and the guys were pretty thrilled about it. The recording process was a matter of going through it once and then capturing it on the second take.

"The guys like to move on pretty quickly. They don't want to stuff around. So it's capturing the raw moment."

The plan is to have the CD on sale at the band's next gig at Rad Bar on June 21.

While Bowker is only a temporary Rocker, he said he's been having fun in the line-up.

"I've really benefited from playing with the guys. It's been really enjoyable for me," he said.

"There's absolutely nothing pretentious about what they do and that's the really refreshing part of working with them.

"They do what they do and they're not trying to project any sort of image at all."

Friday Night at the Oxford

Party honours Belinda's life, rather than one dark moment

July 2, 2016

Fifteen years ago Peter Conran's partner Belinda Deane committed suicide.

Every year since, he's organised a big party to celebrate her memory and invited stacks of bands to play.

That party – known as HOPE – has become an iconic event on the Illawarra music scene's calendar.

The event also serves to raise awareness and funds for suicide prevention.

As well as that it gives Deane's family and friends a chance to remember her through something she loved – music.

Deane was a bassplayer in several bands, including local legends The Unheard, so for Conran it made sense to mark her memory with music.

The result is a night that celebrates someone's lifetime, rather than focusing on one dark moment of it.

"You could spend your whole time mourning someone's passing or you could spend your time being glad that you got to meet them in the first place," Conran said.

"Let's face it, the world is huge and there's a lot of people – the majority of those people we don't get to meet in our lifetime let alone be friends with or anything like that.

"So the chance of meeting someone and having them make any sort of impact is relatively minor in the overall scheme of things."

On the first anniversary of Deane's death, Conran decided to organise a benefit night in her memory, and bands who knew her volunteered to play.

From there it became a fundraising show and, to Conran's surprise, has been held every year since.

"I thought I'd still do it every year but I didn't realise that it would become such a necessary thing or such a well-loved thing throughout the community," he said.

Part of the reason for the continued success of HOPE is that many people know someone who has taken their own life, so the event offers special resonance for them.

That's evidenced by the fact some of the bands and the punters turning up didn't know Deane. But they do have an empty space in their life that someone left.

"Some of them have lost people in the past, so it becomes a way for them to celebrate those lives that they knew," Conran said

"We don't just keep it to Belinda even though she's – for want of a better word – the figurehead of the advertising and she was the prime reason for us starting it up.

"There are other people who have lost people – through natural causes, or cancer or road accident or something else – who use the night to meet up with their friends and celebrate those lives as well."

That first HOPE show – and so many more – was held at The Oxford Tavern, Deane's favourite place and the home of the Wollongong music scene for many years.

Following the Oxford's closure, the event moved to The Patch for a few years and has been at Dicey Riley's for the last three years.

Some may find organising a concert each year to mark the death of a loved one to be too much to handle, too much of a reminder of what is no longer there.

But HOPE is different for Conran – it's actually a bright spot in what has become a tough time emotionally.

"It doesn't get any easier throughout the years, it's always been the same sort of impact," he said.

"It's just a case of dealing with the day as it comes up. This is part of the way of dealing with it, organising this and trying to help people not be in the same sort of situation that we're in.

"Around that time the days are a numb time anyway but because of what it is, it's a case of trying to get through the day. And this kind of helps in a way, it helps make a difference to other people."

The HOPE show may have had its origins in a moment of sadness but Conran says the night wasn't a somber affair.

Friday Night at the Oxford

"A lot of people who go there who still remember Belinda don't go out very much anyway, they're older people," he said.

"But they tend to turn up for this. It's become part of their social calendar and they run into people they haven't see for years. In a sense it brings people together."

As well as allowing for old friends to reunite and remember, Conran said HOPE's importance has increased in recent years.

"It's becoming more of a necessity because there's been a lot of cutbacks in mental health and the suicide statistics are going up, so it still feels like something that's necessary," he said.

"For most people it's putting [the issue] in their mindset. Even though they don't attend, they know that there's something going on. It's keeping it in everybody's mind."

Conran, who wears a constant reminder on his upper arm in the form of a "HOPE" tattoo, said suicide can leave powerful feelings of guilt in loved ones.

They can spend a lot of time looking for signs that something was wrong, thinking about things they could have done that might have saved a life.

"Whenever anyone dies, it doesn't matter whether it's suicide or anything else, everyone always questions how they treated that person," he said.

"Could they have treated them better? Could they have done this for them? That plays on their mind – that's a human condition, we always do that.

"For most people who commit suicide, there wasn't anything really you could do because it was that person's decision.

"They're thinking solely of their own decision, they're not thinking of anyone else at that point, so they're not doing it primarily to attack people, they've just had enough."

One thing people can do is work to break the taboo that surrounds suicide. Talking about it more can break the stigma and make it easy for someone to come out and ask for help.

"I think it's becoming a much more open conversation that people are having," he said.

"That's a good thing but it's also a hard thing when you don't know people are struggling, so you don't know whether to ask a question or not.

"Most people who commit suicide don't tend to tell you they're going to do it. They don't tell anyone because they don't want anyone to stop them.

"The people who do say that they're feeling suicidal, it's good that they say that because it means that they're asking for help.

"It really comes down to the people who are suicidal asking for help. And that's why we have to remove the stigma from it. If you keep it in the background it's still a taboo subject and it needs to be talked about a lot more."

For suicide prevention support, please call Lifeline on 13 11 14 or visit lifeline.org.au/gethelp.

Fifteen Years of HOPE is on Saturday night at Dicey Rileys from 3pm. The suicide prevention fundraiser is free and features nine bands including Chainsaw Mascara, Topnovil, Babymachine and Patrick Lyons and the Band of American Creek. Fundraising items like caps, armbands and a limited edition CD will be available on the night.

Hy-voltage rock'n'roll
December 3, 2016

Back in February 2011, Luke Armstrong was turning 30 and wanted to hear a lot of music on his birthday.

So the bassplayer and singer in HyTest organised a music festival at the Cabbage Tree Hotel to mark his third decade on the Earth.

He convinced more than 20 of his favourite bands to turn up and play but didn't send out birthday party invitations – turn up at the door with $10 in your hand and you could join the fun.

And that was supposed to be it for HyFest – it was never supposed to happen again.

"The idea was that it would just be a one-off thing, but it just seems

Friday Night at the Oxford

to have snowballed every year," Armstrong says.

"By the third year we did it we didn't even have to try and pick the line-up and call and ask them to play – we had so many people hassling us to play."

Held every year since, HyFest has become very much a Wollongong institution. Despite the fact it no longer coincides with Armstrong's birthday, it's still a gig he and the other bandmates in HyTest look forward to.

Partially because it's one of the few guaranteed times of the year they get to play a gig.

As they get older, work, families and drummers make it harder to make time to play.

"As we were getting older, the other members of HyTest were all doing different things and playing in different bands," Armstrong says.

"Neil, our drummer, he plays in about half a dozen bands, so any time we try and book something we have to try and work around his schedule.

"Also we're all working full-time so it's hard to tour like we used to. We used to leave Wollongong every second weekend and go out and do stuff.

"We've had kids in the last couple of years as well so it all makes it difficult to get everyone together and do it.

"But this show is the one gig of the year we all look forward to, for sure."

Playing the show is great for Armstrong. But organising it? Well, that became a pain in the backside.

Such a pain, in fact, that he was about ready to throw in the towel.

"The last two years I've said, 'nah, I'm not doing it this year'," Armstrong says.

"It really is quite a logistical nightmare to put together – getting so many people together, finding the right venue. After having kids I found it really hard to find the time to book it."

That's where Warren Wheeler, from Helter Smelter Booking and Promotions, stepped in.

"Warren's been a champion," Armstrong says.

Glen Humphries

"He's just jumped on board and said 'you don't have a choice – I'm taking it out of your hands, this has to happen'."

Wheeler felt HyFest needed to happen, as it had become much more than a birthday celebration, and more than an excuse for a HyTest gig.

"I offered to help because I love loud rock, punk and metal music and know plenty of others do too," Wheeler says.

"HyFest is as much about that community as it is about getting your eardrums shattered into a million pieces.

"Not that this compares with the Yours & Owls festival at all, and look, I love those guys and they've got a good thing going.

"But there's another demographic that gets left out of that scene a bit. HyFest caters for those that love their rock 'n' roll a little louder, a whole lot uglier."

As well as a chance for Wheeler to shatter his eardrums, keeping HyFest going was about nurturing the local music scene for tomorrow's singers, guitarists, bassists and drummers.

"We have some great heavy bands here doing some awesome stuff," Wheeler says.

"Maggot, for example, are tearing up stages and legends like Babymachine and HyTest fly the flag well.

"HyFest is an opportunity to bring bands in who wouldn't ordinarily play Wollongong, giving young bands something to aspire to."

Someone else might be organising HyFest but one thing remains unchanged – HyFest get to pick all the bands.

"HyTest still have the final say over what bands play," Armstrong says.

"Warren put a list together of bands that he thought should get up. It got down to the point of us saying 'we really like those bands but they're not really mates of ours, and we've got mates of ours who are hassling us to play'."

One band who were mates and did make the cut are headliners King Parrot from Melbourne.

Lead singer Matt Young says HyFest definitely has a reputation in independent music circle outside Wollongong.

Friday Night at the Oxford

"I think there's definitely a buzz about, especially in Melbourne," Young says.

"I think there are four Melbourne bands playing on it this year. Definitely the Melbourne guys know about it and look forward to making the trek up there.

"They've done a really great job of promoting it, making sure it's a bit of a national fixture."

Young says those in the crowd at HyFest can expect "total and utter chaos" from King Parrot's headlining set.

"We like to make a mess, we like to get involved with the crowd and we like to get the crowd involved with us," Young says.

"I know by the time that we get on stage people will probably be a bit messy, so that suits us perfect.

"You can expect nothing but craziness from us."

Reformation gets the Nod
December 23, 2016

It's not often you hear about public transport's effect on the Wollongong music scene.

But Steve Abrahall from the "reforming for one night only" Mutated Noddys remembers the early 1980s in Wollongong as a lean time for the local music scene – and the trains didn't help.

"In '83 we were still a bit isolated," Abrahall remembers.

"There were no electric trains at that stage, so going out in Sydney wasn't the easiest."

So that meant heading to places like Dapto Leagues or Collegians to see bands who played top 40 covers of the same songs you heard on 2WL or 2OO (now Wave FM and i98 respectively).

"When you'd go to see certain bands you'd see a lot of the same faces but not many people were into the idea of starting their own band," Abrahall says.

"A lot of people would talk about it but I think there wasn't a great deal of reward in having a band together because there wasn't really anywhere to play."

But, in mid-1983, Abrahall started the Mutated Noddys anyway, a band channelling the Detroit rock sound espoused by the likes of MC5, The Stooges and Radio Birdman.

While The Oxford Tavern is spoken of as the iconic Wollongong music venue, Abrahall says, back in those days, it was another pub that changed things – especially for those bands and punters who liked it loud.

"The biggest difference was when the North Gong started getting great indie acts, such as the Lime Spiders, Hummingbirds, Exploding White Mice, Died Pretty and The Hitmen," he says.

"Wollongong indie bands were able to gain exposure supporting them and, in some case, do their own headlines.

"That was a great scene – everyone hanging out the front in summer, drink in hand, between bands. Just magic."

The band broke up in mid-1994 and guitarist Abrahall, bassist Gary Uren and drummer Brett Bradley went their separate ways.

That was until longtime fan and Wollongong musician Ronny Van Dyk asked if the band would reform and play a gig for his birthday.

"Ronny just asked, 'I suppose I've got a snowball's chance in hell of the Noddys reforming for my party'," Abrahall says.

"I asked our drummer who lives in Nimbin and Gary who lives in Chicago what they thought."

And they felt it'd be a bit of fun.

"It was just by sheer coincidence that Gary was coming back for Christmas for about a week."

The Mutated Noddys play at Jane's on Friday night supported by Crapulous Gee Gaw and OCDeeDee. The bands kick off at 8.30pm and tickets are $5 at the door.

Friday Night at the Oxford

It's a Tragic 10th anniversary for band
January, 30, 2017

After being together for a decade, Crash Tragic are in it more for the love these days than the chance to make it big.

But they wouldn't knock back a bit of fame if it came their way, says bassist Paul Ditton.

"Making it big would be lovely but at this point I don't think there's too much chance of it," Ditton says.

"Although we could be like that old racehorse that one day might surprise everyone."

With people getting married and having kids, it can be hard to keep a band together, but Ditton says he and guitarist Anto Kalsow and drummer Scott Campbell still like playing together.

"The band is still important to the three of us and that's why we make time for it," he says.

"It's kind of like a marriage. We know each other's idiosyncrasies and we just like the music that we play together."

The band celebrates the 10th anniversary with a gig at Dicey Riley's on February 11.

"There will be a giveaway of CDs and T-shirts and other than that we're going to go hard like we always do."

Evol unearthed again
February 18, 2017

Evol haven't played a gig in 20 years but it seems all someone had to do was ask them.

The Wollongong fourpiece are back for a show at Dicey Riley's on Saturday – their first since the band broke up way, way, way back in 1997. Back when there was an all-ages venue called Sunami upstairs near Dicey's and no-one had even thought about knocking down the Oxford

Tavern.

The band have never performed a real gig since the break-up. And perhaps they never would had local music maven Warren Wheeler from *Steel City Sound* not asked them to reform for a show. A show that also features a rare performance from Shifter.

"We got asked by Warren Wheeler to do this gig – that's it really," says singer Flavia.

"We thought 'okay, let's give it a try'. It doesn't mean that we've reformed it just means that we're going to do this gig. "I don't know what's going to happen from there."

Perhaps the band's biggest moment was winning the Wollongong instalment of the Triple J Unearthed contest in 1997.

That was back when the competition was a big deal and there wasn't a new Unearthed winner announced every week.

Flavia said they entered the contest without much thought to winning it. But when they did, there was a bit of a tongue-in-cheek sense of "cool, we've made it".

"There was an element of that, in a joking way," Flavia says.

"But I think when we realised the enormity of it was when we were asked to play with Silverchair at Wollongong uni.

"That when it really hit us that this was pretty big. "We didn't really think that we'd made it. It was just nice to be recognised. We were even given the keys to the city by the mayor at that time."

For Saturday's show, Flavia says they're playing "all the old favourites" and have been getting together and play whenever they can.

"I think we've had two practices," she says. "So that equates to three hours of practice after 17 years but it's coming back."

Evol and Shifter perform at Dicey Rileys on Saturday night from 8.30pm. Also on the bill are Garry David and Space Boys.

Friday Night at the Oxford

Big price tag for rare songs from Wollongong band
February 29, 2018

In an era where so much music is free, asking someone to pay $500 for three songs from a local band may seem a bit steep.

However, that's the starting price a mysterious Helensburgh seller on eBay has set for a handful of songs on a vinyl seven-inch.

That seven-inch – *Three Kinds of Escapism* – is from Sunday Painters, a Wollongong band from the late 1970s and early 1980s, that was making weird and strange sounds in an era where most local acts were cranking out covers of top 40 songs.

The band is largely unknown to people in Wollongong – and elsewhere – but has a cult following around the world. And that's a cult following eager to snap up any of the band's absurdly hard-to-find vinyl or cassette releases

Which is why Wollongong music historian Warren Wheeler reckons our mystery Helensburgh seller will have no trouble finding a buyer keen to part with $500.

"I don't doubt it will sell for that – if not a lot more," Wheeler said.

"I suspect that someone somewhere will be wanting that. Sadly it's not going to be me."

If $500 is too steep, then the same seller – who did not respond to emails – also has the rare Sunday Painters' first single going for $299 and an album and EPs going for $149.95 each.

The cheapest item – a seven-incher called *Painting By Numbers* – will set you back $100.

Wheeler says the band's original releases do appear on auction sites from time to time and they're always snapped up quickly because of their scarcity.

"Over the years as I've been watching those auction sites, I've seen those prices go up," Wheeler says.

"To see this particular item at $500 is part of that ongoing trend and I'm not surprised that they're getting to those prices."

Not even the fact a US indie label put out a CD re-release of the band's first three singles – including the one with the $500 price tag –

will put a dampener on the desire for the original articles.

But why are these releases from a little-known band so sought after?

Part of it is that most of the releases are designed as works of art with multiple covers, handwritten sleeves and – in one case – drops of a band member's blood.

In terms of the music, Wheeler says their discordant fuzzed sound were ahead of their time.

"The sounds that they produced were very much a reflection of growing up in an industrial city, which Wollongong very much was back when they existed," he says.

"They were able to draw inspiration from their immediate environment and turn it into an art form."

Here Comes the Sundial
March 31, 2018

It's a sign of Tumbleweed's enduring popularity that there is so much excitement about the re-release of an album that is 26 years old.

In 1992, the band released their debut self-titled album that featured crowd favourites like *Sundial*, *Acid Rain* and *Healer*.

While it was part of a larger CD compilation of their early work released in 2013, it's been impossible to find the album itself.

Illawarra record label Farmer and the Owl is changing all that. Next month, to mark Record Store Day on April 21, it's re-releasing the *Tumbleweed* album on blue vinyl, as well as a seven-inch single of *Daddy Longlegs*.

The news has already got Tumbleweed fans in the region excited, with people planning on how to get their hands on a copy when record store Music Farmers opens its doors on April 21.

They'll have to be near the front of the line; with just 400 copies of the album being pressed, they're sure to sell out fast.

Tumbleweed singer Richie Lewis says it's comforting to know that something the band created almost three decades ago still strikes a chord

Friday Night at the Oxford

with so many people.

"The fact that our thing has lasted this long, is testament to it being pretty okay and meaning something to a lot of people at one time," he says.

"So I'm very grateful for that. For me it's like a lot of people have been asking for it to be on vinyl for a long time so I'm very happy that we've finally got the opportunity to deliver it to them."

Formed in Tarrawanna in late 1990, the band broke through when grunge changed the music scene forever.

Quickly – but not entirely accurately – pigeonholed as "stoner rock" because of their long hair and apparent proclivities of some members, the debut peaked at No48 on the Australian charts shortly after its December 1992 release.

That was an especially busy year for the band, which also saw the release of two EPs.

Lewis says having to come up with songs for three releases in a year stretched the band's creativity a bit thin at times.

"The way I feel about it when I look back at it now, *Theatre of Gnomes* and *Weedseed* came out in rapid succession," Lewis says.

"We put all of our great songs into those two EPs and we had a few left over, like *God*, *Atomic*, *Sundial* and I think *Healer* was left over too.

"So we had to come up with some more songs, so there's a couple I think were rushed into, like *Starseed*."

Recorded in a pre-digital era where tracks were recorded to tape, Lewis recalls long streamers of segmented tape stuck on the studio walls with masking tape explaining what part of which song each came from.

Rather than recording a complete song in one shot, the tracks on *Tumbleweed* were made up of a chorus from one take, an intro from another, a guitar lead from a third, all cut apart with a razor and put back together.

"So a song like *Acid Rain* was pretty much cut to bits and reassembled in the studio from bits of tape," Lewis says.

"It was an amazing process to see how a big American producer [Doug Olson] did things in those days. I was a young 18-19 year-old who was fresh to the scene going 'wow!'.

"There was a lot of technique in studio practice back then that now has been made very easy with technology and Pro Tools. So seeing that physical aspect was really cool."

The surprising downside to that tape-splicing approach is that it changed the nature of at least one song. *Acid Rain* actually ended up a bit longer than it once was, forcing the band to listen to their own album to learn the new version.

"That song in particular we had to relearn from the pieced-together edit of the song, because it had the addition of a few bars going into a chorus and a few other things," Lewis remembers.

Over the next few weeks before Record Store Day, the whole band has been listening to that first album to prepare for an in-store performance of *Tumbleweed* from the first track to the last.

"Songs like *A Darkness at Never Never* with acoustic guitars in it, with the layering and texturing in it, I don't think we ever tried it live, which is a shame because it's amazing," Lewis says.

"It's one of the ones I'm really, really looking forward to doing.

"In the set now that we've been doing there's only one song that we're doing from that album, which is *Sundial*.

"So it will be really interesting to be doing a completely different set and I'm looking forward to the challenge."

Listening back to that first album in preparation for the gig has been a mixed bag for Lewis.

On the one hand, he feels a bit self-conscious about listening to his old stuff. But on the other hand, enough time has passed that he can almost trick himself into thinking it's someone else he's listening to.

"Time is an amazing thing and looking back on it from 26 years on you can hear it with fresh ears," he admits.

"You can almost view it as if it's not really you, you listen to it as if it's somebody else."

Jeb Taylor from both Music Farmers and Farmer and the Owl said he'd been talking with the band about a vinyl version of *Tumbleweed* for a few years.

He said it gave old fans the chance to have the album on a new format and let a new generation who grew up after Tumbleweed's

Friday Night at the Oxford

heyday "a chance to go back and discover the most important band to emerge from this region".

While he says you can hear the Tumbleweed influence in plenty of other bands – from HyTest and Dropping Honey, to Hockey Dad, Shining Bird and The Vans – the five-piece from Tarrawanna also influenced him.

"Personally I probably wouldn't be working in music if it wasn't for Tumbleweed," Taylor says.

"As a very young teenager I discovered a couple of songs from the band and when I realised they were a bunch of guys from a few suburbs down the road, doing well on a national stage, it was inspiration first to start a high school band and play shows.

"From doing that, it led me into the music scene and with that booking venues, managing bands, opening a record shop and starting a record label."

Lewis says Tumbleweed has plans to release new material. He says they plan to head to the Austinmer home of bassplayer Jamie Cleaves one weekend and record some tracks.

The result is more likely to be released on limited-run seven-inchers rather than a studio-produced album.

"What we want to do is go back to where it was when we first began," Lewis says.

"There was a real fruitful period, a real productive period where other people didn't really matter.

"It wasn't really a part of what we were about – we just wanted to see who we were and see what we could create and just enjoy the process of writing and recording and experimenting."

Record Store Day is on April 21 at Music Farmers. The Tumbleweed vinyl and other limited releases go on sale from 9am. Entertainment starts at noon with DJ sets from Honeybear and Farmer and the Owl Sultans Of Spin. The bands – Tumbleweed and Los Tones – start from 3pm.

Glen Humphries

Not everyone feels good about Born Lion's new video
June 28, 2018

It's no surprise to John Bowker to suggest the new video from his band Born Lion might make some people feel sick.

"Yeah, we got a bit of that feedback," laughs the singer and guitarist.

The video is for *Old Days*, the third single from the band's *Celebrate the Lie* album.

The reason it makes some people feel ill? That's due to what Bowker calls the "glitchy camera effect", which he says had no effect on him.

The video was filmed using a row of five GoPro cameras mounted on a hand-held board and held in place with gaffer tape.

The result is each scene is shot from five slightly different angles which, when edited together, make for a stuttering but somewhat disorientating video.

"We just wanted something really simple and easy to put together for hardly any money," Bowker says.

He came up with the idea for the video's storyline, which sees him walk from the pub to the band rehearsal room.

As for the jerky footage, the inspiration for that came from Bowker "mucking around" with a stop-motion app on his phone.

"I showed that to [label] FourFour," he says.

"They had a young guy there who was really quite good at a range of different video options. He was right into stop motion and he thought of that whole GoPro situation. So we hired the GoPros and he used a bunch of gaffer tape and rigged it all up."

The *Celebrate the Lie* album comes three years after the release of the ARIA-nominated debut *Final Words*.

Bowker says there were a few reason for the three-year wait between albums.

"It could have been a lot quicker," he admits.

"The gap between finishing the recording and having it released was

Friday Night at the Oxford

considerable.

"There was some massive hold-ups in terms of mixing and stuff.

"We had it mixed completely, which took a long time and when we got it back we weren't happy with how it sounded so we had to remix it.

"That took another few months. Then we were going to release it last year but the label decided it would be better to do it at the start of the New Year."

Having been nominated for that ARIA in 2015, there was a chance to really gain some momentum. Bowker says the lag time may have made it hard for them to capitalise on that recognition.

"I think the band was frustrated about the process of this whole album," he says.

"We were really happy with the music but that delay is really quite stifling for any artist. To have that big a gap ... by the time it's been released we're already thinking about new music and other songs and other directions. So it feels like what you've done is slightly redundant by the time it's out there.

"I think it's important to do stuff and get it out there really quickly. That's something we've learned, we just need to do that."

For an album that took longer than expected, it kind of makes sense that the album launch happens a few months later too.

Celebrate the Lie was released in February this year, but the band is playing a Wollongong launch this Saturday.

"The theory behind waiting a little while was to give people a chance to listen to the album," he says.

"It's so it gets out there and circulates a little bit before we did a proper tour for it so there'd be some greater recognition of the new stuff when we played."

Bowker says the lyrics for the new single *Old Days* came out of a dark time in his life.

"Lyrically it's a personal reflection about where I was at that point in my life," he says.

"I'd been through some pretty heavy events, like a divorce and was starting to come out the other side of all that. It's a reminder to myself that even though things may seem all doom and gloom, it can change for the better if I keep working at it."

Pulling those dark moments out of his head and getting them down on paper is cathartic for Bowker, especially when he can turn them into a "high-energy pop-rock song".

"It's good to turn something that's a bit depressing into some art, or a piece of music that you put out there," he says.

"It's twisting it, turning it around from something that's quite solitary and that you're processing on your own into something else.

"I like that about it, it's sort of repackaging it."

Born Lion play the Servo Food Truck Bar at Port Kembla on Saturday night.

Friday Night at the Oxford

Index

The listings here include all bands mentioned in *Friday Night at the Oxford*, whether they were the subject of a story or just listed as a support band. In the case of any band whose name started with "The" that first word is ignored (eg "The Culprits" can be found under C, rather than T). Solo performers are listed by surname.

Also, there are no listings for individual band members mentioned in these pages as indexes are a huge pain in the butt to compile and that would have made way too much extra work.

2Vox FM 95-96
5x5x5 exhibition 172-73
7th Freak 61

A Comedy of Errors 123
Abe 90
Acoustic Tally Room 24-25
Agent Pecan 115
The Alohas 112
Arnold, Patrick 86
ATE 72-73, 123-24
Awakening 104

Babymachine 151-52, 171, 212, 213, 220, 221, 231, 234
Bah Humbug CD 85-86
The Balkan Club 194
Beniuk, David, 12-13, 20-22, 24-25, 25-26, 26-27, 43-47, 49-50, 59-60, 127-129
Blind 65
Born Lion 181-82, 221, 223, 227, 243-45
Boys on Bex 42, 70

Brackish 86
Bracode 68
Brazen Hearts 152
Bridge Tavern (Nowra) 209
Bruce! 179-80, 185, 213, 216
Bulb (magazine) 93, 94, 173
Bulldoze all Bowlos 172
Bulli Hotel 124
Bulli PCYC 91, 115
Butane 15

Call to Arms 216-17
Chainsaw Mascara 231
The Chargers 113, 147, 148, 153-54
Cherrypickers 65-66, 96-97, 134, 146-47
Cicada 24
Cikim 95, 98-99, 134
Citizen Dog 159
Collegians 235
Compressed Heads 15
Cooneys 28, 145, 156, 157
Corrimal Hotel 197, 202, 217

Cosby 129-30
Countersunk 95
Crapulous Gee Gaw 236
Crash Tragic 236
Crown the King 195
The Culprits 1, 12 49, 59, 60, 193-96
Cult 45 17
Cyndustry 152

Dapto Leagues Club 235
David Challenger and the Insiders 201-02, 225
David, Garry, 238
The Dawn Collective 138-39, 152-53
Dawn Patrol 14, 117
Dead Records 158
Decode 110
Delaite, Danielle 65
Dettol 6, 135
Devlin, Johnny 125-27
Dicey Rileys 194, 211, 226, 229 237
Dinky Crash 17
The Dodgy World of Adam Buckland 24, 28, 40-43, 61-62, 70-71, 76, 85
Doubled 65, 86, 139
Dragster webzine 2
Dropping Honey 24, 38-40, 62, 83-84, 107-09, 113, 114, 199-201

Ebb 31

Eezee 113
El Sanchez 77
Elia 209
Empty Bed 76
Engineer Brains 201
Emmitt 15
Erika's Jive 22, 24
Evol 198, 237-38

Faded Underground 95, 113, 129
Farmer and the Owl 239, 242
Farmer and the Owl Sultans of Spin 243
The Figurines 114
The Fists of Righteous Harmony (aka The Fists) 135-36, 157-58
Flying Colours 75-76, 181
Frank's Plastic Monkey 73
Fugg 16-17, 22-24, 28-30, 42, 57, 58-59, 61, 62, 68, 74-75, 77, 89-80, 137-38
Fly Agaric 150

The Gangsters 188
Generic 76, 84
Generic Bungi Cord 36
Glab 209-11
Golgotha Method 85, 95
Gong Tribute Band 113-14
Gordo 50
Gravitron 104
Greene, Paul 105, 118-19, 161

Friday Night at the Oxford

Hampson, Noah, 73
Happy Noodle Boy 113
Headlands Hotel 56
Hee Haw 77, 82-83
Hell City Glamours 159
Helter Smelter (website) 178
Helter Smelter (bookings and promotions) 233
Heritage Hotel 141, 149, 188
Hideaway Café 6, 25, 26, 62
High Beam Music 57-58, 77-80, 82, 112, 117, 131-32
Hirst & Greene 139-41, 154-55
Hockey Dad 190
Honeybear 243
Hoon 212
HOPE 67-68, 228-231
How Machines Work 111-13, 142-43
Hybrid Earth 64
HyFest 179, 196-97, 232-34
HyTest 2, 147-48, 152, 175, 179, 185, 196, 198, 213, 232, 2334

Illawarra Brewery 226
Illawarra Singers Union, 22
Illawarra Sound(s) 93-94
Impasse 104, 110
Infotainment Lifestyle Band 26, 27, 43
Infusion 143-45, 155-57
Inscape 195
Intercontinental Playboys 149
The Inland Sea 128

Ireland, Tim, 26, 39, 114, 159-61
The Ironworkers 189, 194

Jane's 222, 236
Jawbox 73
Johnny Johnson and the Rebels 191
Jordan 19

Kaleidoscope 176, 212, 213
Karma 181
Kemblastock 112, 152, 167
Klub 53 (venue) 76, 83, 84

Lady 86
Landers, Scott, 19
Lariat 35-38, 56-57
Larynex 76, 181
Lawler, Andy, 19
Leadfinger 172
Life Adjustment Order 180
Lint 216
Log 106-07
Love Buzz 221
Los Tones 243
Lucky Charm (record label) 149
Ludo 85, 110

The Marksmen 174, 189
Machine Translations 90-91
Me Jane 113, 115
Merry Widows 12, 13, 22, 49, 59, 128, 200, 224-26

MFS 115, 152
Mind at Large 110-11, 113
Miner's Elbow 99
Mojo Hands 198
Monstrous Blues 77, 86-87, 90-91, 112, 118, 152, 167
Mudlungs 6
Music Farmers 191, 198, 240, 242
Musicoz 65, 66, 101, 130
Mutated Noddys 234-36
Mustard 13, 202

Nabilone 62-63 80-82, 110, 113
Naiad 63, 104, 113
Nether 113
Neveready 33-35, 48, 55-56, 64-65
The Nice Folk 172, 202-04, 213
Nichamin, Tania, 86, 129-30
The Night Fans 221
North Gong Hotel 14, 15, 19, 20, 195, 235
Nowra School of Arts 155

Obsidian 83
OCDeeDee 236
Ohana 115
Omusic 94
Optic Nerve 999-100
Origami Paradise 76
Oxford Tavern 3, 13, 28, 31, 32, 36, 40, 50, 56, 58, 61, 64, 66, 69, 72, 75, 82, 85, 86, 87,

90, 91, 93, 96, 99, 103, 105, 111, 121, 124, 129, 143, 154, 159, 189, 194, 197, 229, 235, 237

Palm Court Hotel 100, 147, 152, 180
Pancake Day 30-33, 60-61, 68, 113
The Passenger Corridor 141-42
The Patch 180, 182, 189, 195, 229
Patrick Lyons and the American Creek Band 202, 231
The Peppertones 84
Phial 94, 101-03, 110, 113, 141
The Pink Fits 167
Pioneer Hall 189
Porcelain 66-67, 149-50
Pounderhound 5, 39, 63, 160
Proton Energy Pills 163
Pulse of the Illawarra (magazine) 173

RAD Bar 201, 204
Radio Shack Five 19
Recliner 64
Red Star Studios 95
Redback Music (label) 5,6
Revilo 115
Rex Hotel, 24
Richie and the Creeps 90, 148-49, 167
Riffter (see also Shifter) 107, 117-18

Friday Night at the Oxford

ROADS (Remnants of a Dead Star) 120-21
Robinson Steven 18-19, 202
Rockafella 88-89, 112, 114-15, 118, 148, 158-59
The Rockers 227-28
RPM 121-23
Rukus 216
Run For Cover 216

The Safety Dance 219-221
The Sandcasters 149
Scalene 113
Second 134
Segression 69-70, 113, 115, 117
Self-Titled 115
Servo Food Truck Bar 245
Schnook 129
Scumm 212, 213
Sh'Mantra 83
Shooters Bar 161
Shifter (see also Riffter) 13-14, 77, 117-18, 237, 238
Side Effect X 113, 115-17
Single Note Theory 134-35
Sleeping at Grandma's 95
Smasheddybash 222
Space Boys 238
Star Café 207
The Start 201
Steel City Allstars 216
Steel City Sound exhibition 1, 2, 188, 189-92, 192-93, 198, 215
Steel City Sound website 173-74, 178, 188, 237

Stifler 152
Stone Ox 121
Strangers 121
Stud Lee Muffin 76, 85, 86
Summer Blast! 114-15
Sunami 237
Sunday Painters 189, 198, 206-08, 214-216, 238-39
Svegies Vegies 187-88, 226

Tea Club (Nowra) 129
Tears Turn Flood 113
Terminal Records 205, 238-39
Three Chimneys 211
Thousand Plane Raid 195
Thumlock 57, 58, 76, 77, 79, 120, 121, 131, 198
Tim Ireland and the Gilded Kiln 62, 63
Topnovil 24, 35, 47-49, 221, 231
Towradgi Beach Hotel 118
Traces of Nut 99
Tumbleweed 75, 101, 113, 148, 158, 161-168, 170-71, 171, 176-77, 182-83, 184-845, 186-87, 192-93, 200, 210, 218-19, 239-43
Turbo Degenerate 112

The UnAustralians 59
Undertow 945
The Unheard 62, 68, 163, 167, 198, 221
University UniBar 56, 120, 155,

157, 176
Unscene (festival) 178-79
Unscene and Unheard (exhibition) 178

Vacant Lot 194
Ventolin 143

Waik 109-10
The Wanderers 190
The Watt Riot 181, 213
Waves 8-9, 170, 172, 173, 174, 195, 219
We Love You Madly 26
Where Did You Sleep Last Night? 211-13
White Trash 188
Whitey, Jed 159
Wollongong Music Round Table 101-02, 113
Wollongongmusicscene.com 94-95
Wollongong Youth Centre 6, 9-10, 70, 110, 130
Woonona Bowls 89, 107

Yallah Roadhouse 161
Ye Luddites 172
Yes/No/Maybe Referendum Gig 25-26
Yours & Owls 178, 189

Zambian Goat Herders 6
Zero 165
Zondrae's 189

www.ingramcontent.com/pod-product-compliance
Lightning Source LLC
Chambersburg PA
CBHW071903290426
44110CB00013B/1255